The Foundations of Early Modern Europe
1460-1559

THE NORTON HISTORY OF MODERN EUROPE

General Editor: FELIX GILBERT, Institute for Advanced Study

The Foundations of Early Modern Europe, 1460–1559
EUGENE F. RICE, JR.
The Age of Religious Wars, 1559–1689, *2nd edition*
RICHARD S. DUNN
Kings and Philosophers, 1689–1789
LEONARD KRIEGER
Eighteenth-Century Europe: Tradition and Progress, *1715–1789*
ISSER WOLOCH
The Age of Revolution and Reaction, *1789–1850, 2nd edition*
CHARLES BREUNIG
The Age of Nationalism and Reform, *1850–1890, 2nd edition*
NORMAN RICH
The End of the European Era, 1890 to the Present, *3rd edition*
FELIX GILBERT

The Foundations of
Early Modern Europe
1460–1559

EUGENE F. RICE, JR.
Columbia University

W · W · NORTON & COMPANY
New York · London

For Geno, John, and Louise

W. W. Norton & Company, Inc., 500 Fifth Avenue, New York, NY 10110
W. W. Norton & Company Ltd., 10 Coptic Street London WC1A 1PU

Library of Congress Catalog Card No. 76-95531

Cartography by Harold K. Faye

PRINTED IN THE UNITED STATES OF AMERICA

3 4 5 6 7 8 9 0

ISBN 0-393-09898-2

Contents

Illustrations

Maps and Charts

Introduction

THE CENTURY OF European history between 1460 and 1559 was a period of rapid, comprehensive change. Like all periods of transition from one firmly contoured civilization to another, its most obvious characteristic is an intricate counterpoint of tradition and innovation, catastrophe and promise. This is why historians of the fifteenth and sixteenth centuries, like historians of the transitional centuries between antiquity and the Middle Ages, have always faced particularly difficult choices of perspective and emphasis. Some historians of fifteenth - and sixteenth-century manners, belief, and institutions have told their story in metaphors of spring and awakening. Others have lingered on the evidence of stagnation, traditionalism, and decay. Their imagery is autumnal. This sort of apparently contradictory appreciation reflects the period's bewildering, and fascinating, mixture of new and old.

Was the shift from old to new a shift from medieval to modern? The answer is yes, though with qualifications. The first concerns the temptation to reduce the medieval to a sociological "type," to find a quintessential medieval science, art, philosophy, religion or system of government and then measure change and innovation by variations from this standard. Such a procedure is not wholly misguided. The selection and ordering of material always stylizes the past to some extent. Otherwise, its history would be unintelligible. At the same time, the comparison of innovation with tradition must remain alert to the diversity of medieval life. For example, it is a common, and sometimes desirable, kind of historical shorthand to use St. Thomas Aquinas' solution of a particular problem to represent the opinion of all medieval philosophers and theologians. To the extent that all or most medieval thinkers shared important assumptions, the views of St. Thomas are typical, and yet Thomism was only one of several thirteenth-century philosophical tendencies. Equally representative contemporaries rejected many Thomist doctrines, and his influence in the fourteenth and fifteenth centuries was largely confined to his own Dominican order; the Church has recognized him as a normative theologian only in modern times. It is also well to remember that claims for innovation in one period often rest on ignorance of the period that preceded it.

The idea of the modern conceals an even greater diversity and ambiguity. Clarity here is important because so many nineteenth- and early twentieth-century scholars saw in the fifteenth and sixteenth centuries—especially in the civilizations of Renaissance Italy and Reformation Germany—the prototypes of modern European civilization. By modern they meant their own day. To later twentieth-century historians, however—self-consciously aware that they are living in another period of transition that is moving even more rapidly than the age of the Renaissance and Reformation—the innovations of Erasmus or Luther, of Henry VIII or Jakob Fugger, of Raphael or Michelangelo look less like the beginnings of the modern world than strands in a fabric of custom and tradition which contemporary innovators have been tearing up for three quarters of a century. Many of the modernisms of the Renaissance and Reformation have become as old-fashioned as medieval Latin or Gothic architecture were in sixteenth-century Rome. It is no longer plausible, therefore, to argue that the Renaissance and Reformation are the beginning of the modern world, if by modern we mean contemporary, or give the word the connotation it has, for instance, in the phrase "modern art," an art, like so much else in twentieth-century culture, based on assumptions and aspirations different from and hostile to those of the Renaissance.

Between modern and fifteenth- and sixteenth-century Europe lie, in any case, the industrial and French revolutions, the development of nationalism, and a profound secularization of culture. Renaissance and Reformation Europe was a pre-industrial, "underdeveloped" society, much closer in its economic life, technology, demographic patterns, communications, and class structure to imperial Rome than to contemporary western Europe or America. Everywhere political and military loyalty was dynastic rather than national. Political ties were overwhelmingly personal and familial, and every man took religion seriously. The age was one of astonishing religious creativity, pullulating with saints, mystics, reformers, and original theologians. Among the laity the temperature of piety was high—for the safety of religious minorities, dangerously high.

In a word, the shift from old to new in the fifteenth and first half of the sixteenth centuries (it had begun earlier in the fourteenth) was not a shift from medieval to modern, but from medieval to *early* modern. Renaissance and Reformation men built the foundations of a new Europe, but one that modern historians now call traditional Europe—Europe before the French and industrial revolutions. It still remains for students of the period to detect the crucial continuities—and discontinuities—in a gradual shift from one mode of perception and of production to another.

CHAPTER 1

Science, Technology, and Discovery

THE DATE 1492 is familiar, and so is 1498, the year Vasco da Gama reached the Malabar Coast of India by sea. Around these dates cluster others hardly less familiar and equally important. During the half century before 1500, Europeans read the first books printed in the West. Firearms created a new kind of warfare between 1450 and 1525. In 1500 Copernicus lectured on mathematics in Rome, and soon after, he began to teach that the earth rotates on its axis and at the same time revolves in orbit around the central sun. Each of these innovations, discoveries, and rediscoveries influenced profoundly the future course of European and world history. Together they transformed Europe's relation to non-European civilizations and to its own past. Until the sixteenth century, Europe was the technical and cultural pupil of Greco-Roman antiquity and of the civilizations of the Near and Far East. The voyages of Columbus and Vasco da Gama coincided with the beginning of the end of that dependence. Europe acquired and exercised, along with political and economic predominance, technical and scientific leadership. Before 1500, Europe imported ideas and techniques; after 1500, Europeans were cultural creditors.

THE INVENTION OF PRINTING

Printing with movable metal type was perfected in Mainz about 1450. Three names recur in the sources, those of Johann Gutenberg (c. 1395–1468), Johann Fust (c. 1400–1465), and Peter Schöffer (c. 1425–1502), Fust's son-in-law. These sources are scanty, often unclear, and sometimes of doubtful authenticity. So it is impossible to determine accurately the contribution of a particular individual to the development of typography and its commercial exploitation. Our relative ignorance about the origins of printing does have advantages, however. It discourages the misguided effort to attribute complex technological innovation to a single man, and forces us to realize that an invention is in any case not the creation of an individual, as is a poem or a painting, but a social

1

product. Like the development of the steam engine or the telegraph, the "invention" of a mechanical process for duplicating texts was multiple and cumulative. It was successfully completed by Mainz printers in the 1450's, but it had important earlier beginnings.

Two Chinese inventions, block printing and paper, are linked with the beginnings of typographic printing in western Europe. Xylography, or block printing, originated in China in the early eighth century. The printer drew in reverse on a block of wood the text or the picture he wished to reproduce, carved the wood so that the graphic pattern stood out in relief, inked the block, and transferred the design to paper. The process is simple in conception; difficult, time-consuming, and wasteful in execution; and ill adapted to the alphabetic writing of the West. Its transmission to the West—probably during the century from 1250 to 1350, when European contact with China was unusually close—had little direct importance for

The Papermaker. *Woodcut by Jost Amman from Hans Sachs' description of the arts, crafts and trades, published in 1568.*

the development of typography. Its indirect importance, on the other hand, was great. It probably suggested the next crucial step: cutting up an old block into its constituent letters and then rearranging these letters to spell out a new text. It certainly diffused the idea of printing and of the printed book, while the lively commercial success starting in the late fourteenth century of printed playing cards (another Chinese invention), religious prints, and crude block books emphasized the magnitude of the market and the potential profit to be got from it.

Paper was indispensable, but for economic rather than technical reasons. Manuscript books were usually copied on parchment (made from split sheepskin) or on vellum (calfskin), and these materials were used also by typographic printers when the aim was magnificence rather than utility. But since a single large book like the Bible required as many as 170 calf skins or 300 sheep skins, the absence of paper soon would have nullified the promise of mechanical duplication: the cheap, rapid production of books in large numbers. Paper manufacture was introduced in Spain during the twelfth century by the Arabs, who had themselves received the technique from China. It spread slowly during the next two centuries to much of Europe: Italy (*c.* 1270), France (*c.* 1340), Germany (*c.* 1390), and Switzerland (1411). In Europe the chief raw material was old rags. Papermakers shredded the rags in a stamping mill driven by waterpower, mixed the macerated flax and hemp fibers with water, and dipped their mold, a large flat wire sieve with a wooden frame, into the liquid pulp. When the pulp was evenly distributed over the wire mesh and the water had run out through the holes, they put the sheets on alternate layers of felt, squeezed them in a press, and then dried and sized them. Hans Sachs (1494–1576), the cobbler-poet and hero of Wagner's *Meistersinger von Nürnberg*, described the process in a poem which accompanies the earliest picture of papermaking:

> I am using old rags in my mill,
> Where flowing water turns the wheel
> That tears the rags and shreds them up.
> Then I soak the pulp in water tub,
> Mold the sheets, on a felt them lay,
> And squeeze them in my press all day.
> I hang them up to let them dry,
> Snow-white and glossy, a treat for every eye.

By the time of Gutenberg's youth, paper was plentiful and sold for approximately one sixth the price of parchment.

Western typography drew upon European methods also, and these were of more immediate technical relevance. Printing, as it was practiced in Mainz by Gutenberg, Fust, and Schöffer, required a suitable ink, a press for transferring the ink to paper, and metal type. To adhere to metal smoothly and evenly, ink must have an oil base. By the early fifteenth century, Flemish artists had begun to paint in oils; a suitable printer's ink, consisting of a pigment (lampblack or powdered charcoal) ground in a linseed-oil varnish, was simply an adaptation of oil paint. The immediate ancestor of the wooden press was also at hand: the press used in paper mills for squeezing water from the damp sheets, a device easily adaptable to printing. Most crucial was the invention of type—the mirror image of each of the letters of the alphabet made in metal by precision casting from matrices. The skills which contributed to the development of typecasting were understandably those connected with the more delicate forms of metallurgy: those of the metal engraver and the designer of coins and medals, of the goldsmith adept at casting small objects, of craftsmen who made punches for stamping letters on bells, pewter vessels, and bookbindings. We must imagine that in many places in Europe during the first half of the fifteenth century ingenious artisans experimented with type, inks, and presses; that many parallel efforts were made to replace the scribe by a mechanical device; that the actual invention of printing—the dramatic fusion (so easy for us to imagine in retrospect, so immensely difficult before it was accomplished) of familiar techniques into a new and workable process—also occurred independently in several places; that, finally, this new process was perfected and first organized as an industry by Gutenberg, Fust, and Schöffer.

What is certain is that the oldest surviving books printed with movable metal type were issued in Mainz. The best among them astonish still by their technical perfection, further evidence that the Mainz printing firms had inherited considerable expertise from earlier experiment and discovery. The great Latin Bible popularly associated with Gutenberg and more cautiously named the forty-two-line Bible by bibliographers (to distinguish it from another early Mainz Bible, printed with thirty-six lines to the pages) was finished in 1455. The craftsmanship of its type and the art of its typesetting and printing are impeccable. Clearly, the Mainz printers had established the technology of printing on firm foundations; and indeed for over three hundred years Gutenberg's successors cut punches, fitted matrices, cast type, composed, and printed substantially as he had done. Nor were later printers to surpass the founders aesthetically. On August 14, 1457, Fust and Schöffer issued the *Psalms*. The volume was printed on vellum. The type, printed in red and black, is noble and fits handsomely on the page. Each psalm, as the printers boasted in a note at the end, is "adorned with the beauty of large initial letters"; the lacy design of these letters, ornamented with flowers and small animals and printed in red and blue, is masterly. Fust and Schöffer's *Psalms* is the oldest signed and dated book printed in Europe that has survived. In its sober magnificence it is also one of the most beautiful.

A page from Fust and Schöffer's Psalms. *The initial "B" begins the second Psalm:* Beatus vir qui non abiit in consilio impiorum: Blessed is the man that walketh not in the counsel of the ungodly.

These first printed books have a further, and curious, characteristic: their pages so closely resemble those of manuscript books as to be virtually indistinguishable to the unpracticed eye. Clearly the printers' technical, aesthetic, and commercial aim was to reproduce exactly the handwritten manuscript. And they did not do so merely through inertia or in order to give their customers a familiar product; the practice suggests rather that the earliest printers had no conception of the unique potentialities of their invention, that they considered printing only a new and particular kind of writing ("the art of writing artificially without reed or pen," as Schöffer put it), and that they thought that what they had to sell consisted simply of less expensive manuscripts in greater numbers. Their difficulty in freeing themselves from traditional conceptions is explained by the fact that although typography was the greatest invention of the Renaissance, its earliest development was shaped almost exclusively by clerical tastes and needs. Its geographical origins were far from Italy, the literary and artistic center of European culture in the fifteenth century. Printing first became a significant business enterprise in a provincial ecclesiastical capital with a population of about three thousand and meager intellectual distinction. Monasteries and cathedral chapters contracted for the Latin Bibles, missals, psalters, and antiphonaries which were the printers' more important productions. The ecclesiastical authorities dominated job printing; for example, a common order was for indulgence forms. The cheaper books, to judge from the earliest publishers' list (that of Peter Schöffer), reflected traditional tastes; biblical digests, works by St. Thomas Aquinas, saints' lives, brief guides to living well and dying well, and for secular diversion, romances of chivalry predominated.

Yet even in Mainz, what was to be the key factor in the astonishingly rapid spread of printing between 1460 and 1500 was clearly evident: the unsatisfied demand for books among the merchants, substantial artisans, lawyers, government officials, doctors, and teachers who lived and worked in towns. The European peasantry was largely illiterate and would remain so for centuries. The needs of the clergy and of those adaptable nobles who were beginning to recognize the importance of a literary education for careers of service to their prince and country had been reasonably well met in the past by workshops where sometimes scores of copyists multiplied books by hand. Indeed, printed books met with a lively resistance for several decades, especially in Italy, from wealthy and cultivated collectors. But among what we must call, loosely but inevitably, the middle classes of the towns, among men who needed to read, write, and calculate in order to manage their businesses and conduct civic affairs, who were being educated in increasing numbers in town and guild schools, and who in the fifteenth century were swelling the arts faculties of the universities, there was a large and ready market for printed books. Underlying the expansion of printing was that expansion of urban population and secular literacy which had begun in the high Middle Ages. As townsmen grew in number, education, wealth, power, and self-consciousness, their intellectual and cultural needs increased. With the unremitting enthusiasm of the bourgeoisie for edification and self-improvement, they eagerly bought entertaining and useful books of all sorts: religious and secular, in Latin and in the vernacular, grammars, dictionaries, and encyclopedias, elementary texts in mathematics, astrology, medicine, and law, local and universal histories, manuals of popular devotion, and Latin classics of proven appeal—Virgil's *Aeneid*, Cicero's *De officiis*, Terence, Pliny, and Seneca. Their demands released the inherent dynamism of typography. The result was a steadily expanding stream of books. Printing spread from Mainz to Strasbourg (1458), Cologne (1465), Augsburg (1468), Nuremberg (1470), Leipzig (1481), and Vienna (1482). German printers, or their pupils, introduced the "divine" art to Italy in 1467, Switzerland and Bohemia in 1468, France and the

THE SPREAD OF PRINTING
THROUGH RENAISSANCE EUROPE

△ Printing centers and dates of first
  occurrence of printing

Printers shown thus: **CAXTON**

NORWAY

Stockholm,
1483

SWEDEN

BALTIC SEA

SCOTLAND

Edinburgh,
1507

IRELAND

Dublin,
1551

ENGLAND

DENMARK

Copenhagen, 1490

Odense, 1482

NORTH SEA

NETHERLANDS

Utrecht, 1470

Elbe R.

Oder R.

POLAND

Leipzig, 1481

CAXTON
London,
c. 1492

GERMANY

Cologne, 1465

BELGIUM

Brussels,
1475

Westminster,
1476

English Channel

**FUST
SCHÖFFER**
GUTENBERG

Mainz, 1450

BOHEMIA

Pilsen, 1468

Nuremberg,
1470

Vienna, 1482

Danube R.

Paris,
1470

Seine R.

Strasbourg,
1458

Rhine R.

Augsburg,
1468

AUSTRIA

HUNGARY

ATLANTIC

OCEAN

Loire R.

Basel,
1468

SWITZ.

FRANCE

Lyons, 1473

Milan,
1471

Venice,
1469

Po R.

ADRIATIC SEA

ITALY

Florence,
1482

Rhône R.

CORSICA

Rome,
1467

PORTUGAL

SPAIN

Tagus R.

Valencia,
1474

SARDINIA

Naples,
1471

Lisbon,
1489

BALEARIC
ISLANDS

Seville,
1478

MEDITERRANEAN SEA

SICILY

0   500 miles

Netherlands in 1470, Spain, England, Hungary, and Poland between 1474 and 1476, Denmark and Sweden in 1482–1483. By 1500 the presses had issued about six million books in approximately forty thousand editions, more books, probably, than had been produced in western Europe since the fall of Rome.

So vast an increase in the quantity of books inevitably had important cultural consequences. Most striking, perhaps, in the years before the Reformation was the influence of printing on scholarship. Manuscripts, totally dependent on the skill, learning, and care of the scribe, had always been inaccurate and unreliable. Furthermore, this inaccuracy and unreliability was becoming increasingly great as successive generations of scribes copied the errors of their predecessors and added their own. The fundamental contribution of printing to learning was that it halted this progressive corruption and made possible the long and continuing effort to restore the great texts of the past to something approaching their original integrity. Printing gave scholars all over Europe identical texts to work on. Referring precisely to a particular word in a particular line on a particular page, a scholar in Basel could propose an emendation which could be rapidly checked by his colleagues in Rome or Florence. Or another scholar might discover, in a monastic library in Paris, a manuscript whose text would be judged, by increasingly precise and objective criteria, better than any known before. From such corrections and discoveries a critical edition would emerge, to be superseded by another and yet another until something approaching a standard text had been achieved, usually only in the nineteenth or even the twentieth century. The past is sometimes a burden. That we know it as well as we do—and so much of it—we owe to printing.

The way printing made textual criticism a cumulative science is only a specific case of a more general phenomenon. Printing turned intellectual work as a whole into a cooperative instead of a solitary human activity. As the steam-powered machines of the industrial Revolution would multiply the productivity of human physical labor, so printing enlarged the amount of intellectual effort applied to individual problems. In no field were the effects of this novel concentration of brainpower more noticeable than in the natural sciences. Copernicus, for example, had adopted the heliocentric hypothesis early in the sixteenth century, but he did not publish it until 1543. Between 1500 and 1543 he worked on this major scientific problem in intellectual isolation. After 1543 Copernicus' printed book gradually drew a few of the best minds in Europe into a cooperative, controversial study of the problem, and a solution was found much more rapidly than it would have been otherwise. Scientific research—and all scholarship—became, through this new tool of the intellect, a public dialogue, a published exchange of novel results controlled by cooperative critical examination and the repetition of experiments. In this context the invention of printing can be compared only with the invention of writing, on the one hand, and of the computer, on the other.

Printing not only made scholarship fuller and more accurate; it also made it less difficult to acquire. Because of the greater standardization of print, learning to read was easier. Now individuals could afford to own books, where before they had normally been owned almost exclusively by institutions—monasteries, cathedral chapters, and colleges. Medieval students had had to compile their own dictionaries and reference books, and much of their time in the lecture room was spent writing out texts dictated by the teacher. To lecture had been to read a book aloud so the student could take it down; now the student could read the text at home. To learn had been to memorize; printing freed the memory. There was less need to keep a fact in the mind if it could more easily be found on the shelf. In 1580, well over a century after the invention of typography, the French essayist Michel de Montaigne (1533–1592) eloquently restated a principal theme of Renaissance educational theory when he defined the end of education not as a large amount of factual knowledge, but as a trained intelligence, sound judgment, and cultivated taste. For Montaigne the walking encyclopedia was a pedant; but he could legitimately brand him pedant only because printed reference books now served the traditional function of the human memory.

Equally striking, particularly after 1500, was the way printing accelerated the diffusion of images and ideas. The visual arts reached a new and wider public. Engravings, the normal means of reproducing works of art before the invention of photography, carried iconographic and decorative motifs from one region to another, from one artist to another; just as the influence of a man of letters like Erasmus of Rotterdam rapidly touched every intellectual circle in Europe through the printed word, so engravings of works by Michelangelo, for example, made the arrangement and postures of the nudes on the ceiling of the Sistine Chapel the common property of his most distant contemporaries. But it was the spread of Lutheranism that first made frighteningly and triumphantly clear the revolutionary significance of printing for the communication of ideas. The Reformation spread with the same astonishing rapidity as printing itself; it could not have done so without it. Indeed, the role of printing in the early sixteenth century already suggests its double role in the future: through its promise of enlightenment and popular education, potentially revolutionary and hostile to the *status quo*; but when controlled by the state, the most effective agent of manipulation until the invention of radio and television.

This is why the systematic censorship of books, little practiced in the Middle Ages, appeared very soon after the invention of printing, and spread with it. By making reading more democratic, printing spawned the modern censor. Both secular and ecclesiastical authorities censored books, for the prohibition and burning of books were designed to maintain political as well as religious orthodoxy. Alexander VI, pope between 1492 and 1503, clearly expressed the attitude of the Church in a bull of 1501. "The art of printing," he said, "is very useful insofar as it furthers the circulation of useful and tested books; but it can be very harmful if it is permitted to widen the influence of pernicious works. It will therefore be necessary to maintain full control over the printers so that they may be prevented from bringing into print writings which are antagonistic to the Catholic faith or which are likely to cause trouble to believers." Such attitudes became concrete in the lists of prohibited books issued to combat the spread of Lutheranism, lists which culminated in the Roman Index of Prohibited Books (1559). Henry VIII of England ordered the publication of such a catalogue in 1526. Other early indexes were prepared by the universities of Paris and Louvain. The Protestant churches protected the minds of the faithful as zealously as Catholic bishops, while secular princes generally considered religious commitments different from their own not only heretical, but treasonable as well. By 1560 censorship of books in all its forms was universal in western Europe. The struggle between author, printer, and publisher, on the one hand, and ecclesiastical and governmental censors, on the other, had become one aspect of the battle for intellectual liberty and freedom of conscience in an age of fundamental ideological conflict.

THE NEW WARFARE

In no period before our own has the technology of violence been more fertile than in the century between 1450 and 1550. During these years the use of gunpowder to propel missiles transformed the art of war. The new warfare, in turn, shaped the pattern of European political and social change as profoundly as printing altered the conditions of its intellectual life.

Gunpowder became known in the West about the middle of the thirteenth century. The Franciscan scientist Roger Bacon (c. 1214–c. 1292) mentioned it as something already widely known. This is his description of a firecracker:

There is a child's toy of sound and fire made in various parts of the world with powder of saltpetre, sulphur and charcoal of hazelwood. This powder is enclosed in an instrument of parchment the size of a finger, and this can make such a noise that it seriously distresses the ears of men, especially if one is taken unawares, and the terrible flash is also very alarming; if an instrument of large size were used, no one could stand the terror of the noise and flash. If the instrument were made of solid material, the violence of the explosion would be much greater.[1]

[1] Quoted by J. R. Partington, *A History of Greek Fire and Gunpowder* (Cambridge, Eng., 1960), p. 78.

Bacon clearly knew real gunpowder—its composition of suitable proportions of saltpeter, charcoal, and sulfur and its explosive combustion in a proper container. He did not invent it. Gunpowder was invented in China, probably as early as the eleventh century, and like paper and block printing was probably transmitted to Europeans by the Arabs.

The technological discovery, however, which turned gunpowder from a toy into a weapon and transformed warfare and society was that of its use as a propellant. This discovery was made early in the fourteenth century, independently in Europe and China. The first mention of a gun in Europe occurs in a Florentine document of 1326, which names two officers to make iron shot and metal cannon for the defense of castles and villages belonging to the republic. The first representation of a gun—a crude "firepot" designed to propel an arrow—is in an English manuscript dated the same year. By the end of the fourteenth century, firearms were being manufactured all over Europe, ranging from twenty-four-pound guns throwing lead bullets and thirty-four-pound guns throwing arrows to guns weighing over a ton and requiring more than a month to make. By the middle of the fifteenth century, artillery had proved of decisive effect against feudal stone castles and the traditional curtain walls of towns. At the siege of Constantinople by the Ottoman Turks in 1453, Sultan Mahomet II (ruled 1451–1481), who had German and Hungarian cannon founders in his service, was able to deploy against the astonished Byzantines fourteen batteries, each of several great bombards, plus fifty-six smaller cannon of various types. Most spectacular of all were two enormous guns which fired stone balls nearly three feet in diameter and weighing over eight hundred pounds. The guns required seventy oxen each and more than a thousand men to move them from Adrianople, where they were cast, to the Bosporus. The bombardment began early in April. By May 28, seven weeks later (the great cannon took two hours to load and could fire only a few times a day), serious breaches had been made in the most formidable defensive walls in Europe. On May 29 the city was carried by storm. In the meantime, in France, the revolutionary effectiveness of artillery in siege warfare became equally apparent during the final phase of the Hundred Years' War, the French reconquest of Normandy from the English. In the twelfth century, French kings had spent months, sometimes years, trying to pry a recalcitrant vassal out of a stone castle. In 1449–1450 Charles VII conducted sixty successful siege operations in a year and four days. The royal siege train became so respected that many fortified places surrendered the moment the big guns were placed in battery. The complete mastery of efficient cannon over the old fortifications was established.

For over a century and a half after these first decisive successes, artillery remained primarily a siege weapon. One major pitched battle—Marignano in 1515—was indeed largely won by artillery fire; more commonly, however, the limited mobility and the lack of accuracy and firepower of Renaissance cannon restricted their role in the field to mutual bombardment before the real battle was engaged. Battles were transformed not by cannon, but by the emergence of infantry as the "substance and sinew" of armies (the phrase is Machiavelli's), and by the gradual equipment of foot soldiers with portable firearms.

The decisive arm in a medieval army had been the cavalry; a medieval battle was a clash of mounted and armored nobles. By 1530, cavalry formed only one eleventh of the French army and one twelfth of the Spanish (some military theorists argued even more radically that the proportions of foot to horse should be twenty to one); and battles had become clashes of plebeian infantry armed with pikes and arquebuses, with heavy cavalry playing only a subordinate role. Early steps toward this new way of fighting had been taken during the fourteenth and fifteenth centuries by the English and the Swiss. The English contributed the longbow. At the Battle of Crécy in 1346, for the first time in over a thousand years, the sky over a battlefield was thick with missiles; for the first time, unassisted infantry won a major victory over enemies who relied on their superiority in cavalry. The achievement of the Swiss was to develop infantry tactics which permitted masses of unmounted troops to maneuver in the open field, defend themselves against cavalry charges, and engage in shock offensive action themselves. It was their practice to form compact squares of as many as six thousand men, trained to move swiftly and precisely without breaking their formation. Their principal weapon was the pike, a shaft of wood about ten feet long with a sharp iron head. In defensive action, the men stood still. The outer four ranks would cross the heads of their protruding pikes and present to charging cavalry a bristling wall. Horsemen who penetrated the phalanx were jabbed with halberds or twisted from their horses and finished off with swords by men of the inner ranks. By such means, men described with aristocratic disdain by a Milanese ambassador as "rude peasants who feed on cheese and curds" routed the chivalrous knights of the Burgundian dukes (at Morat in 1476) as efficiently as English yokels armed with longbows had defeated the mounted mobility of France at Crécy. Even more important was the fact that Swiss pikemen, unlike English archers or Italian crossbowmen, who were incapable of offensive action, could also attack, becoming charging squares of almost irresistible momentum. In the Middle Ages only cavalry had been able to charge; the Swiss pike phalanx made it possible for infantry to come out into the open and charge as well.

The reinforcement of pikemen with large numbers of foot soldiers carrying firearms was the last and decisive step by which the infantryman succeeded to the position formerly held by the mailed knight. Inefficient handguns (miniature cannon strapped to pike handles) were in use by the beginning of the fifteenth century; but only toward the end of the century did a true infantry firearm, the arquebus, become common, and only in 1521 did the Spaniards introduce the improved arquebus that came to be called the musket. It consisted of an iron barrel sunk in a wooden butt, was about six feet long, weighed fifteen pounds, and fired lead bullets to an effective range of about two hundred yards. After 1500, an ever-increasing number of troops were equipped with arquebuses and muskets. The arquebus supplemented rather than displaced the pike. Pikemen, to be sure, were extremely vulnerable to arquebus and musket fire. On the other hand, the arquebusier was helpless against cavalry once he had fired the single shot he normally had time to get off before the horsemen reached him. He needed the pike to protect him against cavalry, as the pike needed the musket to clear a path for his advance.

The tactics suggested by the mutual dependence of pike and musket were worked out between 1520 and 1525 by the father of modern infantry, the Spanish general Fernando de Avalos, marquis of Pescara (1489–1525), and scored their most dramatic early success at the Battle of Pavia (1525). On this occasion a French army commanded by the king, Francis I (ruled 1515–1547), met a Spanish Imperialist army in a contest for the mastery of northern Italy. The Imperialists had about seventeen

The Capture of Francis I at the Battle of Pavia, February 24, 1525.

le Roy François 1 fait prisonnier a la Bataille de Pavie le 24 febrier 1525.

thousand infantry and less than a thousand heavy cavalry. The French forces, especially the cavalry, were more numerous. The battle was a disaster for the French cavalry, a triumph for the Spanish musketeers. The slaughter among the French nobility caused by the steady shooting and maneuvering of Pescara's musketeers was fearful. Francis himself was captured. The French are said to have lost eight thousand men; the Imperialists reported their losses at seven hundred. On that day the superiority of the arquebusier to the mailed knight was proved as decisively as three quarters of a century earlier the vulnerability of medieval fortifications to cannon had been proved by the fall of Constantinople.

Between 1450 and 1525, then, a new era in warfare began, the age of gunpowder, or more precisely, the age of missiles (cannonballs and bullets) propelled by gunpowder. The rapid development and spread of these novel methods of destruction were made possible by an exactly contemporary increase in European metal production. Artillery consumed and wasted enormous amounts of metal. In the 1530's a large cannon required three to four tons of bronze. Although gun carriages were made of wood, they were armored with bands of iron and carried heavy iron bolts, chains and hooks. Together, a gun and its carriage weighed over two tons. By the end of the fifteenth century, iron had replaced stone for cannonballs. The barrels of arquebuses and muskets were made of iron. Moreover, the familiar metal weapons and defenses of the past—swords, lances, daggers, arrows, and above all, plate armor for both men and horses—continued in use. Armor, which had been getting heavier since the middle of the fourteenth century, was an effective defensive reply to the arrows of the English longbowmen. But the elaborate, often very beautiful, metal plates which encased the body of the rider and partially shielded his horse were ultimately useless as a defense against the bullet. The first age of gunpowder was also the last, and most extravagant, age of armor.

A supply of metal adequate to meet these accelerating military needs became available in the years after 1460, when a series of technological innovations combined to increase very substantially the output of Europe's mines. More efficient machines to drain mines, and blast furnaces fanned by water-driven bellows (furnaces which for the first time could refine ore into an iron pure enough to be cast as skillfully as bronze), contributed to a fivefold increase of iron production between 1460 and 1530. New techniques for removing silver from the argentiferous copper ores that abounded in central Europe increased the supply of copper even more rapidly, a fact of particular importance because copper was the essential element in cannon manufacture until cast iron came into use in the late sixteenth century. Just as the spread of typography depended on an adequate supply of paper, so the spread of firearms required an adequate supply of copper and iron.

But although the availability of sufficient metal accelerated the extensive adoption of the new weapons, it hardly explains it. We tend, of course, to assume that the inherent purpose of gunpowder is the destruction of human life. Yet it is by no means self-evident that gunpowder should of necessity be employed primarily for war. It was used for firecrackers and for peaceful economic purposes like blasting in mines before it was used to propel bullets. In China, where gunpowder had been known long before it reached Europe, its military uses were not developed to the extent they were in the West. This difference suggests the existence in Renaissance Europe of a very powerful pressure to exploit the new invention for military purposes. This pressure, becoming acute about 1450, came from the larger territorial princes and derived its force from a fundamental political reality of the age: the consolidation in Europe of what would remain the dominant political form of the modern world, the sovereign territorial state. The new weapons and the new warfare benefitted the ruler seeking to organize a large territory. They armored his aggressions at home and abroad. Gunpowder technology became normal in the West because it royalized warfare and helped the prince to establish a monopoly on the use of organized force within his territory.

If in one perspective the effect of firearms was to royalize warfare, in another perspective the effect was to proletarianize it. Contemporaries seem to have been more struck by the second than by the first. "Would to God," wrote a French noble taken prisoner at Pavia, "that this unhappy weapon [the arquebus] had never been invented. I myself would not bear the scars it caused me and which still cripple me today. Nor would so many brave and valiant men have died by the hands of cowards and shirkers who would not dare to look in the face the men they bring down from a distance with their wretched bullets." Gentlemen with pretensions to chivalry were disturbed not so much by the fact that fighting with missiles propelled by gunpowder was making war bloodier than it had ever been before, as by the fact that firearms enabled a base-born man to strike down at a distance the bravest knight. The poet Lodovico Ariosto (1473–1533), who sang of "ladies, knights, arms and loves" at the court of the duke of Este in Ferrara, lamented the evil, devilish invention of the gun: "O wretched and foul invention, how did you ever find place in a human heart? Through you the soldier's glory is destroyed, through you the business of arms is without honor, through you valor and courage are brought low, for often the bad man seems better than the good; through you valor no more, daring no more can come to a test in the field."[2] Here is the reverse of royal profit, the nostalgia for a past when only aristocrats had really fought, and did so—at least in theory—according to a code of honor. Now foot soldiers with pikes and arquebuses fought more decisively, if not better; and they attempted to win not by valorous clash of arms

[2]*Orlando Furioso*, XI, 26, trans. by Allan Gilbert (New York, 1954), Vol. I, p. 156 .

or acts of individual courage, but by disciplined industry and cunning, by ruse, surprise attack, and fraud. "Although in all other affairs it is hateful to use fraud, in the operations of war it is praiseworthy and glorious," wrote Niccolò Machiavelli (1469–1527).[3] In war the amorality of the state supplanted the personal honor of the knight. Gunpowder hastened the decay of chivalry. Its end is symbolized by the death in 1524 of Pierre Terrail, Seigneur de Bayard, *chevalier sans peur and sans reproche*, the last great representative of Christian knighthood. It was his amiable practice to execute on the spot every arquebusier he captured; he was killed by a bullet.

By royalizing warfare, on the one hand, and by proletarianizing it, on the other, the gun helped to tip the balance of power within each European state away from the nobility and in favor of the crown. The process was gradual and complex, and its rate varied in the different parts of Europe. But the long-range effect was everywhere the same: gunpowder technology curbed, and finally extinguished, the freedom of landed magnates to exercise significant independent, organized military and political power. In earlier centuries private armies had been commonplace and private war endemic. In an age when no weapon but starvation or treachery could reliably prevail against a well-placed stone castle, and when the only effective warriors were armored horsemen, the feudal nobles had monopolized the military profession. The new weapons weakened this military basis of independent aristocratic power. Warfare in the age of gunpowder demanded a siege train of hundreds of cannon and thousands of well-equipped and well-trained infantrymen. Both defensive and offensive operations became enormously expensive, technically and financially beyond the means of any private individual—beyond the means, indeed, of all except the rulers of important states. To be sure, noble magnates still went to war. Their numbers, training, and bellicosity remained the most reliable measure of a country's military competence. In some cases with reluctance, in others with cynicism, most commonly with prudent foresight, they adapted themselves successfully to technological change and continued to lead Europe's armies in the sixteenth century as they had in the past. What they could rarely do was to own or control directly an artillery train, or with their own resources, organize, pay, and field effective contingents of foot. This progressive loss of their former direct and independent control over men and arms—a loss qualified by their kings' continued dependence on their military talents, traditions, skill, and experience—was to influence profoundly the relation of magnates to rulers, and more generally, the development of the early modern state.

Gradually the increasing use of firearms modified even men's moral responses to war. A handful of sixteenth-century intellectuals were pacifists

---

[3]*Discourses*, III, xl.

Mars and Venus. *Painting by Veronese. The goddess of love and concord subdues the god of war and discord. Their coupling produced a daughter, Harmony. Metropolitan Museum, New York.*

and condemned the brutish immorality of all war. A few Christians opposed war on religious grounds, notably the Anabaptists, who quaintly believed that the commandment "Thou shalt not kill" was meant to be observed literally. Everyone agreed that soldiers were detestable. "The whole science of warfare," wrote a Florentine theologian, "has been turned into brigandage, and there is no faith or piety in the men who pursue martial service. They are full of treachery, theft, sacrilege, perjury, blasphemy, cruelty toward even innocent prisoners, drunkenness, gambling, and sodomy."[4] But most men of substance, as they have in every age, defended "just" wars, that is, wars necessary for the preservation of peace, the repelling of aggressive foes, and the prevention of acts of injustice. Commonly, too, war was glorified, for man was thought to possess a balanced capacity for both action and thought, arms and letters. The ideal man developed both. Venus and Mars were a favorite subject of Renaissance painting, their conjunction suggesting the necessary, indeed

[4]St. Antoninus of Florence, *Summa sacrae theologiae.* Quoted by Edward Surtz, *The Praise of Wisdom. A Commentary on the Religious and Moral Problems of St. Thomas More's Utopia* (Chicago, 1957), p. 271.

desirable coexistence of tenderness and violence. War was regarded as the most fitting subject of epic, pageant, romance, and history. War even had an ethical relevance, since it encouraged noble virtues like courage, fortitude, and loyalty. But as the horror of firearms spread, men began to picture war in a more fearful image. In art they revived the Roman war goddess Bellona, associated her with gunpowder, provided her with an arsenal of cannon, muskets, mines, and grenades, and lamented her ruinous brutality. The slow transformation of sensibility by a military technology that erases the poetry of war had begun.

THE ORIGINS OF MODERN SCIENCE

The sensibilities and values of western men were to be even more profoundly molded by the method and pursuit of science.

Only modern western civilization has produced a fully developed science. The breakthrough to such a science, so different and so much more successful than the sciences of the ancient Greeks, the medieval Arabs, the Indians, and the Chinese, occurred between the publication of Copernicus' *On the Revolutions of the Celestial Spheres* in 1543 and the appearance of Newton's *Principia* in 1687. We call it the scientific revolution. This fundamental intellectual mutation, rapid and dauntingly complex, rested, of course, on earlier work. Specifically, it was the fruit of a novel and sophisticated methodology created in the late Middle Ages and in the Renaissance. The new method combined three procedures, one logical, one experimental, and one mathematical. Each of these procedures had been the intellectual tool in a distinct social or scholarly milieu. Their separate histories in the fourteenth and fifteenth centuries form the prehistory of the scientific revolution. Their gradual combination in the early sixteenth century into a fruitful method of discovery laid the foundation for the unparalleled enlargement of man's understanding and mastery of nature achieved by the generations of Galileo and Newton, and is the most important contribution of the Renaissance to the development of modern science.

The logical component of modern scientific method was given its initial form by fourteenth-century scholastics, teachers of logic and philosophy in the arts faculties of the universities of Paris and Oxford, and perfected in the Renaissance by teachers of philosophy and medicine at the universities of Bologna and Padua. They named it the method of resolution and composition. "Resolution" was an inductive movement from observed effects to their cause, a demonstration *a posteriori*. "Composition" was a deductive movement from cause to effect, an *a priori* explanation.

Jacopo Zabarella (1533–1589), the greatest sixteenth-century logician, admirably defined the purpose of this procedure: to lead us in "syllogistic form from known principles by a necessary movement to the knowledge

of an unknown conclusion."[5] For example, an investigator observes the
phenomenon of shadows, From his empirical observations he constructs a
hypothesis to account for them. This is the *a posteriori*, inductive movement from effects to a tentative statement of their cause. But this is only
half his task. He must now prove his generalization by checking it against
the observed phenomena, more precisely by deducing effects which must
follow if the generalization is true and by testing these effects empirically.
This is composition, the *a priori* deductive movement from cause to
effect. The demonstration took the form of an Aristotelian syllogism
reshaped for purposes of scientific investigation. An eclipse of the moon is
a striking shadow effect. Describe it as the major term of a syllogism:
"The moon in eclipse has an opaque body interposed between it and its
source of light." The generalization or cause, previously induced from this
and other observations of shadows, follows as the middle term: Whatever has an opaque body interposed between it and its source of light
loses its light." Therefore—the syllogism's conclusion—the moon loses its
light *because* an opaque body has interrupted its source. The middle term
is thus shown to be the cause of the major term in a tight, logical
structure of hypothesis and observation.

The method of resolution and composition produced some remarkable
results. Fourteenth-century French and English scholastics defined uniform speed. They discovered a form of the theorem describing uniform
acceleration: "a moving body uniformly acquiring or losing that increment
[of velocity] will traverse in some given time a magnitude completely
equal to that which it would traverse if it were moving continuously
through the same time with the mean degree [of velocity]."[6] They probed
weak points in Aristotle's theory of motion. Aristotle had believed that
rest was natural and motion a disturbance of nature. In order for a thing
to move, something else must push or pull it. This is mistaken common
sense. The difficulty is to explain projectile motion. Why does a rock
continue to fly through the air after it has left the thrower's hand?
Aristotle had unconvincingly supposed that the rock was moved along by
air pushed apart by its progress and forcefully reuniting behind it. The
scholastics revived a superior hypothesis, first suggested by a sixth-century
Byzantine critic of Aristotle's mechanics, and explained the continuance of
projectile motion by a force they called *impetus*, an intrinsic qualitative
power infused into the projectile by the projector. Most scholars thought
that this force was gradually dissipated like heat, but one or two argued
that it was destroyed only by resistance of the medium or by the object's

[5]*In Libros Aristotelis Physicorum commentarii.* Quoted by Neal W. Gilbert, *Renaissance Concepts of Method* (New York, 1960), p. 168.
[6]Marshall Clagett, *The Science of Mechanics in the Middle Ages* (Madison, Wis.,
1959), p. 284.

weight, an intimation of the modern definitions of momentum and inertia.

For a century and a half, scholastic physics got no further. One reason for this arrested development was the limited knowledge of mathematics during this period. The late medieval scholastics were far below the highest level of Greek competence in mathematics, and they tended to deny that the abstractions of geometry had any significant link with physical reality; for, they said, there are no observable circles or triangles in nature. Moreover, their method was too exclusively logical. They were reluctant, in practice, to subject their theories to the test of experiment. They considered a hypothesis established if they had logically refuted any argument brought against it. At the same time, many of their more attractive hypotheses were advanced simply to show that a non-Aristotelian explanation was, in fact, logically possible, while they themselves, with an exaggerated respect for authority, continued to believe that Aristotle's explanation was the true one. They were disputatious, and too often preferred the sophistical victory of debate to the empirical search for truth. They calculated, but saw little need to measure.

The habits of experiment and measurement evolved in a social and intellectual milieu wholly different from that of university and clerical scholarship: the studios of Italian artist-engineers of the fifteenth and sixteenth centuries. These men were laymen and superior craftsmen, mechanics who had begun as apprentices educated in a master's workshop. Their thinking was quantitative and causal. Their observation was trained to precision by painting and carving. In order to reproduce nature more accurately they studied birds, flowers, and foliage; learned the optical laws of perspective; used the scalpel and recorded their dissections in brilliant anatomical drawings. In the course of analyzing the proportions of antique ruins and planning their own buildings, measurement became for them a conscious professional discipline. Besides being artists in the limited sense, they were mechanical, military, and hydraulic engineers. They designed cannon, laid out canals and elaborate fountains, built machines for princely theatricals. They made clocks, lutes, and maps, nautical and astronomical instruments. They experimented constantly. They were the real pioneers of empirical research, and their rules of thumb constituted the modest beginnings of the physical laws of modern science.

The greatest of the Italian artist-engineers was Leonardo da Vinci (1452–1519). We know a great deal about him because an impressive collection of his manuscript notes has survived. The notebooks give us a close view of his experimental method and expose both the virtues and the limitations of his scientific work. They record hundreds of experiments. They prove eloquently that for Leonardo experimentalism was a habit, even a philosophy of knowledge. "Wisdom," he wrote, "is the daughter of experiment." "Experience is never at fault." And again: "I

Anatomical Studies (The Shoulder). *Drawing by Leonardo da Vinci. Leonardo dissected more than thirty corpses in his exploration of the human body. Windsor Castle, Royal Library.*

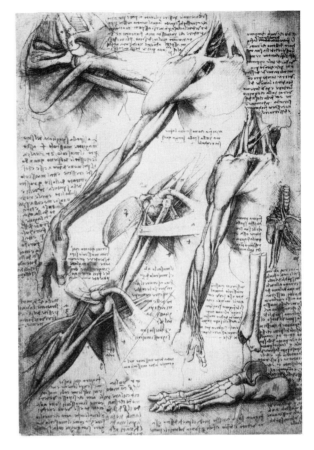

know well that because I have not had a literary education there are some who will think in their arrogance that they are entitled to set me down as uncultured—the fools. . . . They do not see that my knowledge is gained rather from experience than from the words of others: from experience, which has been the master of all those who have written well." The notebooks show him testing his theories by making small scale models and seeing if they work. He knew that experiments must be repeated. His techniques and apparatus were ingenious. But he was a naive empiricist. The scholastics had too much theory; he had too little. And he knew no more mathematics than they. He mentions Archimedes, but he knew him more as a magnificent legend than as a fruitful influence in his work. He was very successful in areas where careful observation and experimental pertinacity are more important than theoretical sophistication—in anat-

omy, for example, or in finding quantitative rules connecting two varia-
bles, one of which can be altered at will and the other observed with
convenience. Thus he conducted experiments on the strength of loaded
beams and struts, placing weights of different sizes on beams of varying
dimensions and on different sites on the beams and observing at what
weight breakage occurred. Ultimately he concluded that the strength of a
beam is directly proportional to its breadth.

Repetitive experimentation alone, however, was not enough, just as the
logical method of the scholastics was not enough. Leonardo's discoveries
explained only a relatively narrow range of phenomena. To organize more
complex experimental results and produce a viable scientific method a
third component was needed: an acquaintance with mathematics, and a
more sophisticated conception of its function in understanding the physical world. Superior mathematical knowledge was the indirect contribution
of a third professional group, the humanist scholars of the sixteenth
century.

By 1500, many Italian humanists knew Greek, and they were prodi-
giously active in discovering, editing, translating, and publishing Greek
texts hitherto unknown in the Latin West. An important phase of this
reappropriation of Greek antiquity was the recovery and renewed understanding of major Greek scientific and mathematical works, those of
Pappus, Apollonius, Diophantus, Hero, and above all, those of Archimedes, which appeared in Latin translation in 1543. Allied to the exploration of these substantive works, knowledge of which transformed sixteenth-century geometry and algebra, was a growing emphasis on the
cultural and scientific importance of mathematics. Humanist educational
practice stressed mathematics at the expense of logic. The professional
teaching of mathematics spread in universities, and there was hardly a
Renaissance writer who did not remind his readers of the sentence
allegedly inscribed over the door of the Platonic Academy: "Let no one
unskilled in geometry enter here." Most important, perhaps, a higher level
of mathematical knowledge and sophistication—encouraged by a widespread enthusiasm for Platonism—began to convince scientists that nature
itself was mathematical in structure, that the circles and triangles of
geometry could, in fact, make intelligible the apparent confusion of
sensible experience.

Why this insistence on the mathematical intelligibility of nature was to
be so important is suggested by Galileo's paradoxical praise of Copernicus
and his supporters for being "able to make reason so conquer sense that,
in defiance of the latter, the former became the mistress of their belief."[7]
Galileo did not mean that the evidence of experience was unimportant.

[7]*Dialogue Concerning the Two Chief World Systems—Ptolemaic and Copernican*,
trans. by Stillman Drake (Berkeley, Calif., 1953), p. 328.

He was suggesting that common sense is deceptive and that the under-brush of empirical fact could better be cleared away by mathematical abstraction than by simple inductions from experience. Almost all science before the sixteenth century had been dominated by naive and direct generalization from sense experience. The result was common-sense expla-nations and empirical rules rather than scientific laws. What was needed in order to formulate scientific laws was the development of a radical habit of abstraction, the will to penetrate the confusing diversity of the visible world and to express its observed regularities in mathematical formulas. This demanded imaginative bravura—the power, for example, to visualize bodies falling in a vacuum or moving in the pure reaches of Archimedean space. It required ruthless simplification and concentration on formulating hypothetical abstractions which could be tested quantita-tively. It meant studying phenomena in their simplest quantitative rela-tions with other phenomena, as mathematical entities rather than as sensible bodies with the inevitable peculiarities and irregularities of nature. It meant a geometrizing of experience. The sixteenth-century recovery of Greek mathematics made this way of thinking possible.

Before 1500 the three components of modern scientific method—the logical, the experimental, and the mathematical—developed in isolation, for the aims, sympathies, intellectual interests, and social positions of the professional groups with which they were connected were too diverse to permit fruitful communication among them. After 1500, the gaps between these groups narrowed rapidly. A successful eclecticism was made possible by interlocking developments of great complexity. One factor, clearly, was printing. The diffusion and wider availability of learned, technical, and mathematical books encouraged the flow of ideas among different professional groups. The cultural ideals of humanism influenced all edu-cated men. Fashion, if nothing else, forcefully imposed newly translated texts on their attention, while an increasing number of scholars learned Greek and began to study Greek science in its original sources. Artist-engi-neers won a higher social position than they had enjoyed before. Their artistic and technological achievements aroused the interests of both liter-ary men and scholastic philosophers and diminished the traditional con-tempt of the academically learned for manual and mechanical operations. Scholars with university training began to write in Latin about gunnery, navigation, and mining. The great mathematician Niccolò Tartaglia (*c.* 1500–1557), for example, devoted much time and energy to problems of ballistics. The physician Georg Bauer (1490–1555), or Agricola, as in humanist fashion he preferred to call himself, was an excellent Latinist, a correspondent of Erasmus and the author both of a book on fossils (*De natura fossilium*, 1546) and of the most important sixteenth-century treatise on mining and metallurgy, the *De re metallica*, published posthu-mously in 1556. Superior craftsmen acquired academic learning. Thus

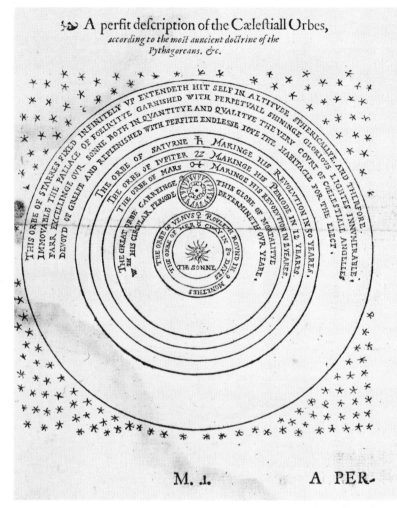

A perfit defcription of the Cæleftiall Orbes,
according to the most auncient doctrine of the Pythagoreans. &c.

THIS ORBE OF STARRES FIXED INFINITELY VP EXTENDETH HIT SELF IN ALTITVDE SPHERICALLYE AND THERFORE IMMOVABLE THE PALLACE OF FOELICITYE GARNISHED WITH PERPETVALL SHININGE GLORIOVS LIGHTES INNVMERABLE FARR EXCELLINGE OVR SONNE BOTH IN QVANTITYE AND QVALITYE THE VERY COVRT OF CŒLESTIALL ANGELLES DEVOYD OF GREEFE AND REPLENISHED WITH PERFITE ENDLESSE IOYE THE HABITACLE FOR THE ELECT.

THE ORBE OF SATVRNE ♄ MAKINGE HIS REVOLVTION IN 30 YEARES.

THE ORBE OF IVPITER ♃ MAKINGE HIS REVOLVTION IN 12 YEARES.

THE ORBE OF MARS ♂ MAKINGE HIS REVOLVTION IN 2 YEARES.

THE GREAT ORBE CARRIENGE THIS GLOBE OF MORTALITYE
WH HIS CIRCVLAR PERIODE DETERMINETH OVR YEARE.

THE ORBE OF VENVS ♀ ROVLETH ROVND IN 9 MONETHES

THE ORBE OF MER ☿ CLAY IN 80 DAYES

THE SONNE

M. I.   A PER-

Copernicus' heliocentric hypothesis. *A sixteenth-century English adaptation of a diagram from the 1543 edition of the* Revolutions of the Celestial Spheres. *Within the sphere of the fixed stars, the orbs of Saturn, Jupiter, Mars, Earth, Venus, and Mercury revolve in circles around the central sun.*

Leonardo learned Latin in middle age and came into direct contact with humanism and traditional university scholarship. From this fusion of professional habits and procedures emerged a new sort of natural philosopher, the *filosofo geometra*, as he was called in Italy, a scientist who combined in his research the syllogistic procedure of the scholastics, the experimental habit of the artist-engineers, and the mathematical knowledge made available by scholars trained in Greek. Nicolaus Copernicus (1473–1543) is a striking early example of this new type. He studied the scholastic Aristotelian tradition at its greatest centers, Padua and Bologna. He learned Greek, and came to believe profoundly in the possibility and importance of discovering simple geometric regularities in nature. And he absorbed the causal thinking and manual dexterity of the artists and engineers; there is some reason to believe, for example, that he painted a self-portrait, and reliable evidence indicates that he built many of his own astronomical instruments.

The same process of decompartmentalization produced a new scientific method. The vulgar empiricist became aware that he could give his multitude of observations theoretical structure by applying to his data the scholastic's method of resolution and composition. The scholastic logician was stimulated to measure and experiment. The mathematician learned to bend his abstract imagination to the demands of the scientific syllogism and the controlled experiment. The result was a powerful intellectual tool, a methodology whose core was the traditional scientific syllogism, but whose middle term now took the form of a mathematical formula, while the consequences deduced from this mathematical hypothesis were rigorously tested by further observation and experiment. With this tool the scientific revolution was made.

Yet even in the middle of the sixteenth century an acute observer could not have predicted revolution. The first major document of the new science, Copernicus' *On the Revolutions of the Celestial Spheres,* appeared in 1543. Those who accepted his views before 1560 can, literally, be counted on the fingers of one hand. Opponents too were few, but they were, like Luther, vigorous: "The fool wants to overturn the whole science of astronomy." The typical attitude was indifference. Yet with the single-minded impetuosity of genius, Copernicus had reconstructed the heavens. Embedded in his largely traditional structure were the novel assertion that the earth rotated annually around the sun and a detailed demonstration that the mathematical consequences of the earth's motion fitted existing knowledge of the heavens. In 1560 most men still pictured the universe as Dante had: closed, tidy, man-measured and man-centered. But with Copernicus' assertion of the earth's status as a planet, the first great step had already been taken toward the Newtonian World Machine.

PORTUGUESE VOYAGES OF EXPLORATION

"The owl of Minerva," said Hegel, "flies only as dusk is falling"; he meant that only toward the end of a historical process can we grasp its full significance. Until very recently the economy and civilization of

Europe dominated the world. The passing of that domination in our own day makes us understand all the more clearly the significance of the Portuguese voyages of exploration. They marked the beginning of European expansion over the world: the political colonization of vast areas, the economic penetration which transformed the earth into Europe's economic hinterland, the Christian imperialism which was only a part of a vast effort to impose European cultural patterns on the whole globe. They began the European age of world history.

At the same time, it should not surprise us that many sixteenth-century Europeans were no more impressed by the importance of the discoveries than they were by the truth of the heliocentric hypothesis. So intelligent a man as Erasmus hardly mentioned them. Luther saw them only as providential channels for the dissemination of the Gospel. Far more books were published about the Turks than about India or China. A French description of the world written in the second half of the sixteenth century does not mention America. As ignorant of their future as we are of ours, the contemporaries of the explorers assessed their discoveries far more narrowly than we do. They measured them in terms of their own immediate personal interest and ambition. Or they judged them by the provincial standards of a closed society intolerant of the foreign values of non-European cultures. In both cases they were blinkered by their particular position in time, at the beginning rather than at the end of an era.

They were all the less likely to magnify the results of expansion because the initial impulse to exploration and discovery was itself narrow and concrete. It is misleading to suppose that important historical events must necessarily have equally important causes. The discoveries are a case in point. They began the extension of European influence throughout the world. But their original motive was more prosaic—a desire, colored by crusading emotion and justified by missionary zeal, to find gold in Africa.

The Portuguese descent of the African coast, which began in 1415 with the capture of Ceuta, was at once an episode in the long struggle of Christianity and Islam and an attempt to reach the sources of an ancient and well-known trade in gold. The capture of Ceuta, a Moslem city at the northern tip of Morocco, was a traditional crusading enterprise; and even after Prince Henry the Navigator (1394–1460), a younger son of King John I of Portugal, had come to see it as the first step in a coherent program of African expansion, hostility to Islam remained a powerful motive behind Portuguese exploration. One of Henry's initial aims, for example, was to measure Mohammedan power in Africa. Another was to contact directly the mysterious Prester John, a Christian ruler of vast and opulent domains whom Europeans had come to identify with the negus, the emperor of Ethiopia, and to draw him into a Christian alliance against the infidel. Later the Portuguese hoped to find Christians in India, the descendants of those traditionally said to have been converted by the

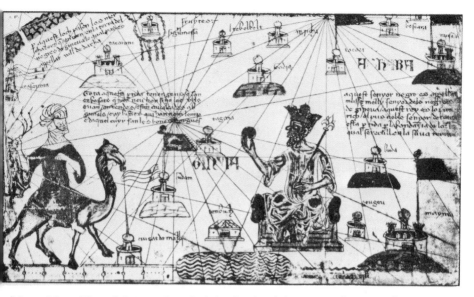

Mansa Musa, King of Guinea. *Detail of the Catalan Atlas, a map drawn on the island of Majorca in 1375. Bibliothèque Nationale, Paris.*

apostle Thomas; while for the more numerous Indians who were not Christians their hope was speedy conversion.

But the hopeful blossoms of conversion were nourished by roots of commerce, and the first commercial lure was gold. In 1375 a Spanish Jew had drawn a map of Africa that was to become famous. At the center of the Sahara the map showed the figure of a Negro monarch with a scepter in one hand and a nugget of gold in the other. The legend read: "This Negro lord is called Musa Mali, lord of the Negroes of Guinea. So abundant is the gold which is found in his country that he is the richest and most noble king in all the land." The cartographer's information was perfectly correct as far as it went. Mansa Musa, to give the king his real name, is known from other sources. He made a pilgrimage to Mecca in 1321 and on the way dazzled the Egyptians in Cairo with a prodigal display of wealth. His kingdom was only one of several organized states in the great bend of the Niger River whose wealth and power were based on profits from the gold trade. This trade was a very ancient one, and from at least the tenth century powdered gold had flowed into the Mediterranean world from the West African Sudan (most notably from the region bounded on the north by the Senegal River, on the west by the Falémé, and on the east by the Niger) and from the territories of the Ashanti north of the Gold Coast. The primitive natives of these regions got the gold from river gravels. They traded it to more sophisticated Moslem Negroes for salt, the one absolutely indispensable product they lacked. These, in turn, carried it inland to the great markets on the southern fringe of the Sahara: Niani, the capital of Mansa Musa's kingdom of Mali; the independent city of Jenné, an important center of trade and culture farther up the Niger; and the prosperous commercial centers of Walata and Timbuktu. Here the merchants of the south met their white coreligionists from the north and east, and the gold began the long journey by camel caravan across the Sahara to the Mediterranean ports of the Maghrib—Algiers, Bône, and Tunis.

For centuries merchants from Venice and Genoa, Marseilles and Barcelona, had traded on the Barbary Coast and bought the goods so laboriously transported across the desert from the distant countries of the Negroes, the area already known as Guinea. Prince Henry's fundamental objective—and it was one requiring great imagination in conception, and courage, skill, and tenacity in execution—was to tap the gold trade at its source, to bypass the Moslem middlemen of the Maghrib and the Sahara, to win control of a trade hitherto in infidel, and often hostile, hands. He was all the more anxious to do this because in Portugal, as in all Europe, the precious metals, and especially gold, were notably scarce in the fifteenth century. A monopoly of one of Europe's principal sources of gold would bring with it power and profit. The voyages sponsored by Prince Henry were not, therefore, leaps into a dark unknown. To be sure, they demanded skill in navigation and cartography and innovations in shipbuilding and naval gunnery. And they necessarily involved exploration and an expansion of knowledge. But they rested on earlier knowledge of Africa gathered by an international group of scholars and seamen—Christians, Jews, and Moslems in Henry's service—and their aim was precise: to seek out the gold of the Guinea Negroes.

Prince Henry's will and imagination directed the first stage of the Portuguese advance. Almost every year, voyages were made down the African coast. By 1460, the year of Henry's death, Portuguese sailors had arrived off Guinea. Between 1460 and 1480 they explored the territory and began its commercial exploitation. King John II (ruled 1481–1495), an enthusiastic expansionist, assumed the title of lord of Guinea. Contact was made with the rulers of West Africa. Forts and trading stations were established. By the end of the century the Portuguese had drawn into their hands a very large proportion of the trade once monopolized by African Moslems. Gold now went to Europe by sea, directly to Lisbon and Antwerp, rather than over the old caravan routes to Algiers and Tunis and ultimately to Genoa and Venice. The result in the sixteenth century was severe economic depression for the cities of the Maghrib and a brilliant prosperity for Portugal. Already by the end of the 1440's Portugal commanded enough gold to issue its first national gold coin, the *crusado*. By 1502, an ordinary shipment of gold weighed two thousand ounces and normally twelve or fifteen ships arrived every year, each bringing a similar quantity. But gold was not all. In the 1470's the Portuguese colonized the island of São Tomé off the Cameroons, planted sugarcane, worked the estates with Negro slaves, and shipped sugar to Europe. In return for cheap, loud-colored fabrics, rings, bracelets, and copper dishes, they acquired ivory, ebony, and melegueta pepper (cruder than eastern pepper, but cheaper). Far more lucrative even than their trade in these tropical products was their commerce in slaves. During the second half of the fifteenth century over a thousand slaves a year reached Lisbon from Africa. The slave trade would continue for centuries, remaining profitable long after the gold and silver of Mexico and Peru had reduced the West African supply to insignificance. Until 1530, gold was more important than slaves; after 1530, slaves were more important than gold, and the Guinea coast became significant chiefly as a source of African forced labor for the colonists of the New World.

At what precise moment the Portuguese raised their sights from the gold and slaves of Guinea to the spices of India is unknown. It is probable that by the last decade of his life Prince Henry imagined reaching India by sea. It is certain that by 1480, when the exploitation of the Guinea coast had become continuous and efficient, the principal objective of Portuguese ambition had shifted to the East. New and rapid progress down the African coast was made in the 1480's, reaching its climax in 1487 when Bartholomeu Dias (c. 1450–1500) voyaged around the Cape, named "Good Hope," for the promise it gave of finding India, so desired and for so many years sought after." Fulfillment of this promise was delayed for ten more years. Then in 1497 the king of Portugal "dispatched four vessels to make discoveries and go in search of spices."[8] On May 20, 1498, Vasco da Gama (c. 1469–1524) anchored off the Malabar Coast.

The twentieth-century American, taking for granted refrigeration, ease and rapidity of transport, and the resulting extraordinary variety of diet, may find perplexing his ancestors' lust for spices. We must remember some of the foods Europeans lacked. They had no rice, no corn, no potatoes; little cheese or butter; fresh fruits and green vegetables only in season, and few of these in the larger cities; almost no sugar. Fresh meat was relatively plentiful at the moment of massive slaughter in the autumn. At other times of the year meat was salted and more than a little high; and since its source was excess work animals, it was hardly of prime quality. The ordinary diet was based on bread and gruel, enlivened by pickled cabbage, turnips, peas, lentils, and onions. The entire art of

---

[8]Álvaro Vehlo, "A Journal of the First Voyage of Vasco da Gama in 1497–9," in *Portuguese Voyages*, ed. by C. D. Ley (London and New York, 1947), p. 3.

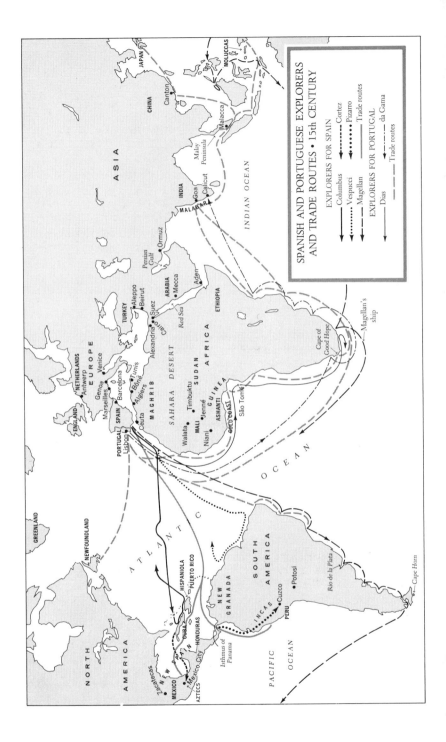

SPANISH AND PORTUGUESE EXPLORERS
AND TRADE ROUTES · 15th CENTURY

EXPLORERS FOR SPAIN
Columbus
Vespucci
Magellan
Cortez
Pizarro
Trade routes

EXPLORERS FOR PORTUGAL
Dias
da Gama
Trade routes

NORTH AMERICA

GREENLAND

NEWFOUNDLAND

ATLANTIC

ZacatecasMEXICO
NEW SPAIN
Mexico City
AZTECS
HONDURAS
Isthmus of Panama
CUBA
HISPANIOLA
PUERTO RICO

PACIFIC OCEAN

NEW GRANADA
INCAS
Cuzco
PERU
Potosí
Rio de la Plata

SOUTH AMERICA

Cape Horn

OCEAN

EUROPE
ENGLAND
NETHERLANDS
Antwerp
Venice
Genoa
Marseilles
Barcelona
SPAIN
PORTUGAL
Lisbon
Ceuta
Tunis
Algiers
Bône

TURKEY
Aleppo
Beirut
Alexandria
Cairo
Suez

ARABIA
Mecca
Aden
Red Sea

ASIA

MAGHRIB
SAHARA DESERT
SUDAN
AFRICA
Walata
Timbuktu
MALI
Jenné
Niani
ASHANTI
GOLD COAST
GUINEA
São Tomé

ETHIOPIA

Cape of Good Hope

Magellan's ship

INDIAN OCEAN

Persian Gulf
Ormuz

INDIA
Goa
MALABAR
Calicut

CHINA
Canton

Malay Peninsula

Malacca

JAPAN

MOLUCCAS

cookery lay in the sauce, and the piquancy of the sauce lay in its spices. Men wanted spices because they teased the palate, disguised the disagreeable or dull, gave variety to the menu. They wanted them for medicines and drugs, for perfumes and for use in religious ceremonies. The result was a most powerful demand for camphor, cinnamon, nutmeg, ginger, mace, cardamon, and above all, for pepper and cloves—all products of Asia and excessively rare in Europe.

When da Gama arrived in Calicut the trade in spices between Europe and the Far East was ancient and well organized. At Malacca, on the western coast of the Malay peninsula, junks from Canton and spice craft from the East Indies met the ships of the Moslem merchants who controlled the trade of the Indian Ocean. The spices were then shipped to the second great area of redistribution and transshipment, the Malabar Coast, especially the city of Calicut. From there the spices took either of two ancient routes to the Mediterranean: to Ormuz, at the entrance to the Persian Gulf, through the gulf, up the Euphrates River to Aleppo and Beirut; or to Aden, through the Red Sea, and then overland to Suez and Alexandria. At Alexandria and Beirut the precious cargoes for the first time passed into the hands of Christian merchants, mostly Venetian, for at the end of the fifteenth century Venice still successfully enforced the monopoly of the Mediterranean spice trade she had imposed during the Middle Ages. Along this vastly extended line of traffic the trade enriched all who touched it, and from the Moslem merchants of the Indian Ocean to the sultans of Egypt and Turkey and the Venetian traders, all had a vested interest in maintaining the old routes.

The arrival of the Portuguese in the Indian Ocean threatened them all; and it became the task of the Portuguese to repeat on a vastly greater scale the strategy they had employed in cornering Sudanese gold—to wrest commercial control of the eastern seas from the Moslems, destroy the Moslem monopoly, divert the traffic in spices from the routes leading to Venice by way of Ormuz, Aden, Beirut, and Alexandria, and instead ship the cargo around the Cape of Good Hope directly to Lisbon. In 1509 they annihilated a large fleet assembled by the Mameluke sultan of Egypt with the connivance of the Venetians. Under the leadership of Affonso de Albuquerque, governor of the Portuguese in India, (1509–1515), they destroyed Calicut, captured Ormuz, and conquered Goa and made it the trading center of the Malabar Coast. Malacca, a commercial nerve center, fell in 1511. These victories of the first twenty years of the sixteenth century laid the foundation of the Portuguese empire in the Indian Ocean and made possible the magnificent flow of spices to Lisbon, and from Lisbon to Antwerp, which began between 1501 and 1504. By 1520 the bridgeheads of European imperialism were firmly planted in the East.

The Portuguese rapidly captured an important share of the European market. In 1515 even Venetians were forced to buy pepper in Lisbon. The opening of a direct sea route to the Indies did not, however, put an immediate end to the Mediterranean spice trade. The flow of spices along the old routes continued. The Portuguese broke the Moslem monopoly of the Indian Ocean, but they never succeeded in establishing a monopoly of their own. Specifically, they failed to capture Aden. It fell in 1538, not to the Portuguese, but to the Turks. The Red Sea became a Turkish lake. In 1560 the amount of pepper and other spices that reached Alexandria and the Mediterranean was still as great as the amount that reached Lisbon. The ultimate triumph of the oceanic route was inevitable; and da Gama's voyage initiated the shift of Europe's center of gravity from the Mediterranean to the Atlantic, from Italy to the Netherlands, England, and France. But the triumph was long delayed. Economic preponderance did not shift decisively to the north until the seventeenth century.

THE NEW WORLD

In 1492, shortly before the Portuguese, having thrust south and east, entered the Indian Ocean, the Spaniards were sailing westward across the Atlantic. The motives of the two were identical: to acquire wealth and save souls. "We came here," said one of Cortes' foot soldiers, "to serve God and the king, and also to get rich."[9] Christopher Columbus (1451–1506), like Henry the Navigator, was touched by the fact that "many people believing in idolatries were lost by receiving doctrine of perdition."[10] He left Spain prepared to smite the heathen, and he did, in fact, convert them in droves to the true and European faith. He also wanted to get rich. His first voyage was a race to India by a mariner convinced that he could reach it more easily and rapidly by crossing the Atlantic than by sailing around Africa. The result was very different from his expectations. The Portuguese had looked first for gold in Guinea, and their search had insensibly led them to the sources of the spice trade. The Spanish looked first for an alternative and better route to the spices, pearls, and treasures of the Indies. They discovered instead a new world, but they found there gold and silver in hitherto unimagined quantities. Consequently, while the Portuguese empire in the East took the form of a loose string of forts and trading stations around the periphery of the Indian Ocean, the Spanish empire in the New World became a vast and settled mining community. Begun in rivalry, the two empires were soon linked by the fact that bullion from America was increasingly used to pay for the spices of the East. The commercial exploitation of Asia was made possible by the discovery of precious minerals in the West.

[9]Quoted by Lewis Hanke, *Bartolomé de las Casas* (The Hague, 1951), p. 9.

[10]*The Journal of Christopher Columbus*, ed. by C. R. Markham (*Works Issued by the Hakluyt Society*, Vol. LXXXVI, London, 1893), p. 16.

After Columbus' first voyage, the exploration and conquest of the New World proceeded with absolutely extraordinary rapidity. As long as he lived, Columbus himself believed that he had reached the Far East. His tenacity of illusion was not shared by many; and as his companions and successors came to realize that what they had come upon was not a goal, but an obstacle, they began a frantic search for a passage to India across or around it. This was the first motive for penetration of the Americas, the spur which led Amerigo Vespucci (1451–1512) to explore the Río de la Plata and Ferdinand Magellan (c. 1480–1521) between 1519 and 1521 to discover the southern strait and head westward across a Pacific Ocean which, with mistaken optimism, he thought was an arm of the Indian Ocean and an easy path to the Moluccas, themselves mistakenly believed to lie temptingly close to the Spanish settlements on the Isthmus of Panama. However, by the time Magellan's voyage had made clear the vastness of the Pacific and the hopeless impracticality of tapping the spices of the Moluccas from the West, gold had been discovered in the Caribbean islands and on the mainland. Henceforth, the lust for gold became the prime motive for exploration and colonization in Spanish America.

The geography and chronology of conquest and settlement were dictated by the location of gold and silver deposits and by the availability of Indian labor to work them. Mining was the first economic activity of the Spaniards in the New World; and the necessities of the mine would shape every detail of the political, economic, and social life of Spanish America throughout the colonial period. Gold was found first on the island of Hispaniola, Columbus' main discovery on his first voyage, then in Cuba and Puerto Rico. The central mountain core of these islands was honeycombed with gold-bearing quartz veins. Extraction was simple; gold was dredged from shallow surface diggings, or more often, worked from the sand and gravel of streams. But because a single person had to wash so long to get so little, only the presence of large numbers of docile Indians who could be forced to mine as virtual slaves made placer mining economically viable. When Columbus landed, over a million Indians lived in Hispaniola. By 1510 smallpox epidemics, famine, and the ruthless exploitation inseparable from placer mining had reduced the Indian population by about 90 per cent, to a hundred thousand. Deprived of Indian labor by the catastrophic decline of the native population, a minority of settlers remained on the islands and turned to cattle raising and agriculture, growing sugarcane with Negro slave labor imported from Africa. The surplus majority crossed over to the mainland, to Mexico and then to Peru, in the hope of finding more gold and the Indians to mine it.

The conquests of the Aztec and Inca empires are the epics of the Spanish appropriation of the New World. In 1519, a quarter of a century after Columbus' landfall, drawn by rumors of a wealthy empire on the

The Cerro Rico of Potosí. *Unknown artist, about 1584. On the nearer flank of the mountain, llamas loaded with silver ore. In the foreground, reduction of ore by the mercury-amalgamation process. Hispanic Society of America, New York.*

mainland, Hernando Cortes (1485–1547) left Cuba for Mexico. By 1532, Spaniards controlled the entire area of high Indian culture in central Mexico, and named it New Spain. A year later, in 1533, a second private freebooting expedition, led by Francisco Pizarro (c. 1470–1541) and recruited, promoted, and financed in Panama much as wildcat mining schemes are organized today, occupied Cuzco, the capital of the Inca Empire. Within fifteen years the two great kingdoms of the New World had fallen to a handful of utterly brave and utterly ruthless adventurers. The rewards were great. Spaniards now controlled the most populous areas of the continent, with twenty to twenty-five million inhabitants, ninety per cent of the population of pre-Columbian Central and South America. Cortes amassed an enormous booty of gold and silver ornaments from the Aztec lands; Pizarro seized the hoard of the Incas. But what made the *conquista* supremely important for early modern Europe was the accidental fact that several of the richest silver deposits in the world were within the newly conquered territories of New Spain and the viceroyalty of Peru:

at Zacatecas and Guanajuato, north of Mexico City, discovered between 1543 and 1548, and at Cerro Rico, the fabulous sugarloaf mountain of silver at Potosí, in the Bolivian highlands, discovered in 1545.

With the exploitation of these Mexican and Peruvian silver deposits placer mining gave way to the more elaborate and technically demanding vein mining as the fundamental economic activity of the New World, and silver replaced gold as the principal export of Spanish America to Europe. In the sixteenth century Potosí was the most important mining town in the world. It lay in the shadow of the celebrated Cerro Rico at an altitude of almost three miles above sea level. No temperature above 59 degrees Fahrenheit has ever been recorded there. At the time of the first census, a quarter of a century after the discovery of the lode, Potosí had a population of 120,000, larger than that of any city in Spain, approaching that of Paris and London, the greatest cities in Europe. The city had eighty churches, crawled with gamblers and prostitutes, and its inhabitants produced, in an uproarious atmosphere of violence, exploitation, and conspiracy, astronomical quantities of silver. Potosí and Zacatecas rapidly became the nerve centers of a colonial economy based on silver. The location of silver deposits determined the centers of population, while the nonmining population worked to house, feed, and equip the miners and scoured the country for the forced Indian labor which did the actual digging; in this economic pattern the development of agriculture, stock farming, manufacturing and trade became functions of mining. The colonists, to be sure, sent hides, copper, tobacco, sugar, and indigo to Europe too. But in amount and value, silver and gold far outweighed all other exports. The New World specialized in mining and exported bullion in exchange for manufactured goods. From the European point of view, treasure so far outweighed all other colonial products that the very fleets which sailed between Spain and the Indies were spoken of as the "fleets going to the Indies to bring back the gold and silver of His Majesty and private individuals."

However rich, the Mexican and Peruvian mines would not have made such a great impact on European civilization if they had not been imaginatively worked. Technological innovation was as crucial for silver production in the Renaissance as it was for the production of firearms and books. The best knowledge of mining and metallurgy in sixteenth-century Europe was German, summed up in the most comprehensive metallurgical textbook of the period, Agricola's *De re metallica*, a work much read in the New World. By the mid 1530's scores of Germans were active in American mines; and it was they who introduced into Mexico in 1555–1556 the mercury-amalgamation process, the decisive event in the history of American mining. In this process the ore, finely crushed in a water-powered stamp mill (also introduced by German miners), was mixed with water, mercury, salt, and impure copper sulphate in a spacious

Sixteenth-century mining. *Woodcut from Agricola's* De re metallica, *published in 1556. Shaft (A, D), tunnel (E), mouth of tunnel (F), and drift, a dark tunnel without a mouth open to daylight (B, C). The larger capital investments required by technological innovation imposed an increasingly capitalistic organization on the mining industry in the sixteenth century.*

rock-floored patio, then heaped into piles and allowed to stand until the silver ion chemically separated out of its compounds was amalgamated with the mercury. The amalgam was then washed, pressed into bars, and heated in a furnace, where the mercury volatilized, leaving bars of silver. Apparently this technique of reducing silver ores had been developed by miners in the territories of Venice late in the fifteenth century, but it was not used on a large scale before its introduction into America. There it proved valuable because it greatly increased the yield of silver ores and permitted the profitable exploitation of ores of a much lower grade than was possible with traditional methods. During the fifteen years after the new process reached Potosí in 1571, production quadrupled. Corresponding increases in production occurred at Zacatecas and Guanajuato.

During the sixteenth century, then, a flood of bullion poured into Europe. In the beginning, between 1503 and 1535, shipments were mostly of gold—from Hispaniola, Cuba, Puerto Rico, and Central America—obtained from placer mines or by collecting the golden objects worked and accumulated over the centuries by the pre-Columbian civilizations. After 1535, most bullion came from Mexico and Peru. Silver predominated to an ever greater extent, until by 1570 only 3 per cent of the treasure arriving in Seville was gold. In amount and value, the bullion Europe received increased throughout the century, forming a graphed curve which ascended slowly until 1535, climbed more sharply between 1536 and 1580 with the spoliation of the Incas, the discovery of Zacatecas and Potosí, and the introduction of the amalgamation process, and after 1580 rose precipitously to its peak in the 1590's. By the 1540's, about 1.5 million ounces of silver a year were pouring into Europe; in the 1590's, over 10 million. These figures take on more concrete historical meaning when we compare them with those of the contemporary European output. Most of Europe's silver was mined in Saxony, Bohemia, the Tyrol, and Hungary. Like iron and copper production, silver production there rose rapidly after 1460, to a peak of some 3 million ounces a year in the decade between 1525 and 1535. Before 1540, therefore, Europe produced about twice as much silver as Spanish America. But while the production of American silver was climbing vertiginously during the second half of the century, European production was declining with hardly less impressive rapidity. By the end of the century vastly more silver circulated in Europe than ever before, but it came from Mexico and Peru rather than from central Europe.

The most important sixteenth-century effect of the discoveries was the impact of the massive importation of American gold and silver on European prices. The increasing quantities of bullion in circulation reinforced inflationary pressures caused by a rising population and rapidly pushed up prices. The great price increase began early in the century. By 1560, Spanish prices had doubled. Elsewhere, inflation was more gradual, and its consequences were not felt acutely until the later sixteenth and early seventeenth centuries. But even in the earlier part of the century it hastened profound shifts in the distribution of wealth and economic power. Its role was the more revolutionary because its beginning coincided with a general, rapid expansion of the European economy between 1460 and 1560. In its early stages, the price revolution both stimulated commercial and industrial development and aggravated the social tensions inseparable from the emergence of capitalist modes of production in industry and agriculture. In this perspective, expansion abroad was itself a prolongation of expansion at home, while aggressive thrusts beyond the traditional boundaries of Christendom sharpened patterns of change inherent in the domestic development of the European economy.

CHAPTER 2

The Economic Expansion of Europe

OVER TWO CENTURIES of medieval economic expansion had ended by the beginning of the fourteenth century. The years between 1310 and the 1340's were a period of scarcity and often of famine. The Black Death—which reached Constantinople and the eastern Mediterranean littoral in 1347; Italy, Spain, and France in 1348; Switzerland, Austria, Germany, and Low Countries, and England in 1349; and Scandinavia and Poland in 1350—transformed this subsistence crisis into demographic catastrophe. Fragmentary evidence makes any estimates of the losses impressionistic. The most reliable suggest a reduction of from 12 to 60 per cent in the population, depending on the region, with a global loss for the period between 1348 and 1377 of about 40 per cent. Until far into the fifteenth century, population stagnated at a level well below that of 1347. In response to the fall in population, both prices and the volume of commerce and of industrial and agricultural production also declined or remained stationary. The long depression ended between 1460 and 1500. During the lifetimes of Luther, Copernicus, and Michelangelo, Europeans enjoyed a remarkable prosperity, a resurgence of industrial, commercial, financial, and demographic growth.

A CENTURY OF PROSPERITY

In the first half of the sixteenth century, population growth was large, generalized, and rapid. In most parts of Europe, population continued to increase, probably less rapidly and less uniformly in the second half of the century, until about 1620. The populations of Sicily and the kingdom of Naples doubled. Rome housed 50,000 people in 1526, 100,000 at the end of the century. In villages in the agricultural region south of Paris, the number of inhabitants doubled, tripled, even quadrupled between the end of the fifteenth century and the middle of the sixteenth. Changes in the rural population of the county of Hainaut, one of the seventeen provinces of the Netherlands, show a similar pattern. From 1365 to about 1470, the

38

population declined. Between 1470 and 1540–1541 it swung sharply upward. Antwerp expanded from 20,000 about 1440, to 50,000 about 1500, to 100,000 about 1560. Calculations of the total population of the Empire are wildly approximate, but studies of particular areas confirm a strong upward trend. Similar evidence of demographic vitality, though with important regional variations, can be found in Spain, Portugal, and Switzerland; elsewhere in the Netherlands and France; and in Scandinavia, Poland, and Russia.

A buoyant expansion of industrial production paralleled this growth in population. The quantities of iron, copper, and silver extracted from Europe's mines quadrupled. Very probably the output of the metallurgical industries expanded as rapidly as mining itself. Wholly new enterprises contributed to industrial prosperity. The production of printed books, for example, already so remarkable before 1500, soared in the sixteenth century, and its progress stimulated older industries like papermaking and the manufacture of spectacles. An increasing urban population encouraged building. Much of Rome as we know it today, to take a single instance, was built in the sixteenth century: fifty-four churches, including St. Peter's, sixty palaces, many villas outside the city, hundreds of buildings to house ordinary citizens, and scores of hotels for pilgrims. Thirty new streets were laid out; most of the old streets were paved; almost a hundred miles of ancient aqueducts were rebuilt to bring in drinking water.

The pattern of growth in textile manufacture, Europe's greatest industry ever since the thirteenth century, was more complex. The preeminence of Italy in the manufacture of woolens faded. Florence, which had produced about 100,000 bolts of cloth a year in the late fourteenth century, produced only 30,000 in 1500; but the decline in woolens was probably more than offset, in value if not in volume, by increases in silk production. The old woolen industry of the Netherlands, centered at Ypres, Ghent, and Bruges, was also in decline; but again the progress of a new industry, the manufacture of lighter, cheaper woolen fabrics, made up for the losses in the old. In the meantime, England, which in the Middle Ages had exported raw wool rather than cloth, superseded Italy and the Netherlands to become Europe's chief producer of heavy woolens of the best quality. In 1503–1509 England exported an average of 81,835 bolts of cloth a year and only 5,000 sacks of wool. By 1540–1548 her average yearly exports totaled 122,254 bolts.

These are only examples. They could be multiplied. Everywhere the evidence is the same; industry was booming, and depending on the commodity, production rose from two to five times what it had been before.

The increases in population and production, and the opening of new trade routes, made it profitable for European merchants to exchange a larger volume of goods over greater distances than they had in earlier

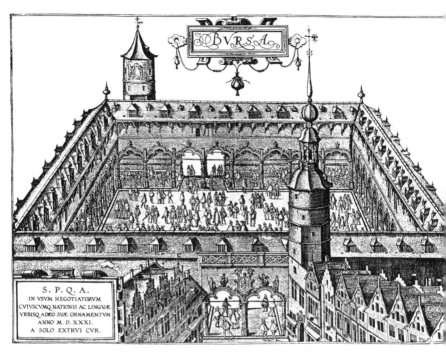

The Antwerp Bourse. *Engraving from Ludovico Guicciardini's description of the Low Countries, published in 1565. The inscription reads:* Erected in 1531 by the senate and people of Antwerp for the use of the merchants of every nation and language and to enhance the beauty of their city.

centuries. Portuguese merchants pushed east from Malacca to the centers of clove and nutmeg cultivation in the Moluccas, and then north to China and Japan. In the West, Seville was becoming the capital of an emerging Atlantic economy. European trade became literally worldwide in 1565 when Spanish galleons began regularly to link Manila and Mexican port of Acapulco. Chinese junks visited Manila every year and traded spices, silks, and procelains for Mexican silver, a traffic reproducing in miniature the exchange forming the basis of intercontinental commerce in the sixteenth century: American silver for eastern spices.

But the romance of intercontinental trade should not obscure the fundamental and more important exchanges of food, raw materials, and manufactured goods among the different regions of Europe itself. England exported its woolens to northern Europe, not to the East. Indians did not drink Portuguese wine; Englishmen did. Spanish wool went to the Netherlands and Italy; Hungarian copper to Germany and France. The market for Venetian goblets and mirrors, Ferrarese ceramics, Flemish tapestries,

Neapolitan silks, the products of the metallurgical industries of Nuremburg and Milan, was overwhelmingly European. And the heaviest volume of trade—economically and in tonnage far more weighty than the domestic trade in luxuries or any extra-European trade—involved the prosaic exchange, by way of Antwerp, Europe's commercial nerve center in the first half of the sixteenth century, of the cereals and forest products of the Baltic for the salt, wine, fish, vegetable oils, fruits, and dyestuffs of France and Spain and of southern and Mediterranean Europe in general. Commercial expansion abroad rested on the vigorous multiplication of commercial exchanges at home.

Bankers too enlarged their field of operations. In the Middle Ages banking had been almost exclusively an Italian monopoly. During the several decades before and after 1500, Frenchmen, Englishmen, and Germans joined Italians in consolidating the position of exchange banking in the economies of France and England, while financiers of many nationalities established banking houses in areas that had had few or none before—in Portugal, in Castile, and above all, in Germany. The organized money market widened, and in most of the great commercial centers, merchant-bankers built exchanges, often called bourses (after the Place de la Bourse in Bruges, a square much older than the banking institution to which it gave its name, and itself named for a Bruges family called, providentially, *de la Bourse, i.e.* "Purse"), where they bought and sold bills of exchange and speculated on currency rates. In 1531 the new Antwerp bourse was opened "to the merchants of every nation and language." The proud inhabitants boasted of its size and beauty and of the thousand merchants who crowded its daily sessions, so colorful in dress and so various in tongue that the bourse seemed a miniature world, a microcosm, bringing together everything to be found in the large one, the macrocosm.

In 1460 the most impressive business organization in Europe was the Medici Bank of Florence. By 1545, the Fugger Company of Augsburg was the largest firm. The Medici Bank (the firm was called a *banco*, but its activities were commercial and industrial as well as financial) had eight branch offices, the Fuggers, twenty-five. The Medici owned three modest textile firms. The Fuggers owned silver mines in the Tyrol and gold mines in Silesia, mined mercury in Spain, and controlled the larger part of copper production in Hungary. The Medici Bank got into financial difficulties—one among several more important reasons for its decline—when its agent at Bruges made a risky loan to the duke of Burgundy. At the time of the imperial election of 1519, Jakob Fugger loaned Charles, the Habsburg candidate, the colossal sum of 543,000 florins with which to bribe the electors, and he got it back with interest. Finally, the capital of the Medici Bank in 1451 was 90,000 florins; that of the Fuggers in 1547 was over ten times as great. The larger scale of economic activity in the sixteenth century is clear.

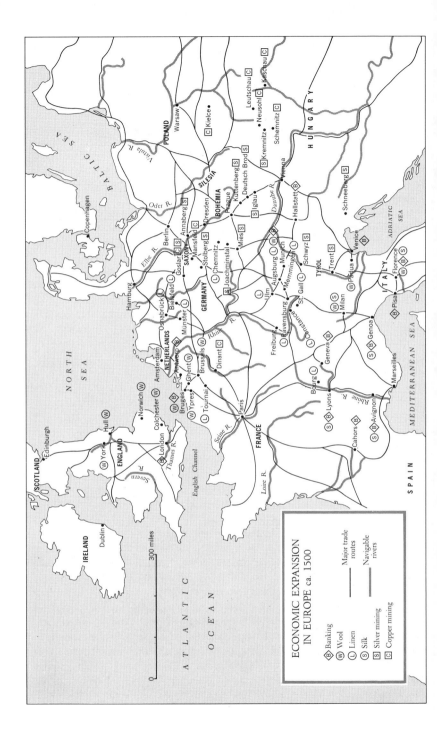

ECONOMIC EXPANSION
IN EUROPE ca. 1500

Legend:
- Ⓑ Banking
- Ⓦ Wool
- Ⓛ Linen
- Ⓢ Silk
- Ⓢ Silver mining
- Ⓒ Copper mining

——— Major trade routes

⫩ Navigable rivers

300 miles

ATLANTIC OCEAN

NORTH SEA

BALTIC SEA

MEDITERRANEAN SEA

ADRIATIC SEA

English Channel

IRELAND
Dublin

SCOTLAND
Edinburgh

ENGLAND
York Ⓦ
Hull Ⓦ
Norwich Ⓦ
Colchester Ⓦ
London Ⓦ
Severn R.
Thames R.

FRANCE
Paris
Tournai Ⓛ
Ⓦ Ypres
Ⓦ Bruges
Ⓦ Ⓑ
Loire R.
Seine R.
Rhône R.
Lyons Ⓢ Ⓑ
Cahors Ⓑ
Avignon Ⓢ Ⓑ
Marseilles

NETHERLANDS
Amsterdam
Ghent Ⓦ
Brussels Ⓦ
Dinant Ⓒ
Osnabrück Ⓛ
Münster Ⓛ
Bielefeld Ⓛ
Antwerp Ⓦ Ⓑ
Hamburg

GERMANY
Berlin Ⓢ
Goslar Ⓢ
Mansfeld Ⓒ
Stolberg Ⓢ
Chemnitz
Joachimsthal Ⓢ
Annaberg Ⓢ
Dresden
Freiburg Ⓛ
Ravensburg Ⓛ
Augsburg Ⓛ Ⓦ Ⓑ
Munich
Memmingen Ⓛ
Ulm Ⓛ
St. Gall Ⓦ
Schwyz Ⓢ
Elbe R.
Oder R.
Rhine R.
Danube R.

SAXONY
Mies Ⓢ

SILESIA

POLAND
Warsaw
Kielce Ⓒ
Vistula R.

BOHEMIA
Prague
Kuttenberg Ⓢ
Iglau Ⓢ
Deutsch Brod Ⓢ
Hallstatt Ⓑ

HUNGARY
Leutschau Ⓒ
Neusohl Ⓒ
Kaschau Ⓒ
Schemnitz Ⓒ
Kremnitz Ⓢ
Schneeberg Ⓢ

TYROL
Trent Ⓢ

ITALY
Venice Ⓑ
Padua Ⓦ
Florence Ⓦ Ⓑ Ⓢ
Pisa Ⓑ
Genoa Ⓢ Ⓑ
Milan Ⓦ Ⓢ
Geneva Ⓑ
Bourg Ⓛ

SPAIN

Copenhagen

THE MERCHANT

The key figure in the expanding economy of Europe between 1460 and 1560 was the merchant. He belonged to an exclusive business elite. The merchant aristocracy of Venice numbered about 1,500 out of a total population of 100,000. In Florence in the same period very probably no more than 2 per cent of the inhabitants were engaged in international trade and banking or held positions of capitalist command in industry. The proportion was not larger elsewhere. In Lyons and Augsburg, Genoa and Seville, London and Antwerp, as in Florence and Venice, most men were shopkeepers, artisans, or wage workers. The merchant's dynamism, economic power, and influence, however, were out of all proportion to his numbers.

Furthermore, the diverse enterprises of the merchant illustrate many characteristics of the economic life of the age. In the high Middle Ages the merchant was usually an itinerant trader who moved his goods in person along the trade routes of the continent. By the early years of the sixteenth century he had been, by and large, a sedentary businessman for many generations. Under improved conditions of transportation, with the greater security for goods and persons enforced by the larger states, with cities like Bruges replacing fairs as centers of international exchange, with the beginning of marine insurance and reasonably rational and enforced codes of commercial law, the merchant became a man in an office. Here a mounting pile of ledgers, with their neat rows of assets and liabilities (recorded in Arabic rather than Roman numerals), informed him at a glance of the conditions of his affairs. From the office he conducted a continuous correspondence with his fellow merchants and with subordinates abroad (his factors), who kept him informed about the state of the market and about the many and varied circumstances, often political or military, affecting the supply and prices of the commodities and currencies he dealt in. Through the factors, who functioned as commission agents, he bought and sold. (Sales were not concluded, as they are today, on the basis of samples. Goods themselves had to be forwarded on speculation to the distant agent for sale, if possible, to local retailers—a system, clearly, that demanded of the merchant the nicest combination of flair and calculation.) He borrowed money and transferred it from place to place by a sophisticated system of bills of exchange. His firm was usually a family partnership, but he often pooled his capital with that of affluent associates for particular ventures: to handle large purchases or loans, to spread the risk in a difficult enterprise, to hire ships and ensure their armed protection. The sixteenth-century merchant was the resident motor of a complex economic machine.

A further characteristic of the early modern merchant, as of his medieval predecessor, was the extreme diversity of his enterprises. For although enough risk had been eliminated from international trade to enable the merchant to stay at home, conditions remained extremely hazardous by modern standards. The merchant therefore sought safety by putting his money into a large variety of separate ventures. Like all merchants until well into the eighteenth century, Renaissance traders dealt in as many commodities as possible, in many different parts of the world, investing only a fraction of their capital in each. Antonio, in Shakespeare's *Merchant of Venice*, expressed a common prudence:

> Believe me, no: I thank my fortune for it,
> My ventures are not in one bottom trusted,
> Nor to one place; nor is my whole estate
> Upon the fortune of this present year:
> Therefore my merchandise makes me not sad.

Even as large a firm as the Medici refused to specialize and dealt in commodities as various as raw wool, woolen cloth, silks, alum, dyestuffs, spices, olive oil, citrus fruits, raw cotton, gold thread, and much else besides.

But in diversifying his business the typical merchant went far beyond simply trading in numerous commodities. The very concept of "merchant" was very different in the sixteenth century from what it is today. We tend to separate industrial, commercial, and financial enterprises and to understand by "merchant" solely a man engaged in trade, commonly retail trade. Few Renaissance merchants engaged in retail trade; that was left to shopkeepers. A merchant occasionally restricted himself to buying and selling on the international market, but such specialization was rare. More often he was also a money changer, and sometimes he was an international banker; he was involved in the economics and problems of transportation; he was an insurance broker; he was an industrialist, large or small; he invested in both urban and rural real estate. In its medieval and early modern usage the word "merchant" implied all of these activities, singly or in combination. The Medici, for example, were merchants. In addition to their purely commercial business they conducted all manner of banking operations, manufactured woolen cloth and silk, and for a time managed the papal alum mines at Tolfa. The Fuggers too were merchants, and the range of their business is even more instructive. The first Fugger came from the country to Augsburg, a free imperial city of southern Germany, in 1367. He was a weaver, but he traded too, and when he died, he left his heirs a modest inheritance. They continued in trade, dealing almost exclusively, like most Augsburg merchants, in the spices, silks, and woolens of the Venetian trade. But the family fortune was really made by the business genius of Jakob Fugger, who became a

Jakob Fugger. *Drawing by
Hans Holbein the Elder.
Kupferstichkabinett, Staat-
liche Museen Preussischer
Kulturbesitz, Berlin.*

merchant in 1478 at the age of nineteen and died in 1525, the richest merchant-banker in Europe. He soon turned from the solid Venetian trade to the risky but more profitable fields of international finance, royal moneylending, and mining. Through his loans to Emperor Maximilian I and his grandson Charles V, he became the leading silver and copper merchant in Europe. Among the original Habsburg lands was the Tyrol—as we have seen, since the middle of the fifteenth century one of the principal regions on the continent producing silver, iron, and copper. The Habsburg ruler had important regalian rights in all the mineral wealth of his possessions. All silver mined in the Tyrol, for example, was taxed. The price of a mark of silver (280 grams) was fixed at eight florins. The producers deposited their silver with an officer of the crown and received five florins per mark; the ruler's profit was three florins. As security for his loans to Maximilian, Jakob Fugger got an option on virtually the entire silver production of the Tyrol. He paid the producers, collected and pocketed the tax to the amount of the principal of the loan and the interest on it, and distributed the silver, at a further profit, on the international market.

But the great enterprise of Fugger's life was Hungarian copper. Here, in the rich mining region centered at Neusohl, on the southern slopes of the Carpathians in what is now Slovakia, Jakob and his successors were not only traders but industrial capitalists as well. The firm owned mines and built copper foundries, forges, and refineries. By controlling both Tyrolese and Hungarian production, Fugger cornered a major portion of Europe's copper supply. But this was not all. The Fuggers were papal bankers for much of Germany, Scandinavia, Poland, and Hungary. They managed the sale of the indulgence that was to provoke the anger of Martin Luther. They amassed extensive landed property. In return for further loans, Charles V turned over to them the revenues of the three orders of Spanish chivalry—income derived from enterprises which included mercury mines at Almaden and the wheat and wool of the orders' vast *latifundia*, or landed estates. Their profits on these varied activities had averaged over 50 per cent in each year between 1511 and 1527. To be sure, only the largest companies could imitate the bravura of the Fuggers. But even modest merchants, as a matter of principle and universal practice, responded with unspecialized interest to any chance for profit, whether it happened to be commercial, financial, or industrial.

THE DEVELOPMENT OF INDUSTRIAL CAPITALISM

In his manufacturing undertakings the merchant was becoming an industrial capitalist.

Definitions of capitalism are legion. Most of them are correct; very few are useful. It is correct, for example, to say that capitalism is an economic system which uses capital. It is also correct to define the goal of the system as profit. But since every economic system in every period of history and in every part of the world has involved the use of capital and the pursuit of profits, these definitions are not useful analytical tools. Nor is it particularly useful to call a society capitalistic because some of its members trade or engage in banking operations. Commerce, too, is as old as written records and so is lending and borrowing money, with or without interest. None of these definitions allows us to distinguish among the different forms European economic organization has taken in various historical periods or to distinguish the peculiarities of European economic arrangements from those of non-European cultures. Indeed, they discourage differentiation, periodization, and analysis.

A more fruitful approach is to narrow the meaning of "capitalism," to associate it primarily with industrial production, to understand it as a mode of industrial production—a particular way of producing goods—and to define it by contrasting it with the craft mode of production.

Craft production has dominated every human society except that of the modern West. A typical craftsman is the shoemaker. He buys his own raw material. He makes shoes in his own shop with his own tools. He himself sells the product of his labor to the consumer. He is economically independent and holds each thread of his enterprise in his own hands. The capitalist mode of production splits the single class of artisans into two distinct social groups: entrepreneurs, or capitalists, on the one hand, and wage workers on the other. The capitalist owns and controls the capital invested in the business. He owns the raw material, and owns and markets the final product. He owns the means of production—the plant and the tools. With the help of managers he supervises all stages of production. The worker is economically dependent; he owns only his labor, which he sells to the capitalist in exchange for wages. Capitalism is the form of industrial organization in which this split between the owners of capital and the owners of labor dominates the productive process. The direction of industrial change between 1460 and 1560 was from the craft mode of production to the capitalist mode of production. But in 1500 capitalist production, at least in its pure form, was still extremely rare. Perhaps the organization of capital and labor closest to it was the Venetian Arsenal. The Arsenal built, repaired, and equipped the warships of the Venetian navy. In 1540 it covered sixty acres of land and water, employed well over a thousand workers, and represented, for the time, an enormous investment. It was probably the largest industrial establishment in Europe before 1560. The ship carpenters and caulkers, the sailmakers, pulleymakers, and ironsmiths employed by the Arsenal worked by the piece or by the day under the supervision of foremen. All the employees were wage workers, and the distinction between master craftsmen and apprentices was hardly more than one of wages. The employer owned the capital invested in the enterprise and controlled the whole process of production. The employer, however, was the Venetian state, not a private capitalist. The government fixed wages and hours. Workers considered the obligation to work in the Arsenal a burden to be avoided if possible, and labor had to be conscripted as for a modern army. It is characteristic of the early modern period that until far into the seventeenth century the best examples of large-scale industrial organization were state-owned factories producing war materiel, enterprises rather closer to the military state factories of the later Roman Empire than to the automobile plants of today. This situation suggests that only governments had the capital necessary to finance the largest undertakings and the coercive power necessary to recruit and control the great number of workers they required. In large-scale industry, state capitalism preceded private capitalism, just as national regulation of industry preceded *laissez-faire*.

The Venetian Arsenal represents one extreme among the various forms of industrial organization in existence during the Renaissance. An independent craftsman, perhaps a shoemaker working in a small cathedral town in the north of France, represents the other. Although craft production in its pure form was less common in 1500 than it had been, say, in the thirteenth century, it remained a very widespread, possibly the most widespread, European industrial type. Tailors, glovemakers, and hatters, like shoemakers, were in most places independent artisans. So were cutlers and coopers, bakers and woodcarvers. They produced for a local market and rarely had more than one or two assistants. Usually they belonged to craft guilds, which set standards of quality, supervised the training of apprentices, and limited competition. Their horizon was limited to the town they lived and worked in. The unit of production was the patriarchal family. Their mentality was that of the shop, the guildhall, and the parish church—traditional, conformist, and petty. Their pride was their independence. They were men of modest property who did not sell their labor to others.

Between the military state factory and the independent artisan stretched a wide variety of industrial types. Three of these intermediate types are of special interest. Two of them had already become important during the later Middle Ages and remained common in the sixteenth century: first, the small industrial enterprise owned by an independent craftsman who, through the gradual freezing of the vertical mobility of the medieval craft guild, had himself become a small-scale industrial capitalist; and second, the larger industrial enterprise, generally for the production of textiles, organized according to the putting-out system and controlled by a merchant who had reduced the master craftsmen in his employ to varying degrees of economic dependence. Both types were located within the walls of towns and were subject to municipal regulation. Both combined elements of craft production and of capitalist production, but craft elements predominated. The particular contribution of the sixteenth century to the development of industrial capitalism was a third transitional combination of craft and capitalist production: a rural putting-out system located outside the walls of towns, beyond the reach of municipal control and regulation. In this type of production, capitalist elements predominated.

In the high Middle Ages the craft guild had been a flexible institution. The master craftsmen who were its members trained apprentices in their domestic workshops. They also employed journeymen, young men who were trained artisans but were not yet ready to set up shop for themselves. The passage from apprenticeship to mastership was regulated but smooth. The average apprentice could look forward to becoming a journeyman and then an independent master craftsman. But increasingly, after 1300, the masters thwarted this expectation. In various ways, especially in crafts where equipment was expensive, they tended to make themselves a hereditary group. In many trades the sons of masters were given special privileges. Guilds raised their standards for the masterwork that every journeyman had to finish as a demonstration of his skill in order to qualify as a master; its production became more and more complicated, time-consuming, and costly. Very high fees were set for those who wanted to become masters. As the mastership became hereditary, so did the condition of the journeyman. A growing number of trained artisans could no longer look forward to becoming masters. Journeymen were being transformed from potentially independent craftsmen into the paid workers of masters who had themselves become small-scale industrial capitalists.

The result was a pronounced class tension in many cities in the first half of the sixteenth century. As the old patriarchal relationship between master and journeyman dissolved, journeymen resisted the exploitation inseparable from their new position in the productive process. They fought for higher wages, better food, shorter hours, and holidays. They went out on strike. In Germany they organized *Brüderschaften* ("brotherhoods"), rudimentary labor unions, and kept in contact with unions of the same trade in other localities. About 1500, when the journeyman tinsmiths in Nuremberg found that the masters of the guild had reduced their wages, they struck and left the city, and through the influence of their union no one was allowed to take their places. In 1503 the journeyman tailors struck in Wesel, on the Rhine, demanding higher wages and better diet and maintaining that "those who work the most should get the most." The masters, on their side, organized against the workers. When the journeyman tailors struck in Mainz, they were fired, and in 1505 the master tailors of Mainz called a meeting of the master tailors of twenty-one Rhineland cities to consider the interest of their trade and the best means of treating with the workmen. They agreed that they would not employ a journeyman who had struck against another master, that a master should not be obliged to give his journeyman more than one helping of meat in the evening, that wine must never be expected in the evening, and at other times must never consist of more than "a small half jug," terms which remind us that the relations between employer and employees in these small businesses were closer to those between a Victorian housewife and her maids than to the struggle between capital and labor in modern industry. Yet there is evidence of really bitter antagonism too. In Lyons and Paris strikes by printing workers occasionally erupted in open violence. The masters won (they always did in this period); and the royal edict issued at Villers-Cotterêts in 1539, forbade "all craftsmen to form brotherhoods or unions, large or small, for any purpose whatever." Royal and municipal authorities considered strikes and unions seditious and regularly suppressed them.

The second form of industrial organization common in the late Middle Ages and combining elements of both craft and capitalist production was the urban putting-out system; it, too, retained much of its former vigor in the early modern period. Textile enterprises producing for the export market, especially numerous in Flanders and in northern and central Italy, normally used this system. Since clothmaking probably employed half as many people as all other industries combined, its predominant form of

A water-powered throwing mill. *Engraving from a volume by Vittorio Zonca published in 1607. The machine was introduced in the thirteenth century and was used throughout the Renaissance to twist filaments of raw silk into long threads that were strong enough to weave. Master throwers owned the machine, employed eight or nine journeymen, and worked for the silk merchant on a piece basis.*

organization is of special importance. The Italian silk industry is a clear illustration of the type.

Silk manufacture had been introduced into Europe by the Arabs as early as the tenth century. Until the middle of the fourteenth century, by far the most important European center of silk production was the Tuscan city of Lucca. In the later fourteenth century the industry began to spread all over Italy, so that by 1450 Florence, Milan, Venice, Bologna, Genoa, and Naples were all major centers of silk production. Between 1450 and 1550 the industry's geographical spread continued, over the Alps to Germany and to France and Spain.

In spite of competition from abroad, Italy remained supreme in the manufacture of silk of the first quality. Italians manufactured sheer veils, heavy patterned silks, and brocade velvets with pile of two or three heights, sometimes in one color with delicate traceries, sometimes in three, four, or five colors, and shot with gold and silver thread. The designs of these fabrics make a lively story of cultural interpenetration. They range from Arabic and Byzantine motifs to lotus plants, clouds, and rays of light adapted from Chinese silks, from feudal castles and hunting scenes in the early period to the classical garlands, vine leaves, and grotesques of the sixteenth century. The invariable effect was one of richness, color, and magnificence. This suggests the first important fact about the industry. It was a luxury industry, producing fabrics, wall hangings, banners, and altar cloths for the rich. And it was an export industry, with a clientele in all parts of Europe.

Similarly, its raw materials could not be got locally. In the thirteenth century most of the raw silk used in Lucca was imported from the region of the Caspian Sea; some came from even farther—from Persia and Turkestan. Starting in the fifteenth century, raw silk was produced in western Europe, some in Spain, but most in Italy itself. So rapid was the spread of silkworm cultivation in Sicily and Calabria, Tuscany, Lombardy, and Savoy that by 1550 Italy was self-sufficient in raw silk. But even in the sixteenth century the local manufacturer of Naples or Bologna had to import his raw materials from a certain distance. Moreover, raw silk and the other materials used in the industry—gold and silver thread, good dyes, and alum, the fixative that made the colors permanent—were expensive and required a considerable capital outlay.

The facts that silks were sold on the international market and that the raw materials needed in their manufacture were expensive and not easily obtainable locally opened the industry to control by merchant bankers. The typical Italian silk firm was a family partnership. The head of the firm was a merchant. He and his partners supplied the capital, bought raw silk from merchants who had imported it from the Levant or from another part of Italy and sold the final product through his agents in London, Paris, Augsburg, or Antwerp. This commercial activity determined his relation to the artisans who actually made the cloth. The dyers, for example, worked in small shops and used fairly expensive vats owned by themselves, and they had their own guild. To this extent they remained independent masters. On the other hand, they did not own the silk they dyed, and they performed only a single task in a complex industrial process over which they had no control. The independence of the weavers, who also had their own guild, was similarly limited. Weaving the complex patterns of a luxury silk required great skill and experience and complicated machines—drawlooms—which were expensive to buy and maintain. The weaver's skill and his ownership of his loom solidified his bargaining position. Yet like the dyer he was not an independent craftsman in the full sense, for he did not own the silk thread with which he worked, or sell the fabrics he wove. Both were dependent on the merchant capitalist, who provided and owned the raw material, marketed the final product, and in a loose way supervised the whole process of production. Master craftsmen were becoming pieceworkers. Merchants were becoming industrial capitalists.

Between 1460 and 1560 the dependence of artisan on capitalist in the textile industries increased, and a new type of industrial organization emerged that was to be typical of the early modern period—the *rural* putting-out system. The entrepreneur tightened his hold on the process of production by moving his operations from the city to the countryside. All over Europe a quite new kind of industrial center grew up, unwalled, straggling haphazardly over the countryside from a central marketplace. Enterprising capitalists in the southern Netherlands met the competition of English cloth by importing Spanish wool (by 1536 over thirty thousand bales a year arrived in Antwerp from Spain); making cheaper, lighter fabrics, serges, and worsteds; and locating the new industry in agricultural areas around Ypres and Armentières. Petty towns in Tuscany challenged the old monopoly of Florence, and rural industry spread through the villages of Lombardy and the Venetian mainland. Rouen merchants deserted the city in order to hire cheaply the spare time of peasants and shepherds and their wives and children. The same thing happened in the Netherlands, Germany, and England.

In England the principal cloth-producing regions were Yorkshire, East Anglia, the Cotswolds, and the area along the Avon. The manufacturer of woolen cloth was called a clothier. He was an economic individualist of a novel type. In the rural village where he had his headquarters he was free of municipal taxes and the burdens of public office, unhampered by the old guild and municipal regulations which formerly limited the number of employees he could hire and minutely regulated the quality of his materials and the nature of his manufacturing methods. Here he could hire or contract with whom he pleased, offer whatever wages or piece rates would secure him workers, order their work in any way he liked. He determined the quality, quantity, and price of what he produced in response to the varying demands of the international market. He was free to experiment with machines (such as the gig mill, which mechanized part of the finishing process) in order to reduce labor costs and increase production. The organization of his enterprise marked the beginning of a new stage in the development of capitalist industry.

Basically, the industrial organization of the English sixteenth-century clothier remained the putting-out system, but the system was profoundly modified by its rural location. His new freedom of enterprise and of risk allowed the clothier to extend still further his ownership of the means of production and to group workers in "manufactories," where he could combine under one roof several stages of production that had been kept apart in the past. Thus the large clothier commonly owned a dyehouse where wage workers dyed the wool under his close supervision. He owned a fulling mill, and workshops for stretching and pressing the cloth.

Spinning and weaving were more often put out to large numbers of rural craftsmen working in their own homes. Spinning was very widely distributed over the countryside and was done mostly by women, on a part-time basis. The relation of clothier to spinner was what it had been in the past: the women worked in their own homes and with their own tools on a piece basis for an entrepreneur who owned the raw wool and the finished yarn. On the other hand, important changes were taking place in the relation of clothier to weaver. Often the rural craftsmen could not afford the capital outlay for a loom, and it became common practice for the clothier to own looms and rent them to the weavers. Sometimes the clothier owned a string of houses along a village street and rented these to the weavers as well, obtaining the further advantage of being able to supervise their work more closely. Less often, clothiers concentrated the weaving under a single roof, against the strenuous opposition of the weavers, who were rightly afraid of losing entirely their already limited independence. Some "factories" of this kind employed several hundred workers. Wage work, clearly, was becoming much more common than it had been in the old textile towns, and the separation of capital and labor was becoming more marked. The urban putting-out system was still closer to craft production than to capitalist production; but in the rural putting-out system of the sixteenth century, the capitalist mode of production predominated.

Yet equally characteristic of the age is the still bewildering variety of the ways in which men produced the articles they needed. The complex shift from craft to capitalist production stretched from the twelfth century to the Industrial Revolution and beyond. The rate of change varied enormously from industry to industry, from region to region, and from period to period. In the sixteenth century, as in any other, there existed a spectrum of industrial types, each one, whether traditional or novel, uniquely important to the men whose working lives were organized by it. The expansive years between 1460 and 1560 are particularly important because the balance of tradition and innovation shifted gradually but decisively. A halfway mark in the long transition from craft to capitalist production was reached and passed. Independent craftsmen remained common. Firms were still small; very few employed more than a dozen men. Most men worked at home with their own tools. An artisanal spirit pervaded industry and gave its products the varied individuality of the skillfully handmade. But by 1560 the cleavage between capital and labor, which is—like scientific method and an art based on perspective—a unique peculiarity of western civilization, was firmly and widely established in many parts of industrial Europe.

Rising prices widened the cleavage. Wages lagged behind prices. By 1560, real wages in Spain, France, England, and Germany had fallen from 20 per cent to 50 per cent below their average levels between 1450 and

1500. For wage workers the price rise meant economic regression and a serious fall in living standards. For manufacturers, however, higher prices meant larger profits, and the price revolution was a profit inflation from which they emerged with a larger share of the community's wealth than ever before.

USURY, MORALITY, AND SOCIAL CLIMBING

Grown rich in commerce, banking, and industry, the sixteenth-century merchant-capitalist was a man of individuality and ambitious resource. His life was motivated by a rational search for profit. He operated, however, in a society whose ideals were overwhelmingly religious and aristocratic. He could justify his way of life only in opposition to a traditional clerical distrust and a traditional aristocratic disdain. Any elite develops values that reflect its mode of life and legitimize its interests and ambitions. A gradual secularization of the economic ethic of the churches and the creation of a bourgeois morality performed this value-making function for the merchant class. The process began in Italy about 1400, the work of liberal scholastic theologians and civic humanists; it was continued in northern Europe by bourgeois publicists, Calvinist divines, and the Jesuit order.

Medieval theologians had commonly respected poverty, emphasized the "glittering wretchedness" of wealth, and distrusted merchants. St. Thomas Aquinas (*c.* 1225–1274) expressed perfectly the prejudices of peasants, artisans, and aristocrats when he wrote, "Properly speaking, commerce is the exchange of money for goods with a view to gain.... It is justly condemned, for it encourages the passion for money [*cupiditas lucri*], which is without limit and almost infinite. Therefore commerce, considered in itself, has something shameful about it."[1] On this conviction, and on the further assumption that business behavior should obey the same Christian rules as private morality, clerical theorists had built a comprehensive economic ethic. Its most striking prohibition was that of usury, which was defined as profit on a loan and forbidden on the ground that to lend money to a man who needs it is a charitable act, while to demand payment for the loan is grasping and unchristian.

To traditional ideals of poverty, Italian merchants and their humanist apologists opposed a positive evaluation of wealth. They quoted Aristotle's *Ethics* and *Politics*, in which wealth is considered a necessary aid to the development of a moral life and a necessary condition for happiness. The proper life for man, they said, is action in the world, not solitary contemplation; and all things are good that increase his power to act for the good of himself, his family, his friends, and his country. Poverty leads not to

[1]*Summa theologiae*, IIa IIae, quaest. LXXVII, art. 4.

virtue, but to pettiness; it restricts the possibility of active virtue; it sordidly limits the mind instead of broadening it. Honorable riches, on the other hand, guarantee freedom of choice and give substance to family and civic responsibility.

Nevertheless, few merchants questioned the Church's prohibition of usury. To have done so openly would have exposed them to serious charges in the ecclesiastical courts. Nor must one exaggerate the economic importance of this prohibition. Usury was not identical with interest, which theologians and canonists defined as "compensation due in justice to a creditor because of loss he has incurred through lending."[2] If a man, it was argued, suffered a loss because he lent money to another, then he might justly claim payment in addition to the principal. By the middle of the fifteenth century, moreover, the progress of financial and commercial capitalism had forced the common acceptance of a further title to interest, called *lucrum cessans,* or profit ceasing. When a man lent money to another, it was now often said, he was kept from using it advantageously for his own benefit. He was therefore justly entitled to interest payments which would compensate him for that loss. A loan purely for profit was usury and continued to be forbidden; it remained legally prohibited in France until the French Revolution. But during the late fifteenth century and the sixteenth century, exceptions and reinterpretations proliferated to the point where interest on loans came to be considered normal and usury the exception. Nobles and widows deposited money with merchant bankers and were regularly paid 5 to 12 per cent on their demand deposits, although merchants still preferred to call this payment a "gift," "reward," or "profit," rather than interest. Merchants regularly operated on credit in international commerce. But these credit transactions were conveniently described as simple sales instead of loans. Bankers lent money to princes, and citizens bought interest-paying government bonds. These practices, like prostitution, were considered necessary in order to avoid evils even worse. A few merchants had sufficiently tender consciences on their deathbeds to instruct their heirs to restore to borrowers the interest on loans they had made for business purposes. But in the end, common practice secularized the problem. By 1560 capitalist interests were bluntly supported by the most influential theologian of the age, John Calvin. Sucking the substance of a poor man without risk to oneself is wicked usury. But on loans to the rich or to businessmen a lender's profit is no worse than a manufacturer's or shopkeeper's profit on a sale. A parson knows little about business. So let the believing banker's conscience be his guide. A few years later, the second Congregation of the Jesuit order approved 5-per-cent interest on loans for business purposes, practically

---

[2] Quoted by John Noonan, *The Scholastic Analysis of Usury* (Cambridge, Mass., 1957), p. 105.

ending the application of usury theory to business finance. The competitive individualism of the merchant had escaped ecclesiastical control and reoriented the ethical teaching of the churches.

The merchant found it more difficult to disarm aristocratic snobbery than clerical suspicion. Everywhere, the nobility retained prestige and status. Nowhere (until the nineteenth century) did manufacture and trade confer the highest social position. In a rigidly inegalitarian society, merchants occupied an honorable but median position, with unskilled manual laborers, peasants, artisans, and retail traders below them, and *gentilshommes*, seigneurs, and princes above them. They agreed with Cicero that shopkeeping was "sordid," but they could not agree with those Spanish nobles who remarked to a Florentine ambassador in 1513 that trade in general was "shameful." So a novel theoretical defense of their own merits, virtues, and achievements was from the beginning inseparable from social climbing in practice.

A popular genre of humanist ethical literature in the Renaissance was the treatise *De vera nobilitate* ("of true nobility") which put true nobility in virtue and personal merit rather than in birth and taught that virtue is acquired, not inherited. The popularity of such works should probably be expained by their usefulness in legitimizing bourgeois pretensions. The idea of virtue, moreover, was itself given a positive middle-class content. In Italy in the fifteenth century, and north of the Alps in the sixteenth, there emerged clearly for the first time the attitudes which we lump together as "bourgeois morality," attitudes which contrasted sharply with aristocratic values. A noble, insofar as he could be precisely defined at all in the sixteenth century, was "a man who lived nobly." Fundamentally, to live nobly meant to fight and not to work. Above all, the noble was thought to derogate from his nobility (this was generally true in northern continental Europe, much less so in Italy and in England) if he engaged in trade. In contrast, bourgeois morality attributed positive value to productive work. The great sin became idleness rather than dishonor. Again, nobility obliged the aristocrat to maintain a certain standard of expenditure and consumption. If his income was insufficient, he borrowed. The bourgeois, however, practiced a willing thrift and was persuaded that he should spend less than he earned. He was willing to live ascetically so that his enterprise might prosper. By insisting that spiritual athletes live in the world rather than in monasteries, Protestantism reinforced this tendency and gave the individual new incentives to plan his life rationally in the pursuit of a worldly success, which was increasingly taken to be the sign of spiritual health. The noble might squander wealth in the idle enjoyment of what it could buy. The bourgeois found his identity in a very different ideal: constant productive activity and the reinvestment of its fruits.

Merchants were pleased to know that true nobility consisted in personal merit and that willing thrift could be a moral imperative—as long as they

The Classes of Men. *Woodcut by Hans Weiditz made about 1530. The European social hierarchy is represented as a tree. Entwined among the roots, two peasants; above them, journeymen, artisans, and merchants; next, bishops and cardinals, nobles and princes; then pope, emperor, and kings; at the very top, again two peasants, a reminder that they fed everybody else.*

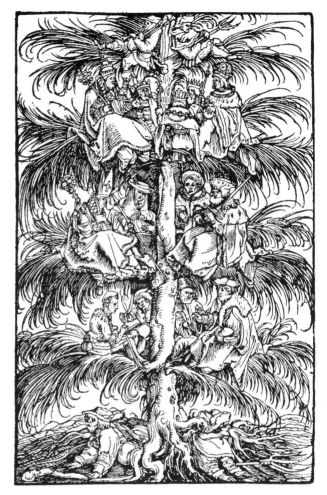

were merchants. In practice, however, bourgeois virtue rarely resisted the attraction of aristocratic status; and the ambition of most merchants was to exchange the social ambiguities of trade for the universally recognized prestige of nobility. The sixteenth-century merchant class was therefore extremely fluid, with trade and industry serving as the chief means by which men moved up in the social hierarchy. The kind of social mobility which had been assured by the Church during the Middle Ages (when the son of a peasant might reasonably hope to be pope) in the Renaissance was assured by mercantile enterprise. To be a noble, craftsman, or peasant was a largely hereditary condition; but few bourgeois fortunes remained invested in trade or industry for more than two or three generations. Normally, the grandson of a successful merchant abandoned the risky enterprises in which the family had made its money and invested more safely. He put his money into land, urban real estate, and government bonds. He bought a seigneury, a title and a government office. He gave his sons a humanistic education. By imitating aristocratic manners and investments, by intermarriage, simply by living "nobly," the bourgeois family displaced or merged with the older nobility.

The phenomenon was universal. In Venice in the sixteenth century the ruling class as a whole was gradually transformed from a purely mercantile oligarchy into an aristocracy whose wealth was in land and government bonds. By the early seventeenth century, the Fuggers were settled on their Swabian estates as imperial counts. In England, men of talent and modest origins made fortunes as clothiers or in the wholesale trade of woolen cloth. Their sons held administrative offices and began to buy up land in their home counties. The grandsons settled on these estates and founded gentry families. The pattern was similar in France. In one case, typical of many, a merchant in a small provincial town bought an office for his son in the royal financial administration. The son made a fortune in government finance and bought land and titles. His sons made brilliant careers in the magistracy and in the Church. In 1600, the family hired a genealogist, who traced their origins to a twelfth-century feudal baron. Success in trade and industry, in short, was the elevator which lifted the most enterprising members of lower social groups into the aristocracy. The process might take several generations; but great merchants, constantly recruited from below, ultimately gravitated to the land. Here they assumed the privileges and authority of nobles. At the same time they took on the economic problems, and opportunities, of agrarian landlords.

LANDLORD AND TENANT

During the Renaissance, as in the Middle Ages, by far the greatest part of human energy had to be devoted to producing food, and men who lived in towns were a small minority in an overwhelmingly agrarian population. The relative size of rural and urban populations naturally varied from region to region. But even in the most urbanized and economically most sophisticated parts of Europe—central and northern Italy, southern Germany, and Flanders and Brabant—over three quarters of the inhabitants were peasants. The progress of industrial capitalism, the expansion of trade, and the widening of the organized money market affected them profoundly.

Medieval agrarian society had been in flux since the early thirteenth century. The mold of manorialism, which bound serfs to work the demesne, or home farm, of their lord in exchange for protection and the hereditary use of a portion of the estate, began to loosen. As the use of money became commonplace and an exchange economy developed, lords wished and needed to buy more commodities from merchants and craftsmen than in the past. They therefore found it advantageous to commute to money some of the traditional dues and services owed them. In order to increase their cash income still more, many landlords abandoned direct exploitation of the demesne and leased it, like the rest of the estate. Where demesne farming declined, serfdom lost its economic importance. For a fee, lords were willing to free their peasants of the dishonorable ties of personal dependence; and the manorial contracts, which had promised personal protection and a subsistence living in return for labor service, gave way to rent contracts. Very gradually, economic individualism began to insinuate itself into rural life.

In the fourteenth century, pestilence and war reinforced the disrupting influences of the money economy on the manorial structure of rural life. The Black Death of 1348–1349 cut the rural population of Europe to a half, in some regions even to a third, of its former level. Wages rose, and landlords were forced to compete for new tenants. In France the devastations of the Hundred Years' War had analogous consequences. By its end the French countryside was ravished, the peasantry decimated and pauperized. Whole regions were desolate and almost abandoned. Powerful nobles reclaimed them, but again the peasants who remained were in a stronger bargaining position than their predecessors had been. The scarcity of labor hastened the abandonment of demesne farming, the commutation of labor service, and the replacement of traditional tenures by rent contracts. Manumissions multiplied, and serfdom disappeared in many parts of western Europe.

Emancipation did not necessarily benefit the peasantry economically. Nor was renting out his whole estate the only means by which a landlord could adjust to a money economy and to the scarcity of labor. In areas where crops like grain or wool could be raised on a large scale and readily sold for cash on the international market, landlords were tempted to evict their tenants and farm the whole estate themselves commercially with hired labor.

The expansion of trade between 1460 and 1560 sharpened this temptation and increased the landlords' freedom of maneuver. Agriculture shared in the general prosperity of the century. Production increased notably in many areas, and opportunities for agricultural profit multiplied as communications improved and a dense network of trade in agricultural produce covered the continent. Grain moved from Sicily to Naples, Rome, and Venice; from eastern Germany and Poland to Scandinavia, the Netherlands, and the Rhineland; from northern Europe to the Mediterranean. Ever more rapidly, the land and its products were sucked into the mainstream of an expanding exchange economy and the subsistence agriculture of the past was transformed into production for near or distant markets. What became decisive for the economic relations between landlord and peasant was precisely whether the market was near or distant,

Peasants. *Drawings by Hieronymus Bosch, about 1558. Kupferstichkabinett, Staatliche Museen Preussischer Kulturbesitz, Berlin.*

local or international. Where the market was exclusively local, agriculture remained of necessity unspecialized and landlords preferred to rent out their whole estates to tenant farmers because this was the easiest way to assure themselves a money income. Under these circumstances, the manorial lord became a rentier. Where landlords could grow wool or grain for export, they preferred to assert their absolute ownership of the estate and engage in capitalist agriculture, the rational exploitation of a large holding to produce a cash crop for commercial profit. Under these circumstances, the manorial lord became a capitalist farmer.

The transformation of the manorial lord into a capitalist farmer is well illustrated by the agricultural histories of the English Midlands and of Germany east of the Elbe River. The decisive factor in England was the expanding manufacture of woolen textiles and the industry's growing demand for wool. This demand was a powerful inducement for landlords to increase their revenues and guard against social and economic decline by raising sheep. To raise sheep they needed a large acreage under their direct control. They got it by a variety of processes called *enclosures*: taking over the common lands of the villages, consolidating scattered strips into compact properties and fencing them with hawthorn hedges, absorbing or "engrossing" small holdings into large farms, and converting arable land into pasture. They then evicted their customary tenants and proceeded to cultivate their holdings themselves. As the great sociologist

Max Weber put it, the "peasants were freed from the land and the land from the peasants." Enclosures, ran a popular proverb, "make fat beasts and lean poor people." The fat beasts were the prospering landlords, while many peasants lost their land and became agricultural laborers.

East of the Elbe, the economic basis of the great landed estates which were in the sole control of the lords included three main elements: rising grain prices (by 1600 three to four times as high as they had been at the beginning of the sixteenth century), the growing demand for eastern grain in western Europe, and the cheap and easy transportation of this grain from grower to market which was provided by the lake and river systems of northeastern Germany. But whereas sheep farming required little manpower and the enclosures therefore led to the creation of a small free agricultural proletariat (ready and anxious to spin and weave for the clothier), the raising of grain required a great deal of labor, and the revival of demesne farming in Pomerania, Brandenberg, and Prussia, (and indeed in Poland and other parts of eastern Europe as well) was accompanied by a growing subjection of the peasantry. Aristocratic landlords, or *Junkers*, grew rich and enlarged their demesnes by buying out or evicting the peasants, and after the Reformation, by appropriating monastic and parish lands. The peasants, who had been freer than those of western Europe in the high Middle Ages, were reduced to serfdom, tied to the land, and burdened with new dues and increased labor services. The great dividing line of the Elbe solidified permanently in the sixteenth century. In the middle of the nineteenth century it still separated a western Europe of small independent peasant proprietors (with the exception of England, where the enclosure movement, reaching its climax in the eighteenth century, had created individual holdings often larger than those of Prussian *Junkers*) and an eastern Europe of serfs and landed magnates. Today it divides communist and capitalist Europe.

On the other hand, in France, much of western Germany, Switzerland, the Low Countries, northern Italy, and the south of England—in the cultural heart of Europe, in short—most landlords secured a money income after 1500 by renting, and agriculture was carried on by peasant farmers working small plots. Landlord and tenant shared proprietary rights in the soil. The old burdens of dependent status were attached to the land rather than to persons, and the peasant was generally a free man. In return for his use of the land he paid rent and supplied equivalents, either in kind or in money, for the traditional manorial services; and the relative prosperity of the landlord and tenant was determined by the movement of prices and rents.

Some landlords found it possible to raise rents at will (a practice tenants called "racking" rents). They thus diverted the bulk of their tenants' profits to themselves, and did well. Many French landlords introduced a short-term contractual lease called *métayage*, similar to the *mezzadria* system common in Italy, especially in Tuscany, since the fourteenth century. Instead of paying an annual rent, peasants paid a fixed proportion of their yearly crop, usually half. This system too increased the landlord's proprietary right in the land and brought him a significant share in the benefits of rising agricultural prices. On the other hand, the long-term leases described by an English observer in 1549 benefited tenants rather than landlords: "The most part of the landes of this Realme," he wrote, "stand yet at the old Rent," unexpired leases cannot be enhanced, though the owners would, and despite raising rents as leases expire, the landlord cannot expect a third of his land to come to his disposition during his lifetime or even during that of his son.[3] In this instance real rents lagged well behind more rapidly rising prices, at least in the short run. Finally, in certain areas, especially in parts of France and western Germany, peasant tenure was heritable. The tenant could farm his holding any way he liked, sell it, divide it among his heirs. He could sell his surplus produce freely on the market. Commuted payments were often fixed in customary law. In such circumstances real rents fell, the landlord was caught in an inflationary vice, and it was the tenant who profited from rising prices.

The aggressive instability of the sixteenth-century nobility suggests that many smaller landlords were caught in the squeeze of rising prices and falling real rents. Hoping to recoup their losses with ransoms, booty, and confiscated land in conquered territory, nobles threw their weight behind royal and princely wars abroad. The pressure exerted by the French nobility was a major force behind the aggressive attacks on Italy that began in 1494. The Spanish nobility had lived for centuries on the reconquest of the peninsula from the Moors. The fall of Granada in 1492 ended the activity and plunder of that long crusade. The arrogant *hidalgos*, or lesser nobles, with small property then turned with alacrity to lead and exploit colonial expansion in the New World. By sailing west, Cortes, an indigent gentleman nourished on romances of chivalry, got a marquisate and vast estates in Mexico. In a pungent autobiography, the German knight Götz von Berlichingen (1480–1562) described how he pillaged peasants and ransomed merchants. Nobles pressured the Church, trying to tap its resources by installing their relatives in lucrative ecclesiastical positions. They pressured their tenants. Like kings, the nobles ultimately resorted to borrowing. But unlike kings, they could not repudiate their debts with impunity, and as their indebtedness grew, they were forced to mortgage and then sell their land. This is when climbing merchants bought it, seizing the opportunity to invest commercial and industrial profit in social prestige and real estate. Most noticeably in France and

---

[3]*A Discourse of the Common Weal of This Realm of England*, ed. by Elizabeth Lamond (Cambridge, Eng., 1893), pp. 19, 38–39.

England, a "new" aristocracy grew up beside the old, mercantile in origin, efficient agricultural managers, adaptable to changing economic circumstance. The bitter resentment of the old nobility exploded in the civil and religious wars of the second half of the century. A lively chronicler of the court of Catherine de Medici, Pierre de Brantôme (c. 1540–1614), writing during the last years of the French religious wars, isolated its role with admirable intelligence: "Rich merchants, usurers, bankers, and other money-grabbers have stolen everything. Gentlemen, having mortgaged or sold their property, can hardly find the wood to warm themselves. But this good civil war (this is what they call it) will put them on their feet again. The fine nobility of France will recover its own by the grace (or rather by the grease [the fat profit]) of this good civil war."

The economic condition of the peasantry was the mirror image of the economic condition of the land-owning aristocracy. Where landlords prospered—in Spain and Portugal, in southern Italy and Sicily, in parts of England, and east of the Elbe—peasants suffered. But from the Elbe to

A Country Wedding. Painting by Pieter Brueghel the Elder, about 1565. A glimpse of peasant life. The wedding feast takes place in a barn furnished with rural stick furniture and crude clay bowls and jugs. The food is bread, gruel, and beer; there is no meat. Kunsthistorisches Museum, Vienna.

the English Channel, from the Apennines to the North Sea, peasants were freer and more prosperous in the sixteenth century than they had been in the thirteenth. We should not be surprised that they nevertheless remained dissatisfied. Real misery more often deadens than sharpens discontent. It is the class on the economic upgrade that finds its burdens, though diminishing, most oppressive. Such a class was the sixteenth-century peasantry in the heart of Europe. Peasant income had risen. Peasants could sell their produce in a rapidly expanding market, while the payments they made their landlords declined in real value. What galled them was that peasant emancipation, in progress since the thirteenth century, stopped in the sixteenth. In an earlier age emancipation had benefited the landlords as much as if not more than, the peasantry. In the sixteenth century, under the pressure of rising prices and the increasing cost of living "nobly," landlords enforced every claim they still possessed and invaded peasant rights whenever circumstances allowed them to. In France, *banalités* survived: fees the peasants were forced to pay for the use of the mill, oven, and wine press, over which the lord had monopolistic control. Lords invaded the old commons of waste, forest, stream, and meadow, all traditionally open to peasant use. German peasants in the sixteenth century complained that "our lords have appropriated all the woods to themselves alone, and when the poor man needs any wood, he must buy it at double price," and that "they have taken over fishing, hunting, and grazing rights as well."[4] Where landlords successfully racked rents or introduced more favorable leases, like *métayage*, peasants actually lost ground. Finally, all peasants felt the sharper financial bite of their political rulers. In Germany, especially in the southwest, many large landlords were becoming the tiny sovereign princelings of their territories. As in much of France, tenures here had generally been hereditary and rents fixed. The new princelings restored the economic balance to their own favor by leveling new dues in the form of taxes, squeezing their tenants not as landlords but as tax collectors. In the larger states what was to be a fundamental maxim of taxation until the nineteenth century—that those who can least afford it should pay most—was already operative. The profit of the peasant became the resource of his king.

As a result, the sixteenth century was an age of permanent agrarian crisis. Where serfdom remained, it seemed a purely arbitrary bondage in a world where lack of personal freedom was no longer accompanied by any economic advantage. Free tenants resented all obligations and tried to escape the dues and services that landlords tried to enforce. Tension between landlord and peasant was endemic, and it occasionally erupted in open violence. There were minor movements in England, scattered risings

[4]Quoted by Günther Franz, *Der deutsche Bauernkrieg,* fourth ed. (Darmstadt, 1956), p. 124.

in France. In Germany there were eleven major peasant uprisings between the early fifteenth century and the great peasant revolt of 1525–1526. The peasants wistfully demanded a return to the good old days and the "good old law." Their mentality was conservative, profoundly religious, and utopian. They dreamed of freedom and a social life regulated by the precepts of the Gospel. Their attitude is perfectly reflected in a revolt of 1476 led by Hans Böhm (c. 1450–1476) the bagpiper of Niklashausen, known as the "holy youngster." He preached to immense crowds that he was going to make them glad with proclamations of the pure world of God. The kingdom of God, he cried, is at hand. When it comes there will be neither pope nor emperor, all class distinctions will be ended, all men will be free and equal, in bondage only to the law of brotherly love. "The princes, spiritual and lay, also the counts and knights are so rich that if all they have were shared by the community we should all have enough; and this must come to pass." Forest, water, meadows, and wastelands must be free for the use of all. It would come even to this, that princes and lords would have to work for daily wages.

The prosperity and dynamism of the European economy in the late fifteenth century and in the sixteenth century was thus inseparable from sharpening tension between landlord and tenant as well as between employer and worker. The fundamental causes of tension were structural changes in production and the organization of labor associated with the development of the capitalist mode of production in industry and, to a lesser extent, in agriculture. These changes produced a widening gap between capital and labor, rich and poor, and forced every group in the social hierarchy to adapt or suffer economic penalties. The price revolution aggravated the crisis. The results were so various as almost to defeat generalization, although certain tendencies seem reasonably clear. Merchant-bankers were coming to enjoy a larger share of wealth and economic power than in the past. Laborers, journeymen, and artisans did less well. In an inflationary period and a preindustrial, "underdeveloped" society, land remained the best and safest form of investment in the long run. For this reason the European nobility, sloughing off its weaker, incompetent members and constantly recruiting from below, did relatively well, and European society was as aristocratic in 1560 as it had been a century earlier. To be sure, the aristocrats paid a price. Gradually they forfeited political and military independence in return for tax exemptions and honorific privileges. Gradually they made service to their prince and state their principal profession, tailoring to this service their manners, mode of life, and education. These developments had important political and cultural repercussions. They form one strand in the intricate patterns of the emergence both of the sovereign territorial state and, equally powerfully though less obviously, of a lay culture based on a revived enthusiasm for classical literature.

CHAPTER 3

Renaissance Society and Humanist Culture

ON DECEMBER 10, 1513, Niccolò Machiavelli wrote a letter that has become famous. Exiled from Florence, he was living in reduced circumstances on a Tuscan farm. In the mornings, he told his friend, he hunted or snared thrushes, stopping occasionally to reread a few verses of Dante, Petrarch, Tibullus, or Ovid. After lunch he would go to the local inn and play dice with the yokels, only to taste again in their brutish company the "malign dregs" of his destiny.

But when evening comes [he continued] I return home and go into my library. At the door I take off my muddy everyday clothes. I dress myself as though I were about to appear before a royal court as a Florentine envoy. Then decently attired I enter the antique courts of the great men of antiquity. They receive me with friendship; from them I derive the nourishment which alone is mine and for which I was born. Without false shame I talk with them and ask them the causes of their actions; and their humanity is so great they answer me. For four long and happy hours I lose myself in them. I forget all my troubles; I am not afraid of poverty or death. I transform myself entirely in their likeness.[1]

Few texts express so movingly the Renaissance admiration for classical antiquity and the effort of many sixteenth-century men to pattern their lives on the image of man to be found in the Greek and Latin classics.

This is a *humanist* attitude. The noun *humanista* ("humanist"), is a Renaissance word, coined toward the end of the fifteenth century in Italy to designate members of a particular professional group: teachers of subjects variously described in the texts as *studia litterarum* ("literature"); *bonae artes, humanae artes, artes liberales* (the "good arts," "human arts," or "liberal arts"); or, most frequently and expressively, *studia humanitatis* (the "humanities"). *Humanitas*, from which "humanist" derives, is a classical word and a classical idea. Cicero used it to translate the Greek *paedeia* ("education" or "culture"). The second-century gram-

[1]*Lettere*, ed. by G. Lesca (Florence, 1929) pp. 88–90.

marian Aulus Gellius defined it as *eruditio institutioque in bonas artes* ("knowledge and instruction in the good arts"). Fourteenth- and fifteenth-century Italian humanists revived the word. "To each species of creatures," wrote one, "has been alloted a peculiar and instinctive gift. To horses galloping, to birds flying comes naturally. To man only is given the desire to learn. Hence what the Greeks called *paedeia* we call *studia humanitatis*. For learning and training in virtue are peculiar to man; therefore our forefathers called them *humanitas*, the pursuit of activities proper to mankind."[2] By "literature," humanists meant Greek and Roman literature; by "learning," classical learning; by "virtue," conduct modeled on the precepts of ancient moral philosophy. "Humanism" (a useful and legitimate word in spite of the fact that Germans coined it in the early nineteenth century) thus denotes something quite specific: an educational and cultural program based on the study of the classics and colored by the notion of human dignity implicit in *humanitas*.

Classical literature no longer commands the enthusiasm it aroused in Machiavelli and his contemporaries. We find it difficult to credit that a young French scholar should have spent three hours on his wedding day studying Greek or that when a visiting Italian lectured on the second satire of Juvenal at the University of Salamanca in 1488, the press of students and professors was so thick, their reluctance to leave the hall so great after two and a half hours, that the lecturer had to be passed bodily over the heads of the audience before he could go home. Yet similar anecdotes could be multiplied. Humanism was the most important single intellectual movement of the Renaissance. Its first great representatives were Francesco Petrarch (1304–1374) and Giovanni Boccaccio (1313–1375). In the fifteenth century a host of celebrated Italians enriched and popularized its program. By the beginning of the sixteenth century, humanist values had begun to refashion the intellectual life of northern Europe. John Colet (c. 1467–1519) and Sir Thomas More (1478–1535) propagated the new ideals in England; Jacques Lefèvre d'Étaples (c. 1460–1536) and Guillaume Budé (1468–1540), in France; Conrad Celtis (1459–1508) and Johann Reuchlin (1455–1522), in Germany. Towering above them all was Desiderius Erasmus (1469–1536), of Rotterdam, who influenced his contemporaries and expressed many of their most important and typical aspirations to a degree and with a lucidity and comprehensiveness unmatched before Voltaire. Caught by the enthusiasm of these men, princes hired humanist secretaries; aristocrats and wealthy burghers entrusted their sons to humanist educators. Humanism transformed literature, art, and scholarship. It influenced medicine, law, theology, and morals. It was the cultural fashion of the day—as

[2]W. H. Woodward, *Vittorino da Feltre and Other Humanist Educators* (New York, 1963), p. 177.

68 / Renaissance Society and Humanist Culture

recognizable, as penetrating, and as subtle as the style of a sharply individual painter or musician.

How are we to understand an intellectual passion and a cultural program apparently so remote from our own twentieth-century sensibility and needs?

THE STUDY OF HISTORY

Renaissance enthusiasm for the classics flowed from a transformation of men's sense of history. Humanists adored the classics because they had learned to read them in historical perspective, a perspective they had established by inventing the idea of the Renaissance, by creating certain of the principles and tools of modern historical writing, and by imagining a new periodization of the past.

The way a man divides the past into periods reveals some of his most basic, and often unconscious, assumptions. Medieval scholars had divided history into an age of darkness and error and an age of light and truth. Between the two ages stood the Cross of Christ. Developing hints from the Old Testament, medieval historians distinguished subsidiary periods within the age of darkness. Some used the scheme of four successive world monarchies adumbrated in the Book of Daniel; others adopted the six ages outlined by St. Augustine (354–430) in *The City of God*. Most agreed that secular history illustrated a providential plan in its movement from the creation to the Incarnation and from the Incarnation to the Last Judgment; that the final period of world history had begun with the simultaneous founding of the Roman Empire and the birth of Christ; and that they themselves were living near the end of that last age.

Humanist historians drew two sharp chronological lines rather than one. The first line divided *antiqua*, or ancient history, from the period humanists now named, for the first time, the "dark ages." The important dates became those of the emperor Constantine's conversion (312) and of the sack of Rome by the Visigoths (410). The second line, dated variously but always placed in the very recent past, distinguished their own period from the dark middle age that had preceded it. This tripartite division of European history into ancient, medieval, and modern was at the same time a judgment of value. By calling the period after the early fourth or early fifth century a dark age and by shifting the moment of crucial discontinuity in historical development from the Incarnation to the conversion of Constantine and the barbarian invasions, humanists reversed the traditional metaphor of light and darkness. Antiquity, so long considered dark because it was the time of pagan error, became in this new vision of the past an age of light; while the period after the decline of Rome was branded an age of cultural decadence and barbarism. Correspondingly, the humanists represented their own age as a new historical

The Conquest of Ignorance. *An engraving after a fresco by Rosso Fiorentino in the chateau of Fontainebleau. King Francis I opens the door of the temple of Jupiter to his blind and ignorant subjects, an allegory of the renaissance of art and letters and of the rebirth of virtue and true learning. Metropolitan Museum, New York.*

epoch of a special kind: a renaissance—an age of light after darkness, awakening after sleep, rebirth after death.

Classical poetry, they complacently maintained, had withered under the chill of monastic contempt and the onslaught of barbarian invaders. For centuries no poet sang; then Petrarch recalled the banished Muses. Ancient art had declined in the time of Constantine, and nothing that was not awkward or barbarous had emerged from the Gothic shadows until Giotto (c. 1276–1337) restored painting to the light. Erasmus discerned the same pattern in the history of religion. The great Church Fathers of antiquity had united wisdom and eloquence in an admirable harmony; but the same barbarian flood that had drowned "good letters" had also muddied the springs of Christian piety. Erasmus attributed the damage to monks and scholastics. Incapable of eloquence, barbarized by a contentious logic, medieval theology—in his view—was arid, presumptuous, and unedifying. Only in his own day, he felt, was sacred truth, in the company of classical letters, beginning to emerge from Cimmerian darkness. In the eyes of Renaissance humanists history was a great arc sadly sagging in the middle. On one side was the greatness of ancient achievement; on the other, the contemporary rebirth of piety, art, and literature. Between them stretched a middle age of cultural and intellectual squalor. The conviction that they lived at the beginning of a new and brilliant period of human history (rather than near the end of the fourth and last monarchy or the sixth and last age) filled the humanists with vivid optimism. Before their hopes faded during the bitter ideological struggles of the Reformation, European intellectuals repeatedly chorused their self-congratulations on living in a golden age. To be sure, much still needed reform and restoration. But grammar, eloquence, painting, architecture, sculpture, and music were being reborn. Like Prometheus, men of genius were "seizing the splendid torch of wisdom from the heavens."[3] There seemed almost no limit to possibility and expectation, and men looked forward to an almost immediate future when all branches of knowledge would recover their pristine beauty; when Roman eloquence would be restored and a beneficial knowledge of Greek firmly reestablished; when the *studia humanitatis,* coupled with a revived and purer Christianity, would become the common treasure of a cultivated elite. Early sixteenth-century men faced the future with confidence and hope.

The humanist periodization of history transformed men's sense of the past in another way. Since the medieval historian had believed that his own historical epoch went back to the reign of Augustus (27 B.C.–14 A.D.), he had been unconscious of the intellectual and imaginative gulf that had to be crossed if the ancient world was to be understood. Apart from the inescapable fact that this world was pagan, it could have for him no special character or style. He regarded the Romans as his contemporaries. The familiarity imposed on him by a theological periodization weakened his ability to see Rome as a culture complete in itself, quite different and separate from his contemporary world. By sharply dividing medieval from ancient history and their own age from the recent past, Renaissance humanists encouraged in Europeans a very gradual development of what Nietzsche was to call the "pathos of historical distance," on which the modern sense of history depends. They came consciously to recognize that a thousand years separated them from classical Rome. They realized too that this past was dead, that it formed a distinct historical period, remote, complete, and over. This sense of historical mortality is the pathos of the past and the price of understanding it. One does not necessarily have to escape the conditioning of one's own epoch, country, and class in order to understand a contemporary. But if one imagines that an ancient Roman is essentially one's contemporary, one can never escape provincialism or be free of anachronisms.

[3]Robert Gaguin, *Epistole et orationes,* ed. by Louis Thuasne (Paris, 1904), Vol. II, p. 26.

A forger needs unusual historical sensitivity in order to avoid anachronisms. It is good evidence of a sharpening sense of history among Renaissance men that a young humanist architect could produce a clever pastiche of a Roman comedy, and that Michelangelo carved a cupid that passed for an antique. The same feeling for style and period shaped a critical method which made possible the exposure of the less skillful forgeries of the past—more evidence of historical awareness. Lorenzo Valla (1406–1457) proved the spuriousness of the Donation of Constantine, a document actually written in the eighth century but purporting to be the legal act by which Constantine recognized the superior dignity of the bishop of Rome and conferred on him extensive properties in various parts of Italy. Valla pointed out (among other less probing arguments) that the word "fief" occurred in it, although both the word and the institution were unknown in fourth-century Rome. Erasmus applied similar critical techniques to the Bible. In his Latin translation of the New Testament, published with his famous edition of the Greek text in 1516, he omitted the verse (the *Comma Johanneum*) in the First Epistle of John that is the scriptural basis of the doctrine of the Trinity. Both in the Vulgate (the Latin translation by St. Jerome, c. 340–420, which was authoritative in the Middle Ages and in the Roman Church) and in the King James version, the text of I John 5:7–8 reads as follows: "And there are three that bear record in heaven, the Father, the Word, and the Holy Ghost: and these three are one. And there are three that bear witness in earth, the spirit, and the water, and the blood: and these three agree in one." Erasmus proved the first of these verses to be apocryphal. He found it in no Greek manuscript. It was missing in several of his oldest Latin manuscripts. He discovered that it was unknown to any Christian writer before the fourth century. He argued, with perfect cogency, that if the text *had* existed, it would surely have been quoted by orthodox writers in a period when the doctrine of the Trinity was the center of theological controversy; and he concluded—modern scholarship confirms him—that the text must have been interpolated into the New Testament after the Council of Nicaea (325) in order to give biblical sanction to the Trinitarian formula adopted there.

Textual criticism of this kind is the concrete embodiment of an historical sense and represents the beginning of modern "scientific" history. It is understandable that the civilization which produced it produced also the early classics of modern historical writing: Leonardo Bruni's *History of Florence* (1420), Machiavelli's *Discourses on Livy* (1516–1517) and *Florentine History* (1525), Francesco Guicciardini's *History of Italy* (1535), and Jean Bodin's *Easy Introduction to the Study of History* (1566). Renaissance historians have obvious faults: a facile moralism, a narrow concentration on political and military narrative, an inconsistent application of the critical techniques they had themselves discovered, a tendency to conceal their sources under a flow of Ciceronian rhetoric and to sacrifice accuracy to elegance. But if there are difficulties in their assumption that history is a branch of literature, there are far greater difficulties in the medieval assumption that it is a branch of theology. The positive contribution of Renaissance historians was to secularize historical writing. History regained its causal autonomy. Recourse to God's providential plan or to direct intervention by God in order to explain historical events became rarer. The explanations advanced by Bruni, Machiavelli, and Guicciardini are usually natural rather than supernatural, involving causes rooted in the appetites of individuals or in the ambitions of particular social or political groups. Renaissance historians also secularized historical writing in another way: by introducing novel principles of selection, new criteria of what was important, of what should and should not be included in a work of history. The most characteristic genre of medieval historical writing was the world chronicle, a universal history of mankind from the creation to the Last Judgment in which the test of relevance was the religious significance of an event and the edification to be drawn from it. The greatest Renaissance historians were laymen of wide experience in law, government, and diplomacy. They wanted to be politically rather than theologically effective. So they normally restricted their narratives to the history of a single state and selected for emphasis events which might help their contemporaries understand and control the political, diplomatic, and military situations in which they found themselves.

Finally, Renaissance historians had a more secular conception of the uses of history, one which fitted it admirably for its important place in humanist education. Instead of being an illustration and justification of God's ways to man, history was, in their view, a guide to life. The study of history incites to virtue and discourages vice. It trains future statesmen in politics and war. It is the mother of experience and the grandmother of wisdom. Old men are said to be wise because their judgment rests on the accumulated experience of a lifetime; a right reading of history builds a vicarious experience that also makes men wise. The new history was thus a secular narrative of past politics or a comparative study of ancient and contemporary institutions, elegantly written, coherently organized, practical in purpose, with causes and motives explained in human terms. The works of historians like Bruni and Guicciardini remained models for generations.

THE REDISCOVERY OF THE CLASSICS

The humanist's secular conception of history and his sense of the historical distance separating him from Greece and Rome transformed the way Europeans read the classics. Renaissance scholars claimed to have recovered ancient literature from the dust and neglect of a millennium.

One must not take their claim literally. To be sure, humanists did popularize certain Latin authors and works little read by their predecessors: Plautus, for example, Cicero's *Letters*, the histories of Livy and Tacitus. They read in the original Greek works that men in the Middle Ages had read largely in selected Latin extracts, epitomes, and translations. Above all, they completed the European appropriation of its Hellenic inheritance. Aristotle had been recovered in the twelfth and thirteenth centuries. Most of Plato's dialogues, all of Herodotus and Thucydides, and the most important works of the Greek dramatists, poets, and Church Fathers became an integral part of European culture only in the Renaissance. Humanist editions and translations of Greek works represent an enormous increment of knowledge. They stimulated intellectual life as profoundly as the discoveries of the explorers stimulated economic life. Nevertheless, it must be recognized that a large body of ancient literature had been conveniently available for centuries. The Latin classics survived at all only because they were copied and recopied in the *scriptoria*, or writing rooms, of medieval monasteries. Virgil and Ovid were universally popular in the Middle Ages. Cicero and Seneca were respected ethical teachers. A tenth-century German nun wrote little plays, imitating the style of Terence (though with a different content). From the twelfth century on Roman law was systematically studied at the University of Bologna. Medieval medical knowledge was a précis of Galen, its physics a reworking of Aristotle. The achievement of Renaissance humanists, then, was not that they read the classics, but that they read them, whether familiar or rediscovered, with eyes newly trained in the perspective of history.

What this could mean is suggested by the novel treatment of classical themes and motifs in Renaissance art. Artists of the high Middle Ages had illustrated classical themes and subjects—Dido and Aeneas, for example, and the antique gods—just as medieval scholars had read and quoted the *Aeneid* and Cicero's *De officiis*. They had often borrowed classical motifs and reproduced, sometimes with great fidelity, the classical images of Hercules, Orpheus, and Atlas. What is striking is that classical motifs were almost never used to represent classical themes, and conversely, classical themes were almost never expressed by classical motifs—a disassociation caused by a lack of historical sense and by an inability, both intellectual and emotional, to grasp the fundamentally secular assumptions of ancient thought. Thus a classical visual image was given a Christian, nonclassical meaning, while pagan themes were illustrated by Christian and medieval motifs. In the one case a depiction clearly based upon the antique figure of Orpheus might be used to portray David, or a Hercules-like figure might represent Christ. In the other case, classical subjects were illustrated by invariably anachronistic images. Dido and Aeneas appeared as a fourteenth-century couple playing chess, Venus as an aristocratic lady fully clothed and plucking a lute. One novelty of Renaissance artists was to close this gap between classical theme and classical motif. For the first time since antiquity, Mercury recaptured his youth and beauty and Venus her naked sensuality. Portrayals of classical heroes, nymphs, and divinities invaded the homes of princes, aristocrats, and bankers, and among the still far more numerous representations of the Virgin and the saints arose pictorial reflections of classical sentiment as fresh and precise as the "Galatea" of Raphael (see p. 85).

The reintegration of classical theme and classical motif in Renaissance art is one aspect of a vaster reintegration: that of the classical text and its classical meaning. Just as medieval artists Christianized classical motifs, so medieval scholars mined classical texts for information relevant to their own concerns and read into these texts Christian meanings. They interpreted Virgil's *Aeneid* as the itinerary of the human soul (Aeneas) to the promised land (Latium) and of its ascension from human love (Dido) to divine love. They identified Aristotle's First Cause with the Christian God. They equated natural law with the ten commandments of the Old Testament. A philosopher, the ancients had said, is a lover of wisdom. Christian theologians identified wisdom with the second Person of the Trinity and defined the philosopher as a lover of Christ. Aristotle's virtue of temperance came to include chastity, and monks understood Stoic detachment from the things of this world as a form of Christian asceticism. Ancient philosophers were often said to have been divinely illuminated, inspired to speak the truth by God as He had inspired Moses, Abraham, or David. Necessarily, medieval scholars found in the classics what they had already assumed to be there.

Allegorical interpretations of the *Aeneid* continued to be published in the sixteenth century, but the great epic poem was also read in historical perspective as a glorification of Augustan Rome. Some Renaissance scholars continued to pillage the ancient texts in the inevitably rewarded expectation of finding pearls in dung heaps. But others passed beyond St. Augustine's injunction that the classics were to be used and not enjoyed. They took pleasure in the melody of Catullus and the epigrammatic thrust of Tacitus, just as they took pleasure in the balance and harmony of ancient orations and ancient temples.

Some Renaissance philosophers defended the divine illumination of the ancients and used as much ingenuity Christianizing Plato as St. Thomas Aquinas had used harmonizing Christianity and Aristotelianism. Thus Renaissance Platonists located Plato's Ideas in the divine intellect. Just as the architect—they argued—has in his mind an image of the building he is erecting, which, as his model, he tries to imitate exactly, so God has in His divine mind the Ideas and patterns of all things, the Ideas of the sun and moon, of men, of all animals, plants, and stones, of the elements, and indeed of everything else as well. This divine mind—and here is the identification on which the Christian Platonism of the Renaissance rested —is the intelligible world, where all things exist, not in a material or sensible manner of being, but in a truer, nobler, more beautiful way, the ideal or intelligible. Man's contemplation of the intelligible beauty of the Ideas is therefore a kind of celestial love, *desiderio intellettuale di ideal bellezza*,[4] (the "intellectual desire for ideal beauty"), and once man has turned to the eternal beauty and light of God, his soul shines with the light of the Ideas in an esctatic vision akin to that of the mystics.

Yet at the same time that Marsilio Ficino (1433–1499), the greatest of the Renaissance Neoplatonists, was discovering this Platonic-Christian vision, other scholars were founding the disciplines of classical philology, classical archaeology, numismatics, and epigraphy, and coming progressively closer to a critical understanding of institutions as different from their own as the Greek games and the Roman senate, of the principles of ancient jurisprudence and political theory, of the distinctive values and moral ideals not only of Platonism, but of Aristotelianism, Stoicism, and Epicureanism as well. Disciplined by the insight that the arts and literature of antiquity were the historical expression of a particular period and a unique society detached from their own, they gradually built up, through the critical and historical study of ancient texts, an image of ancient thought and institutions more nearly approximating ancient reality than any achieved before.

This more objective knowledge of the admired civilizations of Greece and Rome had an impact on the European mind analogous to that of the discoveries. Renewed contact with the cultures of antiquity, like serious contact for the first time with the Aztecs and the Incas, the Indians and the Chinese, encouraged in sixteenth-century Europeans a new freedom from temporal provincialism (the conviction that the culture of one's own age has a peculiar virtue and validity) and a more self-conscious understanding of their own society. Montaigne has described the provincialism of a society whose values are unquestioned: "We all call barbarism that which does not fit in with our usages. And indeed we seem to have no other standard of truth and reason but the example and model of the opinions and usages of the country we live in. There we always see the perfect religion, the perfect government, the perfect and accomplished manner of doing things."[5] That Montaigne could make such a statement is itself an excellent demonstration of how contact with foreign cultures widens the mind's horizons and undermines the ignorant self-satisfaction characteristic of every society that considers its values absolute.

Correspondingly, it was no accident that the first utopia since

---

[4]Pico della Mirandola, *De hominis dignitate, Heptaplus, De ente et uno e scritti vari*, ed. by Eugenio Garin (Florence, 1942), p. 500.

[5]*Essais*, I, xxxi, ed. by F. Strowski (Bordeaux, 1906), Vol. I, p. 268.

antiquity—that of the English humanist Sir Thomas More—appeared in 1516 and was inspired in part by an account of the voyages of Amerigo Vespucci (1451–1512) to the New World and in part by first-hand knowledge of Plato's *Republic*. For utopias, as Robert Burton (1577–1640) later put it in his *Anatomy of Melancholy*, are "witty fictions" describing the supposed effects which would result from imagined institutions different from one's own. By playing the utopian game, More made explicit what had been implicit in the discoveries of explorers and historians from the beginning: the extraordinary variety of possible institutions and beliefs. Just as Copernicus had shown that the earth was not necessarily the center of the universe, as Vasco da Gama and Columbus had shown that Europe was not necessarily the center of the world, as Luther was to prove that Rome was not necessarily the center of Christian Europe, so More's *Utopia* suggested that the perfection of European standards and European values could no longer be taken for granted. His point was not that foreign societies or his fictional utopian society were better than his own. On the contrary, he was certain that many of their beliefs and practices were worse. More's purpose, like that of Machiavelli and Bodin in their comparative institutional studies, was rather to exploit the variety of possible and actual societies as a means of forcing his readers to reexamine their own convictions in an unexpected perspective—from the outside as it were, across a distance analogous to the historical distance from which the humanist regarded Rome—and then to accept, reject, or modify them consciously in the light of this comparative knowledge. Knowledge of other worlds and of the past thus fostered a more detached comprehension of the virtues and corruptions of the present; while the comparison of foreign laws and customs with those of Europe suggested the revolutionary possibility of conscious choice among institutional, moral, and religious alternatives.

THE DIGNITY OF MAN

Yet the achievement of historical distance, the realization that antiquity constituted a period and a culture detached from their own was not the only reason for the humanist's ability to understand the classics more perceptively. Equally important was the fact that transformations in European society were creating objective parallels between the problems of Europeans and those of the ancients. These changes made many ancient solutions relevant to contemporary needs. Here perhaps we reach one root both of the Renaissance enthusiasm for the classics and of the sense of history with which fifteenth- and sixteenth-century men read them. They grasped again the Roman idea of sovereignty because they no longer lived in a feudal society in which public office and public powers were owned as private property, because the fact of sovereignty was again a real part of their daily lives. The English gentry had no difficulty with the Roman idea of absolute property in land because they had begun to enclose their fields and assert their sole proprietary rights to their estates. Italians could more nearly understand Plato's *Laws* and Aristotle's *Politics* because their communal life too was centered in city-states. The idea of *humanitas*, the ancient definitions of wisdom and virtue, Cicero's conception of the orator and of eloquence, the physical perfection of the classical gods—in short, the humanist ideal of man and the educational program that embodied it—attracted men of substance because they seemed to find their own conception of themselves reproduced there more nearly than it was in the ideal human types created by the priestly feudal society of the past.

The humanist philosophy of man was a complex reweaving of traditional ideas. Its novelty, like that of most innovations in intellectual history, is one of selection, arrangement, and emphasis. Professors of theology in medieval universities had normally defined man by what he lacked, by the gulf that separated him from God. (Protestant theologians would unequivocally do the same.) Humanists preferred to praise him and to define him in terms of the positive capacities generously granted him by God when He created him in His own image. "God clearly and especially manifested his wisdom in the creation of man," wrote a German humanist in 1512. "Making man the link between [the sensible and intellectual worlds], he endowed him with magnificent gifts, attributing to him reason and free will, a most excellent gift and noble vestige of that supreme liberty with which God created all things." Not all humanists trusted reason. They were suspicious of the metaphysical and logical subtlety of medieval scholastic philosophy and of the theological rationalism that had created intellectual structures like the *Summa theologiae* of St. Thomas Aquinas. Caution in scrutinizing the divine mind was usual among them, while their attitude to the claims of metaphysicians and logicians was a certain skepticism. An early fifteenth-century Italian humanist condensed the common view in an epigrammatic formula: *Scire nostrum nihil aliud est quam rationabiliter dubitare*[6] ("all our knowledge is no more than rational doubt"). But if many humanists set limits to the competence of reason, very few set any to that of the will. Indeed, they minimized the power of the speculative intellect precisely in order to emphasize the greater importance and freedom of the will. "The will alone is really ours and in our power. The rest—understanding, memory, imagination—all this can be taken from us, altered, troubled by a thousand accidents, but not the will."[7]

Man can know and will the good. On this assertion more humanists

[6]*Epistolario di Coluccio Salutati*, ed. by Francesco Novati (Rome, 1891–1905), Vol III, p. 603.

[7]Pierre Charron, *De la sagesse*, I, xviii, ed. by A. Duval (Paris, 1820–1824), Vol. 1, p. 142.

agreed than on almost any other. They repeated Aristotle's eloquent words in the third book of the *Ethics*, his statement that since it is in man's power to do good or evil acts, "being good or vicious characters is in our power." Man is the "originator or generator of his actions as he is the generator of his children." They revived the story, unused in the Middle Ages, of Hercules at the fork of the road, and made it a favorite subject of Renaissance painting. Arrived at the parting of the ways, Hercules could take either the road of vice or the road of virtue. So man at each important moment of his life is free to choose. Inspired by encomiums of man in classical literature and in the Greek Church Fathers, the Florentine philosopher Pico della Mirandola (1463–1494) wrote an *Oration on the Dignity of Man* (1498) in which he located human dignity in man's freedom from any fixed or static place in the chain of being that links him to the angels and to God above him and to the animals, plants, and inert matter below him. Man is an autonomous moral agent, containing in his own nature the possibility of the most varied development, who can by free choice become akin to any being, become like a rock or plant or beast if he turn toward evil, like the angels or like a mortal god if he turn toward good. Nature seeks to realize that perfection of which it is capable. Since human nature is free, its progress toward perfection is an offered choice. This idea of human freedom was given a coherent statement by the French humanist Charles de Bovelles (1480–1533). Our actions, he wrote in 1509, have three causes or principles: intelligence, will, and power. Through his intelligence man can know what should be done; he can will to do what should be done; he has the power, finally, to act according to his knowledge and desire because he is all things and can become all things. All three causes are necessary for a free and efficacious act. For even if one understands an action and has the power to perform it, that action will be vain if one does not want to do it; similarly, one may know and desire an object, but the knowledge and desire are vain without the power to acquire it; and if one desires something and has the capacity to get it, yet has no clear understanding of what one wants, again action is neither efficacious nor free. Freedom is the harmonious union of knowledge, capacity, and will, and this freedom is a human conquest, the result of the gradual development, through education and a long series of appropriate choices, of the habit of virtue.

The identification of human dignity with moral freedom suggested an ideal of man different from those of the Middle Ages. Medieval admiration had focused on three human types: the saint, the monk, and the chivalrous knight. The humanist conception of a desirable human being was less specialized. The ideal man was noble, but his nobility, his *gentilezza*, as Dante had called it, unlike the knight's was based not on birth but on virtue, and his virtues, unlike the monk's, were not exclusively ascetic and contemplative. The humanist idea of perfection included both mind and body, contemplation and action, the good of the soul and what contemporaries called the goods of fortune—wealth, physical beauty, and health. "Man is a mortal but happy god," wrote the humanist architect Leon Battista Alberti (1404–1472), "because he combines capacity for virtuous action with rational understanding," thus echoing a wonderful passage in Cicero's *De finibus*: "Just as the horse is born to run, the ox to plow, the dog to scent a trail, so is man, as Aristotle says, born to two things: to know and to act, and in this he is almost a mortal god." Contemplation to the exclusion of all else is the prerogative of angels. Man contemplates to the extent that his soul is divine and separate, but as a man, a composite of soul and body living in the world, he exercises the moral virtues and is useful to his family, friends, fellow citizens, and prince. Humanists quoted another famous line from Cicero: *Virtutis laus omnis in actione consistat* ("the true praise of virtue lies in doing"); and Alberti summed up the argument in a sentence equally memorable, "Man was born to be useful to man."

HUMANISM AND ART

"The good painter," wrote Leonardo da Vinci, "must paint principally two things: man and the ideas in man's mind."[8] Because Leonardo's contemporaries did indeed choose these as their subject, few sources make so attractively explicit the humanist philosophy of man as do Renaissance works of art. The poems, orations, moral essays, histories, and educational treatises of even the greatest humanists are little read today except by specialists. Since most of them are written in Latin, only specialists *can* read them. The paintings, statues, and buildings of Renaissance artists are more accessible, even to moderns more easily moved by African masks than by the Cnidian Aphrodite.

Renaissance art was a humanist art in its sources, its content, and its style. Consider the "Allegory of Philosophy" by Albrecht Dürer (1471–1528). The woodcut illustrates, perhaps with more learning than charm, a volume of love poems written by the German humanist Conrad Celtis and published in 1502. Celtis himself devised its complicated program, wrote the verses included in it, and provided the artist with a sketch showing the general arrangement of the figures. Artistic activity in the high Middle Ages had normally been an anonymous, communal enterprise controlled by the clergy and directed by ecclesiastical authority to orthodox religious ends. By the sixteenth century, humanists had replaced clerics as the typical "inventors" of the subject matter of works of art.

Dürer's woodcut is humanist in another way. It illustrates a humanist

---

[8]Quoted by Anthony Blunt, *Artistic Theory in Italy 1450–1600* (Oxford, 1940), p. 34.

Allegory of Philosophy. Woodcut by Dürer illustrating the Amores of Conrad Celtis, published in 1502.

ideal of knowledge. The central figure is a woman, sumptuously gowned and jeweled, wearing a crown and seated on a throne. A tag identifies her as Philosophy. The literary source for both Celtis and Dürer is the opening paragraphs of the popular *Consolation of Philosophy,* by the late Roman moralist and scholar Boethius (*c.* 480–524). In a dream, Boethius saw a majestic woman: "In her right hand she had certain books, and in her left hand she held a scepter," while on the lower part of her dress was "placed the Greek letter Π, and on the upper Θ, and between the two letters, like stairs, there were certain degrees made by which there was a passage from the lower to the higher letter." Celtis made one change. He replaced Boethius' Π by the letter Φ, probably intending it to represent *phronesis,* or prudence, defined by Cicero as "practical knowledge of things to be sought for and of things to be avoided." The two Greek letters therefore stand for the two great divisions of philosophy, ethics and metaphysics (Θ denotes *theoria,* speculative or contemplative philosophy). The "stairs" between them are the seven liberal arts: grammar, logic, rhetoric, arithmetic, geometry, astronomy, and music.

Celtis spelled out the meaning of the picture in verses at the top and bottom. "Everything in heaven and on earth, in the air and sea, all things human, everything the flaming god [the sun] brings to pass in the whole world [of nature], by philosophy I hold them all in my breast." And again: "The Greeks call me *sophia* [wisdom], the Latins *sapientia* [wisdom]. The Egyptians and Chaldeans discovered me, the Greeks wrote me down, the Latins translated me, the Germans have added to me." In medallions fixed to the wreath around the central figure are portraits of the "Egyptian" astronomer Ptolemy, Plato the Greek, the Latins Cicero and Virgil, and to represent the wisdom of the Germans, Albertus Magnus, the teacher of St. Thomas Aquinas. His inclusion is a touch of German nationalism, but a reminder too that the great scholastics of the Middle Ages continued to be widely read and admired throughout the sixteenth century. In each corner is one of the four winds, with accessory objects symbolizing one of the four elements (fire, air, water, and earth), one of the four humors (the choleric, the sanguine, the phlegmatic, and the melancholic), one of the four seasons, and one of the four ages of man. Finally, on each of the arms of the throne is a Greek inscription: on the left, "First honor God," on the right, "Be just to all." Celtis took them from an obscure didactic poem, actually by a first-century Hellenistic Jew, which Renaissance humanists mistakenly attributed to an early Greek poet named Phocylides of Miletus. Equally mistakenly, they believed that the poem shone with Christian doctrine, one more example of a heathen poet who had preached monotheism and Christian ethics centuries before Christ.

The wise man, clearly, should know something about everything, have some knowledge of all things divine and human. He must be both humanist and encyclopedist. For the word "encyclopedia," as more than one sixteenth-century scholar pointed out, is made up of the words *kyklos* ("circle," "orb") and *paedeia* (*humanitas*) and denotes therefore an all-embracing *humanitas*. Dürer has made his central figure the symbol of that ideal.

The idea of *humanitas* included virtue as well as knowledge; and virtue, as we have seen, was thought to be the more important. In 1502, the year that Dürer's "Allegory of Philosophy" appeared, Andrea Mantegna (1431–1506) finished his "Minerva Expelling the Vices from the Grove of Virtue," which he painted for Isabella d'Este, marchioness of Mantua, according to a program supplied by one of her humanist advisers. In it he pictured the kingdom of the will and of moral choice as fancifully and pedantically as Dürer portrayed the realm of intellect.

Vice has entered the grove of virtue, deranging a garden ordered by art. The pool has become an infected swamp. Venus, represented here as the mother of the vices, has imprisoned the mother of the virtues in a rock. (Mantegna records her call for help on the ribbon at the right: "O Gods!

Minerva Expelling the Vices from the Grove of Virtue. *Painting by Mantegna. The Louvre, Paris.*

Come to my aid. I am the mother of the virtues.") Standing on the back of a centaur, emblem of a humanity more beast than man, Venus surveys her conquest. In the venereal pool wallow Sloth, Ingratitude, Ignorance, Avarice, Hate, Suspicion, Fraud, and Malice. A female satyr with her satyr children stands for lasciviousness. A little monkey woman carries bags of seeds labeled "the bad," "the worse," and "the worst." Behind the garden the mountain seems to explode, in a natural catastrophe which comments on the destruction by vice of the order, beauty, and harmony of the moral world and of the human soul. The spirit of the grove, a ghostly olive tree at the left, joins its prayers to those of the imprisoned mother of the virtues, and lifting imploring arms, calls out to the gods—in Latin, Greek, and Hebrew—to expel the vices from the land and accompany the heavenly virtues back to earth. (The Latin inscription is correct; the Greek reproduces the Latin in a Latin script meant to look deceptively like Greek; the Hebrew is an arbitrary arrangement of letters. Study of Greek and Hebrew was more preached than practiced, even in the sixteenth century, and the Renaissance remained a fundamentally Latin culture.)

Answering these prayers, Prudence, or moral wisdom, in the guise of Minerva, rushes in from the left, preceded by Diana (with her bow) and Chastity (carrying an extinguished torch). In the sky on a cloud, waiting for their sister to open the way for their return to earth, are the three other cardinal virtues: Justice (on the left with sword and scales), Fortitude (wearing a lion's skin as a helmet), and Temperance (holding two jars). The fierceness of the fight is emphasized by a fantastic confrontation in the clouds, where an attentive eye can discern heads in profile facing each other, some light, some dark, personifying the combat of vice and virtue and giving it a cosmic resonance.

The theme of the battle of virtues and vices was an old one. But Mantegna has treated it with a typically humanist sensibility. The battle is secular, without specifically Christian references. It records the recurrent struggle of man to order his soul, to subordinate his passions to the rule of reason. It assumes freedom of choice and a significant degree of moral autonomy. As Pico della Mirandola had taught, man can become all things. Virtue is as natural as vice. Both are in man's power. The battle within him is hot and continuous precisely because the stakes are high and the choice is real.

It has been argued that the humanist emphasis on man's dignity and moral freedom weakened religious sentiment. Despite the absence of overtly Christian allusions in such works as Mantegna's painting, this is not true. No serious evidence exists that any fifteenth- or sixteenth-century European was an atheist. It is most unlikely that any Renaissance humanist was a pagan. Humanists were good Christians, quite as good Christians as thirteenth-century professors of theology had been. They were not necessarily the same *kind* of Christians. There are styles in religiosity as there are styles in art; and the one tells us a good deal about the other. The particular flavor of humanist piety is perhaps best caught and expressed in Renaissance church architecture, and especially in its greatest innovation, the circular church.

A church is the house of God. In order to be worthy of God's perfection, it must be built in God's image; that is, it must embody (and so define for us) the particular qualities that an age or culture attributes to God. The humanist architects of the Renaissance believed that the ideal church should be located at the center of the city, stand isolated and elevated on a pedestal in the middle of a spacious piazza, and be sublimely beautiful. How did they propose to achieve staggering beauty? By geometry—because only geometry can create that perfect harmony of proportion which is beauty itself. Since the noblest and most beautiful geometrical shape is the circle (an unquestioned assumption architects shared with philosophers, poets, and astronomers) and since, because of its divine simplicity, uniformity, and equality, the circle of all shapes most adequately mirrors God, the ideal church must be circular. The circular

Tempietto. *Designed by Bramante in 1502. S. Pietro in Montorio, Rome.*

temple, wrote the great architect Andrea Palladio (1518–1580), "is enclosed by one circumference only, in which is to be found neither beginning nor end, and the one is indistinguishable from the other; its parts correspond to each other and all of them participate in the shape of the whole; and moreover every part being equally distant from the center, such a building demonstrates extremely well the unity, the infinite essence, the uniformity and the justice of God."[9] As an example of what he meant, Palladio picked one of the smallest and loveliest churches in the world, the Tempietto in Rome by Donato Bramante (1444–1514). It fulfills virtually every requirement of the humanist church: it is perfectly round and domed; it stands freely on a high platform; it is virtually without decoration, perfectly simple and perfectly proportioned.

The qualities of Bramante's Tempietto are also the qualities of humanist piety: simplicity, sobriety, serenity, equilibrium. Its form and proportion make a clear statement about God, man, and nature. The harmony and symmetry of the church reflect the harmony and symmetry of the world. God has created and ordered the world according to immutable mathematical laws. The structure of the universe is therefore mathematical and harmonious.

[9]Quoted by Rudolf Wittkower, *Architectural Principles in the Age of Humanism* (London, 1949), p. 21.

In the view of the humanist, this harmony is best and most easily perceived in the human body, "because from the human body," in the words of an Italian mathematician who also wrote an early and important treatise on double-entry bookkeeping, "derive all measures and their denominations and in it is to be found all and every ratio and proportion by which God reveals the innermost secrets of nature."[10] Indeed, man is able to build a church in God's image only because God created men in His image and made him the center of a rational and harmonious world. Admiration of the harmony of his body and of the world arouses man's admiration and love of God, while the harmonies of nature teach him something about the nature of God—the one infinite, perfect, generous creator of a geometrically harmonious universe.

Since the harmony of man's body was regarded by the humanist as the measure of all other terrestrial harmonies, it is not surprising that in the Renaissance the human body, particularly the nude, became the central subject of art; art itself, in the first decade of the sixteenth century, became the harmonious arrangement of ideal forms in a rationalized geometrical space. The "Galatea" of Raphael (1483–1520) is a ravishing example.

Agostino Chigi (c. 1465–1520) a Sienese merchant who made his fortune and that of his family as a papal banker, commissioned this fresco about 1514 for his villa on the Tiber. Here he entertained artists, poets, cardinals, and the pope himself. After dinner in the garden he liked negligently to invite his guests to toss into the river the golden plates they had just finished eating off—only to retrieve them later in the night from nets cunningly deployed under the water.

In the fresco, Raphael chose to represent the milk-white sea nymph Galatea, the beloved of Acis, sung by Theocritus and Ovid among the ancients and by the Italian poets Angelo Poliziano (1454–1494) and Pietro Bembo (1470–1547) among contemporaries. Galatea rides a conch shell pulled by two dolphins. Against a background of sky and sea veined like an antique marble, nereids and tritons, hippocamps and cupids, celebrate her triumph. The scene is a vision of antiquity consciously disciplined by historical and archaeological expertise: the figures come directly from a nereid sarcophagus. Raphael's successful effort to make the figure of Galatea an image of ideal beauty represents a conscious revival of the similar effort of ancient art. "To paint a beautiful woman," he wrote about the "Galatea" to his friend and patron Baldassare Castiglione, "I need to see many beautiful women. . . . But since there is a dearth both of good judges of what is beautiful and of beautiful women, I use as my guide a certain idea of the beautiful that I carry in my mind."[11] This idea

---

[10]Quoted by Wittkower, *Architectural Principles*, p. 14.

[11]V. Golzio, *Raffaello nei documenti, nelle testimonianze dei contemporanei e nella letteratura del suo secolo* (Vatican City, 1936), pp. 30–31.

The Nymph Galatea. *Wall painting by Raphael in the Villa Farnesina, Rome.*

of the beautiful he derived in practice from the canons of classical art and from the example of ancient sculpture. The same idealizing impulse controls the tight geometry of the composition. Like every Renaissance artist, Raphael intended to imitate nature—but he regarded nature as ordered, harmonized by geometry, just as Copernicus, and later Johannes Kepler (1571–1630), were certain they would find ideal geometrical patterns behind the confusing particularity of observed experience. Thus Galatea's head is at the apex of a triangle. The horizon divides the picture space into two equal parts, locked together in a musical harmony by intersecting circles; the three flying *amors* outline the circumference of the upper circle; the figures around Galatea mark the lower circumference of the other. In the center of rational nature is a beautiful human being.

Use of the nude to determine harmonious ratios and of geometry to rationalize nature are intimately related to the greatest artistic innovation of the Renaissance: the systematic development of the techniques of perspective. The use of perspective enables the artist to project a unified three-dimensional space upon a plane. The painting surface becomes a window through which we look into a world of rationally related solids. The objects represented seem to have the same sizes, shapes, and positions relative to each other that the actual objects located in actual space would have if seen from a single point of view. The perfection of exact perspective construction in Florence about 1420 was an extraordinary accomplishment. Unknown to any previous culture, these techniques of perspective were to dominate European painting from 1420 until the end of the nineteenth century, giving it, despite the succession of schools and styles, a remarkable cohesion and humanity. Their discovery is a chapter in the prehistory of the scientific revolution. It took place just at the time that men were developing the definition, also in Florence, of the educational and cultural program of humanism. Their abandonment—first apparent in such works as the paintings of the Postimpressionists and Picasso's "Demoiselles d'Avignon" (1906–1907)—is one aspect of the collapse of humanist values in the decades before the First World War.

THE THEORY AND PRACTICE OF EDUCATION

Because humanists believed that man's free will could be trained to virtue and that the piety and the active civic and moral virtues they particularly admired could be taught, education was central to the humanist program. The curriculum was designed to educate laymen rather than priests, to form citizens rather than monks or scholars, to produce free and civilized men, men of taste and judgment rather than professionally trained doctors, lawyers, merchants, philosophers, or theologians. It therefore concentrated on the three subjects humanists considered most suitable for achieving these purposes: Latin and Greek (including classical literature and the principles of effective discourse—rhetoric—to be learned from it), history, and moral philosophy, or ethics. These studies formed the "good and liberal arts," the *studia humanitatis*. Humanists made them the core of education because rhetoric, ethics, and history are disciplines of doing, uniquely appropriate for training useful scholar-citizens. Moral philosophy teaches the student the secret of true freedom, and defines his duty to God, family, country, and himself. It draws him from the abstract preoccupations of physics and metaphysics to fruitful activity in the world. History offers him concrete illustrations of the precepts inculcated by moral philosophy; it teaches ethics by examples. The one shows what men should do; the other what men have said and done in the past and what practical lessons we can draw for the present day. Eloquence, finally, is indispensable not only because a beautiful style is pleasurable in itself, but also because it enables us to persuade our fellow men to follow the lessons of history and the duties of ethics in their private and public lives. Literature, history, and ethics remained the core of the liberal education until the end of the nineteenth century. These studies are called liberal, wrote a humanist educator and statesman, "because they make men free," and they are called humane "because they perfect man." And again: "We call those studies liberal which are worthy of a free man; those studies by which we attain and practice virtue and wisdom; that education which calls forth, trains and develops those highest gifts of body and of mind [honor and glory], which ennoble men, and which are rightly judged to rank next in dignity to virtue only."[12]

The humanist emphasis on physical training reflects a similar human purpose. Medieval educators, suspicious of the body, had been reluctant to assign any place to physical exercise in the schools under their jurisdiction. Renaissance educators, reviving the antique ideal of a healthy mind in a sound body, wished to develop fully all an individual's potentialities, the strength and grace of his body as well as his intellectual and moral virtue. An age which redefined happiness, with Aristotle, to include money, beauty, and health as well as virtue; which redefined wisdom, with Cicero, to include knowledge of the human as well as of the divine; which, for the first time since antiquity, reestablished the portrait as a major genre and used the nude to express its image of perfect beauty—such an age was inevitably concerned to educate the body as well as the mind, to prize as peculiarly liberal and humane the harmonious cultivation of every admirable human potentiality. Thus the training of aristocratic boys in riding and fighting, which in the Middle Ages had had a strictly utilitarian purpose, acquired a new and more general signifiance when fifteenth-century schoolmasters made gymnastics and organized sports an integral part of a liberal education. "As regards a boy's physical training," wrote Pius II, pope from 1458 to 1464, "we must bear in mind that we aim at implanting habits which will prove beneficial through life. . . . Games and exercises which develop the muscular activities and general carriage of the person should be encouraged by every teacher."[13] A kind of football, for example, was very popular in Italian schools; and a member of a great Florentine family wrote a book describing its virtues: it made the body dexterous and robust and caused the sharpened mind to desire virtuous victory. This emphasis on sports was not common in northern Europe before the middle of the sixteenth century. In England, where competence in sports was ultimately to bulk so large in the ideal of the gentleman, football was considered base and mean. Football, wrote an English humanist in 1531, ought to be utterly rejected by all noblemen because there is in it "nothing but beastly furie and exstreme violence; whereof procedeth hurte, and consequently rancour and malice do remaine with them that he wounded."[14] The ideal, nevertheless, in both Italy and

---

[12]Woodward, *Vittorino da Feltre*, p. 102.
[13]*Ibid.*, pp. 137–138.
[14]Sir Thomas Elyot, *The Boke Named the Gouvernour*, ed. by H. H. S. Croft (London, 1880), Vol. I, pp. 295–296.

Erasmus of Rotterdam. Woodcut by Hans Holbein the
Younger, 1535. The old humanist rests his right hand on
the head of Terminus, a Roman
god whom Erasmus understood
as a symbol of death.

the north, was the man who excelled in both arms and letters, who
combined contemplation and service to the state, *humanitas* and physical
excellence.

Such a conception of man, the humanist believed, found its highest
expression in ancient literature. A humanist education; therefore—aside
from the fact that Latin was the indispensable language of the Church,
diplomacy, scholarship, and the professions of law and medicine—was
necessarily classical and literary. The study of letters meant the study of
Latin letters. Latin, and later Greek, literature formed the core of
education because, as Erasmus bluntly put it, "within these two literatures
is contained all the knowledge which we recognize as of vital importance
to mankind." Ancient literature was the voice itself of *humanitas*, the
civilizing force which made man free and whole, refined his sensibility,

molded his moral attitudes. A man was liberally educated who had achieved self-knowledge through the accurate understanding of ancient literature, whose imagination was stirred by the ideal pattern of classical humanity, who modeled his life on the image of man in the Greek and Latin classics in just the way as Scipio and Caesar had kept before their eyes the image of Alexander. The very idea of *humanitas*, indeed, suggested that a classical education was peculiarly human, that it, preeminently, civilized the rude and uncultured, that it made a human being more fully and perfectly a man. In the Renaissance a liberal education was invariably classical.

By the early sixteenth century, humanist schools were attracting students in every country of Europe. Overwhelmingly, recruitment was from two groups: the nobility and socially ambitious merchants. This particular pattern of recruitment suggests a final explanation of the Renaissance enthusiasm for the classics: a humanist education fashioned a ruling class trained to govern the early modern state in cooperation with the sovereign prince.

The declining economic resources of some of the nobility and the diminishing military and political independence of them all forced aristocrats to adapt to changing circumstance. They needed to read, write, and calculate if they were to manage their estates with the rationalism and efficiency demanded by a competitive agricultural market. They needed new standards of manners and more realistic values than the ideals of a decaying chivalry could supply if they were to become courtiers, at ease in the behavior and attitudes demanded by an evolving ceremonial. Above all they had to have adequate formal education if they were to compete successfully for royal offices and favors and represent their prince abroad or serve him profitably at home. Humanist propaganda tirelessly insisted that nobles could claim no office simply by right of birth. Only education—a humanist education—could fit a man to be a judge, councillor, governor, or military commander. Education had, in fact, become an avenue to power and influence for laymen, and many among the nobility recognized this novel situation. Adaptable nobles met the need of king and prince for educated service by sending their sons to humanist schools or adding a humanist tutor to their household. By 1500 the phenomenon was no longer unusual in Italy. Between 1500 and 1560 the reeducation of the nobility made rapid progress north of the Alps. A great Flemish noble, Jean de Lannoy, pointed out to his son what a disadvantage it had been to him not to have a Latin education: "No day passes that I do not regret this, and especially when I find myself in the council of the king or the Duke of Burgundy, and I know not nor dare to speak my opinion after the learned, eloquent legists and scholars who have spoken before me."[15] He was determined that his son should have what

---

[15]Quoted by J. H. Hexter, "The Education of the Aristocracy in the Renaissance," in *Reappraisals in History* (New York, 1963), p. 63.

he had lacked. Many of his peers sent their sons to a humanist college in Louvain. Nobles appeared in ever larger numbers at the universities of Salamanca, Oxford, and Paris, and at the German and Italian universities. In 1500 a humanistically educated young noble like Erasmus' pupil Lord Mountjoy was a rarity. By 1560 a modicum of cultivation was commonplace among the nobility at least in the politically more sophisticated states; and the new conception of the gentleman had been codified in one of the most important and agreeable books of the century: the *Courtier*, by Count Baldassare Castiglione (1478–1529), written between 1507 and 1510 and a best seller in Italian, French, Spanish, German, and English versions throughout the sixteenth century. A humanist education became the formal device which helped transform the members of a feudal aristocracy into diplomats, provincial governors, even customs officials. "To receive favors of princes," Castiglione wrote, "there is no better way than to deserve them." And how does one deserve them? "I would have the Courtier devote all his thought and strength of spirit," Castiglione continued, "to loving and almost adoring the prince he serves above all else, devoting his every desire and habit and manner to pleasing him."[16]

The second important source of students for the humanist educators was the urban bourgeoisie. In France, humanists educated the most active segment of the high bourgeoisie, the "Fourth Estate" of royal officers, the core—under the king—of the ruling group of the country, men who were investing their wealth and talent in the highest ecclesiastical, legal, and administrative posts, buying land and titles, and by intermarriage and the heredity of office creating the first bureaucratic nobility. Humanist schools in England and Germany showed similar patterns of recruitment. In 1496, for example, the town council of Nuremberg founded a *Poetenschule*, a humanist school distinct from the other town schools (which were run by the canons of local churches or by the Dominican order). The students were the sons of the local patriciate. They were taught the humanities in the expectation that this education would make them better citizens and rulers and would equip them for wider careers as lawyers, councillors, political secretaries, or ambassadors in the service of neighboring territorial princes or of the emperor. When the humanist John Colet founded St. Paul's School in 1509 his purpose was the same. The headmaster and teachers were married laymen and the students were sons of the London middle class. He put his school into the charge not of the church, but of "the most honest and faithful fellowship of the Mercers of London," one of the great guilds of the city. Just as the new education made courtiers out of nobles, so it made gentlemen out of merchants. The old aristocracy and the new rich were molded to a common end: royal or princely service in the sovereign territorial state.

[16]*The Book of the Courtier*, trans. by Charles Singleton (New York, 1959), pp. 110, 114.

CHAPTER 4

The Formation of the Early Modern State

THE POLITICAL ORGANIZATION of the European states reached a new level of efficiency in the century between the end of the Hundred Years' War in 1453 and the Peace of Cateau-Cambrésis, which in 1559 brought to a close the Habsburg-Valois wars. Administrative centralization had begun long before 1453, with the first efforts of medieval rulers, after the political fragmentation which had characterised the feudal age, to establish a minimum of order in their domains and to build a more widely respected authority. These efforts achieved an early partial success during the twelfth, thirteenth, and fourteenth centuries in the institution of feudal monarchy. The process was to continue long after 1559, to culminate in western Europe in the administrative reforms of the French Revolution and Napoleon and in the final unification of Germany and Italy after 1850. But it was during the late fifteenth and the sixteenth centuries that state building was most concentrated, rapid, and dramatic. Before 1453, European states were more feudal than sovereign; after 1559, they were more sovereign than feudal. Before 1453, we properly speak of the feudal state or feudal monarchy; after 1559, we speak more properly—though, as we shall see, with qualifications—of sovereign states.

The sovereign state is still the characteristic form of political organization in the contemporary world. It is our familiar reality. To understand feudalism therefore requires an act of conscious historical imagination. We must escape our temporal provincialism and imagine a society which knew no state in the modern or Roman sense; we must picture a system of government in which the normal prerogatives of the state—the authority to wage war, to tax, to administer and enforce the law—were privately owned as legal, hereditary rights by members of a military landed aristocracy. The system rested on a confusion of public power with private property. In the feudal age kings were very weak, while over much of Europe private persons exercised state powers as rights derived from their ownership of property.

By the beginning of the thirteenth century, monarchical authority had again become a significant political force. Kings passed from the defensive to the offensive. They consolidated their power and their holdings. But Europe was still clearly a feudal society and a king's great vassals continued to own important elements of public power as hereditary and legally recognized property rights. This division of power between monarch and magnate, royal lord and great vassal, was the central characteristic of feudal monarchy, an intermediate political type, standing between decentralized feudal government on the one hand and the sovereign state on the other. The feudal monarch shared with the magnates of his realm many of those powers which a Roman emperor had held intact. His relationship to all others in his realm was not that of a king to his subjects or of a republic's executive to its citizens; instead, he was linked to them by the network of personal loyalties and obligations created by the feudal bond between lord and vassal. He was chief lord, or suzerain, of a feudal hierarchy which included all members of the ruling class, and he enjoyed few powers or resources not dependent upon his position at the apex of this hierarchy. From his position in the hierarchy the king derived certain rights, privileges, and obligations—more rights, privileges, and obligations, indeed, than fell to anyone else in the hierarchy. But his vassals also had rights and privileges. In the high and late Middle Ages the forces of feudal decentralization and monarchical centralization were in precarious balance. Between 1453 and 1559 this balance tipped in favor of the crown.

THE EMERGENCE OF THE SOVEREIGN STATE
IN WESTERN EUROPE

The pretensions of French, Spanish, and English kings in the sixteenth century were absolutist and sovereign. In 1527 the president of the highest court in France assured the reigning monarch, Francis I, that "we do not wish to dispute or minimize your power; that would be sacrilege, and we know very well that you are above the laws."[1] *Princeps legibus solutus* ("the prince is not bound by the laws"). The text is from the Roman law. Jurists cited a second ancient text: *Quicquid principi placuit legis habet vigorem* ("the will of the prince has the force of law"). These are definitions of absolutism; they also define the fundamental attribute of sovereignty: the power to make the law. The political theorist Jean Bodin (1530–1596) is explicit. *Maiestas* ("sovereignty") is the power to make law. By definition, a sovereign authority is unbound by human law and above it, for what the sovereign can make he can also unmake or change. "It is the distinguishing mark of the sovereign," wrote Bodin, "that he

---

[1]Quoted by Gaston Zeller, *Les institutions de la France au XVIe siècle* (Paris, 1948), pp. 79–80.

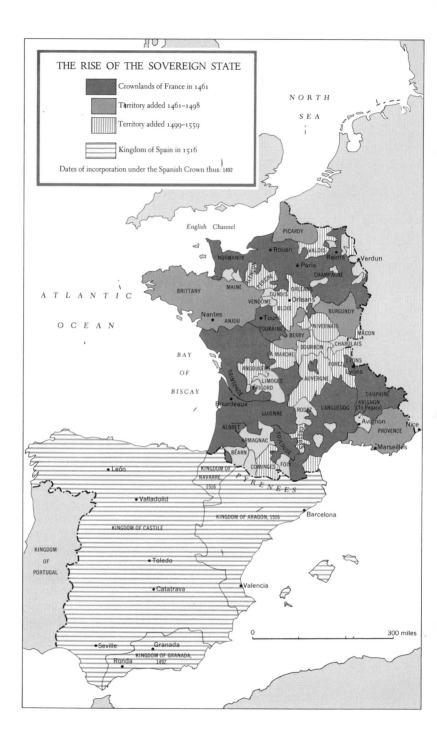

THE RISE OF THE SOVEREIGN STATE

- ░ Crownlands of France in 1461
- ▒ Territory added 1461–1498
- ▓ Territory added 1499–1559

- ▤ Kingdom of Spain in 1516

Dates of incorporation under the Spanish Crown thus: 1492

NORTH

SEA

English Channel

PICARDY

Rouen   VALOIS
NORMANDY   Reims   Verdun
            ★ Paris
                    CHAMPAGNE

ATLANTIC   BRITTANY   MAINE
                              DUNOIS   ORLÉANS
OCEAN   VENDÔME   BLOIS   BURGUNDY
              Nantes   Tours   MÂCON
                    ANJOU TOURAINE NIVERNAIS
                         BERRY   CHAROLAIS
BAY   BOURBON   LYONS
                    MARCHE   FOREZ Lyons
OF   ANGOULÊME   AUVERGNE
                 LIMOGES
BISCAY   SAINTONGE PÉRIGORD   DAUPHINÉ
         Bourdeaux   AVIGNON
                    GUIENNE   RODEZ LANGUEDOC (To Papacy)
         ALBRET   Avignon   Nice
         ARMAGNAC   TOULOUSE   PROVENCE
           BÉARN   Marseilles

León   KINGDOM OF   COMINGES FOIX
                  NAVARRE
                  1516   PYRENEES

Valladolid

                   KINGDOM OF ARAGON, 1516   Barcelona
KINGDOM OF CASTILE

KINGDOM
OF   Toledo
PORTUGAL
                         Valencia
         Catatrava

                                0   300 miles
Seville   Granada
Ronda   KINGDOM OF GRANADA,
              1492

The Emperor Maximilian I (1493–1519). *Engraving by Lucas van Leyden, 1510. Around the emperor's neck is the chain of the Order of the Golden Fleece.*

cannot in any way be subject to the commands of another, for it is he who makes law for the subject, abrogates laws already made, and amends obsolete law."[2] The sovereign prince is an absolute ruler limited only by divine and natural law. He monopolizes all power and justice in the state. He has drawn back into his own hands those public powers usurped from him by the magnates of the feudal age. Theoretically, he should be able to tax regularly and without consent; face his unarmed subjects with a permanent army under his sole control; command an efficient bureaucracy; dispense his justice in every case and to every subject, sharing his jurisdictional prerogatives with no one; and dominate the rival authorities of parliament, estates, and church.

Theoretical claims are one thing; practice is another. To what extent did the "new monarchs," as the Renaissance kings of France, Spain, and England have traditionally been called, exercise in fact the attributes of a sovereign ruler? To what extent had the balance of effective power shifted in their favor and away from their greater subjects? To answer these questions one must look first at what we would call today the bureaucracy—the administrative structure of the new monarchies—and more particularly, at the king's officers.

The King's Officers

At the top of the governmental hierarchy the king was supreme both in theory and in fact. He ruled through his council and great officers of state; by the middle of the sixteenth century the council was an instrument of

[2]*Six Books of the Commonwealth*, trans. by M. J. Tooley (Oxford, n.d.), p. 197.

absolute government dependent on him alone. Its composition was entirely in the king's hands. Members had no security of tenure. Their function was to carry out the wishes and policies of the king. They advised a monarch who was in no way bound by their advice. They enabled a king to do what he wished to do; they did not determine what he ought to do. Royal "ministers" could become immensely powerful; but their authority reflected exclusively the power of their royal master. They were instruments.

At the local level, on the other hand, though the king was supreme in theory, he was not always so in fact. The Castilian *corregidor* was the officer of local government most nearly approaching the bureaucratic type. The crown appointed and paid him. To prevent him from identifying himself with local interests, his term of office in one locality was limited to a maximum of five years; he was never sent to the area where he had his home; and he was forbidden to mingle in local factions, buy property, or build a house where he served. The royal council bombarded him with instructions. At the end of his term a special judge was sent down to his district to receive complaints and to prepare for the council a full report on his administration.

Justices of the peace served the Tudors of England just as efficiently as the *corregidors* served the Castilian kings. The crown appointed them and the council supervised them closely. But unlike the *corregidor*, the justice of the peace was selected for his burdensome and responsible job from among the men of substance of his own locality, and he was not paid. English local government rested on the unpaid voluntary service of wealthy amateurs. It worked remarkably well under Henry VIII (ruled 1509–1547) and Elizabeth I (ruled 1558–1603) and helped establish a valuable tradition of public service and political activity among the economically powerful. Its weakness lay in the independence implicit in voluntary service. As long as the local official was asked to enforce regulations that benefited his locality and furthered the interests of his class, he enforced them effectively and gladly. But when royal orders conflicted with his interests and convictions, he seldom resisted the temptation to disregard them.

In France, theory and practice diverged more strikingly. The principal officers of local government were the *baillis* and the *sénéchaux*, equivalent terms for the same office. They had few bureaucratic characteristics. Most were recruited from the highest nobility. They were usually absent from their administrative districts, at court or with the royal armies abroad, and the real work of administration was done by a subordinate, *the lieutenant du roi ès bailliage*. Like the *corregidor*, the *lieutenant* was an expert, a university graduate in civil or canon law, usually a bourgeois not immediately identified with the interests of the landed aristocracy. But on the crucial question of appointment bureaucratic principle, according to which an official is appointed by the sovereign authority, was constantly infringed. Sometimes the *bailli* alone appointed the *lieutenant*. Sometimes the *bailli* chose him on the advice of the notables of the district (the *gens de bien*). Sometimes the notables actually elected him themselves. Elsewhere, they selected three candidates, and the king appointed one of them. A royal edict of 1531 tried to limit the appointment of *lieutenants* exclusively to the king. In vain. The most important royal officer at the local level remained a local appointee—the client of local magnates and local interests.

It is in the context of this ambiguous relationship between the king and his officers that the selling of royal offices, the most important administrative innovation of the period, assumes its full importance. Venality of royal offices first became common in France and Spain in the early years of the sixteenth century. In return for immediate cash, kings sacrificed some of their control over the appointment of financial and judicial officers. For although the first result of the traffic in offices was an increase in royal revenue, a secondary and permanent effect was the reappearance in a new form of the feudal tendency to confuse public office and private property. This became the more obvious where venality of office led, as in France, to the inheritance of offices, and on the payment of a suitable fee they passed from father to son like feudal fiefs. The king found it very difficult to dismiss a subordinate who had bought his office and expected to pass it on to his son. Ownership of office encouraged independence of royal policy as well, and kings faced a growing inability to enforce their orders, a situation clearly indicated by the constant reiteration of commands so noticeable in any collection of sixteenth-century ordinances. By generalizing the venality of offices continental princes themselves erected obstacles to the effective exercise of royal power.

This limitation of the effective exercise of the royal will by bureaucratic inadequacy should not obscure the equally significant fact that kings were becoming noticeably stronger precisely because their officers were more numerous and more powerful. No longer were the king's officers excluded from the fiefs of powerful vassals. Royal justice touched directly, if not exclusively, each of the king's subjects. For the first time, effective political power was largely concentrated in the hands of the king and his officers instead of being fragmented among a multitude of spiritual and temporal lords. Venality itself was an essentially royal form of corruption. Its positive function was to attach thousands of magistrates to the crown by the most direct financial ties, to create indeed a "Fourth Estate" whose *esprit de corps*, ambition, and thirst for power and wealth magnified royal power at the expense of the traditional liberties and jurisdictions of the clergy, the nobility, and the towns. In this perspective, a proliferating corps of royal officers is an infallible sign of administrative centralization and the most direct institutional expression of a transfer of power from feudal magnate to sovereign prince.

The Army

A second characteristic of the new monarchies was the existence of a permanent mercenary army. Under feudalism the means of violence were privately owned and the magnates enjoyed the legal right to wage private war. In a modern sovereign state, ownership of the means of violence is a monopoly of the sovereign power, and the right to make war is limited exclusively to the state. Between 1460 and 1560 the rapidly growing wealth of Europe and the technological innovations associated with gunpowder enabled several European rulers to create armies of a new, though still intermediary, type.

The French army during the reign of Francis I is a typical example of such a force. The first steps to create it had been taken by Charles VII (ruled 1422–1461) during the last years of the Hundred Years' War. By an ordinance of 1439 he founded the *compagnies d'ordonnance,* units of heavy cavalry supported by mounted archers. The *compagnies d'ordonnance* were staffed by volunteers from the nobility, but these nobles entered the royal army in a new capacity—not as vassals performing the traditional *auxilium,* or military aid they owed their lord, but as paid volunteers in the regular and permanent service of the crown. Removed from their seigneuries, incorporated into royally recruited units where their place in an abstract military hierarchy rather than the number of feudal dependents who accompanied them to war determined their effective influence, the nobles were broken to royal discipline. They ceased to be knights and became mounted mercenaries.

In the fifteenth century, infantry was commonly conscripted by means of a semidraft. In 1448 Charles VII ordered each parish to train and furnish one archer for the royal army. These rustic reserves were not a success, and by the time Francis I became king the infantry was no longer conscripted, and had become a professional mercenary force. Captains appointed or hired by the French king organized foot soldiers—by now far more numerous than cavalry, and equipped with pikes and with arquebuses or muskets—in companies of from three to five hundred men. Recruitment was royal but not national. Some infantrymen were French, recruited in provinces like Picardy and Gascony, whose inhabitants were noted for their military brio; the majority were foreign. The archers of the king's personal bodyguard were Scots. Under a permanent agreement with Francis I, the Swiss Confederation supplied from six to sixteen thousand pikemen for each of his campaigns. After the Swiss, German *Landsknechte* were the best and most easily available mercenaries in Europe, and several thousand served regularly in the French army, reinforced by Englishmen, Italians, Poles, Greeks, and Albanians.

In France and Spain armies of this type provided the sanction of force behind royal efforts to build centralized sovereign states. Like the corps of administrative officers, however, they were imperfect mechanisms of royal control. When they were left unpaid, they became pillaging mobs, mercilessly sacking cities and ravishing the countryside. Even when paid, they did not accept their discipline from, or give their loyalty to, the crown exclusively. Although the heavy cavalry was no longer feudal, it continued to be almost exclusively aristocratic and was therefore potentially unreliable in internal struggles involving aristocratic interests. Foreign infantrymen were politically safer, but real authority over them was wielded by their captains rather than by the states that hired them. Northern monarchs, to be sure, could not be blackmailed by their mercenaries the way the Italian city-states were blackmailed by the *condotieri*; but they often found that their troops had inconveniently changed sides at the moment they needed them most.

Nor were any European king's subjects totally disarmed. The individual castle had become an anachronism, but innovations in urban fortifications soon enabled a resolute town to defend itself successfully against anything but a costly siege. Most towns retained their own militias. In the middle of the sixteenth century, even quite small places like Troyes and Amiens could field over three thousand admittedly unmartial men. The greatest nobles, finally (this was especially true of France, much less so of England), remained the centers of complex webs of patronage, famly ties, and clientage relationships with lesser nobles. Such ties enabled a Montmorency, member of one of France's greatest families, to arrive at court in 1560 with a retinue of eight hundred horsemen. The continued political and military importance of these relationships is clearly shown by the ease with which the dukes of Guise and William of Nassau, prince of Orange, raised opposition armies during the civil wars in France and the Netherlands in the second half of the century. Sixteenth-century monarchs commanded military machines far more effective than those of their medieval predecessors; but Valois and Habsburgs continued to rely on the willing support of their more powerful subjects in war as in administration.

Finances

The nature of the particular balance of power between the prince and the ruling class which was characteristic of Renaissance monarchy appears even more clearly in its financial institutions.

Renaissance princes were desperate for money. Their largest expense was warfare. Although armies were small by modern standards (the average size of the French and Spanish armies engaged during the Italian and Habsburg-Valois wars was between 20,000 and 25,000 men), war was as expensive, relatively, as it is now. "No money, no Swiss" was a sixteenth-century axiom. When Louis XII (ruled 1498–1515) was preparing to invade the duchy of Milan in 1499, he asked one of his Italian commanders what was necessary for success; the reply was blunt: "Money, more money and again more money." Peace never relieved the pressure for long; war was almost continuous. Major campaigns were mounted by the important powers in three out of every four years between the beginning of the Italian wars in 1494 and the end of the sixteenth century. To military expenditures must be added the costs of diplomacy, the sums, for example, paid by the French between 1525 and 1546 to secure the friendship of the Swiss, the German Protestant princes, and Henry VIII of England, the salaries of royal officers; the pensions given to nobles, a financial aspect of that process by which a feudal nobility was being transformed into an aristocracy in the service of the crown; the spiraling expenditures of royal households on magnificence, display, and luxury in buildings, artistic patronage, and sport (Emperor Maximilian I kept two thousand hounds)—and all this in an age of rapidly rising prices.

To meet these mounting expenses, rulers obtained revenues from a variety of sources. One, the largest in the past but of dwindling importance in the sixteenth century, was the royal domain, which yielded rents and dues owed the king in his capacity as a great landed proprietor and chief of the feudal hierarchy. A second source of revenue was indirect taxation. For all governments, the major sources of indirect taxes were customs duties and sales taxes on wine, meat, cloth, and a growing list of other commodities. To these, individual governments added others. France had the *gabelle*, the famous salt tax, collected by forcing each householder to buy a fixed minimum of salt each year from government warehouses at prices which assured the crown an enormous profit. The *alcabala*, a cornerstone of Spanish royal finance, was a tax of 10 per cent on the amount of all commercial transactions, a heavy burden on merchants and probably a contributing cause of the declining vigor of Spanish economic life in the later sixteenth century.

Kings tried to meet their expenses in a third way—by borrowing. Some loans were forced, constituting a form of disguised and extralegal taxation. The bourgeoisie of the larger cities were the most frequent victims. The case of Toulouse is typical. Louis XII asked the citizens for a "gift" of ten thousand livres. Francis I obtained twenty thousand livres from them in 1537, in 1542, and in 1544. Henry II raised seventeen thousand livres there in 1553 and again in 1555. Borrowing from the great merchant-bankers was a more orthodox but more onerous way of raising money. The French expedition against Naples in 1494 was largely financed by émigré Italian bankers in Lyons. Charles V paid for his wars during

the last years of his reign with loans from Antwerp bankers. His debts
there rose from half a million livres to over six million between 1551 and
1555. When royal credit fell so low that it became difficult to borrow
from merchant-bankers, monarchs turned to the public and initiated two
of the most interesting novelties of sixteenth-century government finance:
the sale of government bonds and the floating of public loans. The Spanish
government sold *juros*, annuities priced at ten to fifteen times their annual
yield. Beginning in 1522 the French issued bonds, called *rentes sur l'Hôtel
de Ville*, bearing 12-per-cent interest paid by the king and secured by the
domains and revenues of the city of Paris, whose credit was stronger than
that of the crown. The most spectacular credit operation of the period
was the loan floated in 1555 by Lyons bankers for Henry II (ruled
1547–1559). This is one of the first examples outside of Italy of public
borrowing on a large scale. Tempted by what a contemporary called the
"sweet expectation of excessive profit," men of every class and fortune,
from Swiss and German nobles to valets and charwomen, hastened to
subscribe. Widows invested their dowers, ladies sold their jewels. From
distant Turkey, pashas subscribed 500,000 écus through their agents. The
speculative bubble burst in the great financial crisis of 1557, when both
the French and Spanish governments suspended payments on their
obligations. In the end subscribers were lucky to recover 30 per cent of
their investment.

Taxation and Representation

European monarchs had a final major source of revenue: direct taxation.
Income from the royal domain was totally inadequate. Indirect taxes were
lucrative, but did not yield enough to meet the costs of war. Borrowing
was a palliative. The crucial problem of every Renaissance ruler was the
universal and critical disequilibrium between income and expenditure.
The only possible basis for sound government finance was a regular system
of direct taxation. But to collect taxes regularly a monarch had to
overcome one of the most deep-seated aversions of his subjects and
abrogate one of their most cherished and most firmly established rights.
The common traditional view was that a king should live "on his own,"
that is, on revenues from the royal domain and from indirect taxation.
These were the *ordinary* revenues of the crown. If a military emergency
should create a need for futher and *extraordinary* revenues, the king's
next step—men even more firmly believed—must be to ask his loyal
subjects for them. In short, taxation was not recognized as an integral and
necessary part of government finance. All direct taxation was
extraordinary. And no taxation could be imposed without the consent of
the subject. Medieval theorists expressed this conviction in another way
when they said that to the king belonged *dominium* ("political
authority"), while to the subject belonged *proprietas* ("private property").

It was unjust for the subject to interfere in political matters like diplomacy or war; the conduct of these was part of the royal prerogative. It was equally unjust for a king to tamper with the property of the subject without his consent. Everywhere in Europe the subject consented to taxation (or withheld his consent) through representative assemblies—the English Parliament, the Castilian or Aragonese Cortes, the Estates-General and the provincial estates of France. Taxation was the subject of periodic negotiation between a king demanding money and representatives of the clergy, nobility, and commons of his realm reluctantly granting it. The dialogue between them—a complex struggle for power in which military necessity, financial need, and the defense of property all played major roles—was ultimately to determine the location of sovereignty in the state. Sovereignty itself was not at issue. More obviously even than their administrative or military institutions, the finances of the new monarchies were those of sovereign states. No one denied that the crown could tax, and only the most determinedly old-fashioned literally expected the king to live "on his own." No private individual still levied and collected taxes as a legal right of his ownership of landed property. Taxation was a government monopoly, an unshared prerogative of the state. At issue, rather, was the future of consent, and through consent, of the representative institutions in each state. In due course, the strength or weakness of the estates would determine the particular constitutional form each sovereign state would take: on the one hand, absolute monarchy, with sovereignty located in the king alone; on the other, limited monarchy, with sovereignty located in the king and estates combined, or as the English would later phrase it, in the king in Parliament.

The kings of France and Spain defeated the principle of consent in practice and seriously weakened representative institutions in their states. French constitutional history is particularly instructive. The most important direct tax was the *taille*, theoretically granted by the national and local estates. From the Estates-General, which represented the kingdom as a whole, the king secured preliminary recognition of his financial needs. Constituents did not empower their representatives in it to vote extraordinary grants, but only to agree that such grants were necessary. Only the provincial, or local, estates could actually consent to taxation. It was the achievement of Charles VII (ruled 1422–1461) to extract from the Estates-General the recognition of the continuing need of the crown for a reliable income. The circumstances are significant—it was a period of military crisis, the time of the final campaigns of the Hundred Years' War against the English. And the immediate purpose of the grant is noteworthy—to finance a royal artillery and pay for the *compagnies d'ordonnance*. Henceforth the crown treated solely with the provincial estates, assemblies much easier to manipulate and awe. Royal ministers negotiated with these provincial estates throughout the sixteenth century. The fiction of consent was maintained, but in fact it became a mere formality. Each year the crown determined unilaterally the amount of the *taille,* and collected it through royal agents. The justification for this action continued to be military necessity—at the beginning the need to repel the foreign army of occupation present in the kingdom, then between 1494 and 1559 the pressing and continuous demands of the Italian wars and the struggle against Charles V. In the meantime, between 1484 and 1560, the Estates-General did not meet. Its decline, and the mounting figure of the *taille,* especially during the reigns of Francis I and Henry II, measure the effective power of the crown, the latent threat of royal arms, the efficiency of the financial bureaucracy, and the tacit submission of the population to a policy which drained all practical substance from the traditional liberty of consent.

Submission was all the easier because the French kings taxed directly only the politically weakest sections of the population. A fundamental characteristic of the *taille* was the inequality of its incidence. Immunities to direct taxation derived originally from the functional stratification of society and the military end that direct taxation was thought to serve. The *taille* was a demand for service from those who were not already serving against the king's enemies in some other recognized and useful way. The nobles served by active participation in the fighting, the clergy by praying for victory, the Third Estate (which included everybody else) by giving money. Each order, in other words, had its special function in society—to fight, to pray, to work. This division of functions theoretically exempted

Francis I, King of France (1515–1547). *Drawing by an unknown artist. Bibliothèque Nationale, Paris.*

the clergy and the nobility from direct taxation, causing it to fall exclusively on the Third Estate. In practice, the situation was more complex. The clergy—and this fact suggests its declining strength and independence—paid a good deal. Conversely, many members of the Third Estate did in fact gain exemption either by serving in some other way—as soldiers or royal bureaucrats, for example—or, more frequently, by obtaining it as a special privilege granted or sold by the king. By paying lump sums the oligarchies of whole towns bought financial immunity. The nobility, however, remained exempt in both theory and fact, so much so that exemption from the *taille* became one of the surest proofs of aristocratic status. In France, and in most other continental countries, aristocratic exemption from taxation became one term of the political transaction at the basis of the early modern state; in exchange for financial immunity the nobility gradually forfeited independent political power. This is why "absolute" monarchies were to live largely on the taxes of peasants.

The pattern of English constitutional development was rather different. England was on the periphery of power politics. While France, as we shall see, was ringed by the territories of Charles V, England was protected by the Channel and, after the middle of the fifteenth century, rarely at war. She had no permanent army and hired few mercenaries. All free men were in theory obligated to military service, but they were recruited and trained by local notables, not by professionals. Like its local government, England's army was amateur, and it was far below the continental level in tactics and armament. As late as the reign of Elizabeth I its principal exercise was shooting longbows on the village green. In England, furthermore, everyone paid taxes, nobles as well as commons; and the universal bite of taxation, along with widespread experience in local government, encouraged in many a sense of political commitment and the ambition to influence legislation and policy. English kings thus had no overwhelming military motive to tax regularly without consent; nor, because they stood disarmed before their subjects, the richest and most powerful of whom were liable to taxation, had they the power to do so.

But the decisive event in sixteenth-century English constitutional history was the religious break with Rome. The English Parliament was able to consolidate its influence in the reign of Henry VIII because the king desperately needed to mobilize opinion and support during the political crisis of his great struggle with the pope. The Reformation Parliament sat in seven sessions between November, 1529, and April, 1536. Under Henry's skillful leadership it legislated the English church's independence of papal control, creating a national church with the king its head. Parliament emerged from the religious crisis with enhanced prestige. The House of Commons had consolidated and widened its privileges, securing freedom from arrest and limited freedom of speech. Its members had played a role in great affairs. The long sessions had helped to establish a tradition of continuity and *esprit de corps*. For the first time, membership began to confer social prestige, access to patronage, and political advantage. Men began to compete for membership. To be sure, Parliament's chief duty was still to supply money and assent to the legislative program of the crown. Under Henry VIII, and even under Elizabeth I, it was no more than a useful adjunct to the Crown's far greater power, an instrument of government, and not, as it would become in the seventeenth century, a check on government. But it existed. It met. It became firmly entrenched in the needs, interests, and ambitions of men of substance. Above all, by using Parliament to give full legal status to many of their political acts, the Tudors tended to make cooperation with Parliament indispensable for their successors. And already in the sixteenth century some members were trying to introduce bills and motions of their own—obscurely demanding, that is, to share in shaping the policy their taxes paid for. The fruitful interplay had begun in which Parliament supplied money in return for redress of grievances, and the crown tailored policy to parliamentary opinion in return for money. The way was open which would eventually lead to quite different interpretations of the nature of parliamentary authority than could be developed under the personal rule of the popular and despotic Tudors.

One should not press the contrast between the constitutional developments in France and in England. They were to diverge remarkably in the seventeenth century: toward limited monarchy in England, toward absolutism in France. In the sixteenth century what was as clear to Englishmen as to Frenchmen was the brute fact of royal power. Wearily advising the English clergy to bend their backs and principles before the king, the archbishop of Canterbury distilled the experience of his age in a lapidary phrase: *Ira principis mors est* ("the anger of the prince is death"). Conversely, it was as clear to a Frenchman as to an Englishman that royal authority rested on the active cooperation of the king's great subjects. French kings bought the cooperation of the ruling class by tax exemption; English kings, by their readiness to use Parliament. In the one perspective, Henry VIII was a "absolute" as Francis I; in the other, Francis' power was as limited by his dependence on the willing administrative service and political support of his subjects as was Henry's.

Like other sixteenth-century institutions, then, Renaissance monarchy was a transitional form, a complex amalgam of tradition and innovation. By 1560, in the key monarchies of western Europe giant steps had been taken toward territorial unification, administrative centralization, and the magnification of royal power. The rapid accumulation of exclusive prerogatives by the central governments of France, Spain, and England—to make laws, to govern through legal, financial, and administrative officers, to tax, to declare war and make peace, to exercise ultimate jurisdiction, and to coin money—defines their transformation from feudal monarchies into sovereign territorial states. Thus we call them the new monarchies not because they broke abruptly with the past or because all feudal remnants had disappeared (we have seen in detail that they did not), but because their structures were sufficiently novel to mark a new period in the history of European political institutions. On these foundations were built the great sovereign monarchies of the seventeenth and eighteenth centuries.

THE EMPIRE OF CHARLES V

Leopold Ranke, the most famous of the early nineteenth-century founders of modern "scientific" history, attributed the pleasure and fascination of historical study to the extraordinary diversity of its human object, the "living variety of mankind." There are few better examples of this variety than the political institutions of Europeans in the sixteenth century. A survey of the new monarchies does not even begin to exhaust it, though their structures are various enough. To sense, even approximately, the complexity of the ways in which kings, princes, cities, and estates exercised, shared, or competed for political authority, one must turn from France and England to the patchwork of territories that made up the empire of Charles V.

Charles of Habsburg (ruled 1519–1556) was par excellence an heir, his empire a classic example of the effects of the accidents of royal marriage, birth, and death in a dynastic age. His paternal grandfather was Emperor Maximilian I (ruled 1493–1519), who had married the only daughter of the last duke of Burgundy, the heiress of the seventeen provinces of the Netherlands and of Franche-Comté. His maternal grandparents were the Catholic kings, Ferdinand of Aragon and Isabella of Castile; their daughter, Juana, married Philip the Handsome, son of Maximilian I and Mary of Burgundy. By 1500, the year of Charles's birth, deaths in the Spanish royal family, unforeseen and untimely, had left Juana heiress of

THE HABSBURG SUCCESSION, 1493–1564

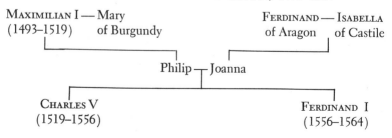

MAXIMILIAN I — Mary
(1493–1519)   of Burgundy

FERDINAND — ISABELLA
of Aragon   of Castile

Philip — Joanna

CHARLES V
(1519–1556)

FERDINAND I
(1556–1564)

The Emperor Charles V (1519–
1555). *Portrait by Titian, 1548.*
Alte Pinakothek, Munich.

the Spanish kingdoms and made the match a political triumph for the
Habsburgs. The result was an unprecedented concentration of territory in
the hands of a single prince. At the death of his father in 1506, Charles
became duke of Burgundy; at the death of Ferdinand in 1516 (the
succession of Juana, now mad, had been set aside) he became king of Castile
and Aragon, and of Naples, Sicily, Sardinia, and the Spanish possessions in
the New World. When Maximilian died in January, 1519, Charles
inherited the Austrian territories of the Habsburg archdukes. In June,
1519, the German electoral princes, moved by tradition, dynastic
sentiment, and bribery, chose him king of the Romans and
emperor-designate. The empire of Charles V stretched from Vienna to
Peru.

Charles inherited political traditions as well as lands and titles. The ducal
court of Burgundy was the European center of decaying chivalry. Charles's
favorite reading consisted of courtly chronicles about his Burgundian ancestors, and his political correspondence is heavy with references to his ambition for "honor," "reputation," "glory," and "perpetual fame." In Spain he
learned that crusades against the Moors were the central obligation and glory
of kingship. His imperial title embodied the medieval idea of the *universitas
Christiana*, a body politic, embracing theoretically the whole of Christian
Europe, of which the emperor was temporal head. "Sire," his grand chancel-

lor wrote to the young emperor after the election of 1519, "God has granted you a most wonderful grace and raised you above all the kings and all the princes of Christendom to a power hitherto enjoyed only by your ancestor Charlemagne. He has set you on the way towards a world monarchy, towards the gathering of all Christendom under a single shepherd."[3] This was rhetoric rather than a definition of policy. No European king recognized Charles as his overlord. The old notion of Christendom as a hierarchy of states headed by the emperor had given way; Europe consisted of independent, competing, equal states. Charles himself had no ambition in practice to be *dominus mundi* ("monarch of the world"), or to win kingdoms in Europe beyond those he had inherited. But he was profoundly moved by his responsibility for the spiritual unity of Christendom, which he tended to confuse with the political prosperity of his dynasty; and in his own eyes (as in the eyes of many contemporaries) he was emperor of the West, reformer of Europe, chastiser of the Turk, and defender of the Christian faith. His ideology, like his inheritance and his temperament, was ecumenical.

Yet even in the territories Charles in fact ruled, the idea of empire was a myth. His monarchy was fortuitous and personal. He ruled not a single imperial state but a heterogenous collection of autonomous kingdoms and principalities united only in the identity of their sovereign; and in each he had a different title and ruled with different powers. A Castilian jurist described the situation neatly: "These kingdoms must be ruled and governed as if the king who holds them all together were king only of each one of them."[4] Charles was conservative. He created no administrative structure common to the empire as a whole. He had no common treasury or common budget. Although his total resources in men and money were larger than those of any other single European prince, the actual power he could mobilize was determined by his strength or weakness as a ruler of separate states, each independent of the other, each with its own laws, customs, traditions, and institutions, each with particular political and economic interests it was reluctant to sacrifice to the larger interest of Habsburg ambition. Charles's empire was less than the sum of its parts.

The Germany of the Habsburgs

The emperor's constitutional position in Germany—the largest, most populous, and richest of his dominions—illustrates his predicament. The Holy Roman Empire (*Heiliges römisches Reich deutscher Nation*) was a congeries of autonomous cities and principalities. As early as the first half of the thirteenth century, the German emperor, weakened by furious struggles with the papacy, by the effort to impose his authority in central and northern Italy, and by civil war at home, had been forced to withdraw his royal officers

[3]Quoted by Karl Brandi, *Kaiser Karl V* (Munich, 1937), p. 96.
[4]Quoted by J. H. Elliott, *Imperial Spain, 1469–1716* (New York, 1964), p. 157.

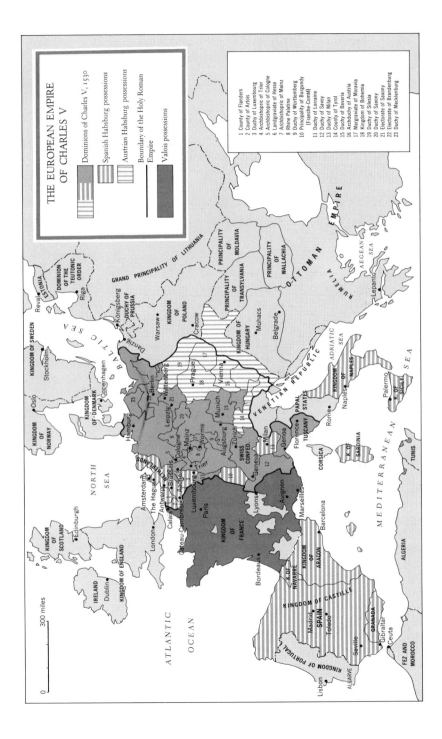

from both ecclesiastical and secular principalities and to grant German princes the exclusive right to coin money and administer justice in their territories. Princely independence of royal and imperial authority was codified in the Golden Bull of 1356, the cornerstone of the German constitution in the later Middle Ages and in the sixteenth century. The bull formalized the election of the emperor by seven electoral princes and confirmed the electors in their exercise of regalian rights and their complete immunity from imperial jurisdiction. In the decades that followed, the same immunities and rights were granted to the other princes, or usurped by them, and to the larger cities, whose patrician governments soon monopolized all power within their walls. By 1500, the princes and the free and imperial cities were the dominant partners of an elected monarch in the government of the empire.

There were approximately three hundred significant political entities in Germany on the eve of the Reformation. At the top of the hierarchy were the electoral principalities—the three archbishoprics of Mainz, Trier, and Cologne, the Rhine Palatinate, Saxony, and Brandenburg. Below them in dignity, but often as powerful, came the greater ecclesiastical and secular princes: the Wittelsbach dukes of Bavaria, the dukes of Württemberg, the landgraves of Hesse, and the dukes of Saxony. Within and around these preeminent principalities clustered in chaotic confusion the territories of several dozen lesser princes and more than a hundred counts, seventy bishoprics and abbeys, sixty-six free and imperial cities, and the minute jurisdictions of over two thousand imperial knights, each the political lord of a dilapidated castle and a few score peasants.

In Germany, in other words, centrifugal forces, curbed in the western monarchies by strong central governments, emerged victorious. The pattern of political development was characterized not by gradual unification, but by solidifying particularism. In France the great fiefs had been absorbed into the royal domain; in Germany they became independent principalities, and entrenched particularism prevented the formation of a single German state. Emperor, electors, princes, and cities recognized the advantages of workable unity for resisting foreign enemies and maintaining a minimum of order and security within the empire. But they could never agree on the means. Electors, princes, and cities, whose interests were represented in the *Reichstag*, or imperial Diet, at the end of the fifteenth century the only national institution of any significance apart from the imperial office itself, wished to have an expanded federal machinery under their own control. The emperor wanted an army and the money to equip and pay it; and if there were to be federal institutions, he wished them to be under his control. At the Diets of Worms (1495) and Augsburg (1500) the estates forced a program of reform on the indigent Maximilian: they proclaimed a public peace (the *Landfriede*) in order to halt private wars and curb disorder, instituted a federal tax (the *Gemeinpfennig*), and established a court of justice (the *Reichskam-*

mergericht) and a permanent imperial governing council (the *Reichsregiment*). On the council sat representatives of the electors, princes, and cities. No act of the king was valid without its consent, and the king had only a single vote. In short, the estates intended drastically to subordinate monarchical authority to that of local rulers. The new machinery did not work. The emperor naturally refused to recognize the authority of the council or attend its meetings. The very princes who had voted the *Gemeinpfennig* at the Diets refused to levy it in their own territories. The larger principalities would not allow appeals from their own courts to the *Reichskammergericht*. The *Landfriede* was a boon, but only because princely, not federal, authority enforced it. The outlines of a federal constitution survived throughout the reign of Maximilian's grandson; but real power in Germany remained focused at the level of the territorial prince until the nineteenth century.

Although feudalism triumphed in Germany at the level of the nation, within the several principalities political change paralleled that in the great western monarchies. German princes faced many obstacles. At the end of the fifteenth century they were still feudal lords, their power and resources those of feudal proprietors rather than of sovereigns. Nobles and towns within their territories had often usurped elements of those public powers they themselves had usurped from the emperor. Few princes had even the beginnings of an effective bureaucratic administration. Their finances were inadequate. They had no monopoly on the use of force or the administration of justice in their territories. Customary law bound every prince, and a *Landtag*, or local diet, limited and rivaled his authority. In 1508, for example, the new duke of Bavaria swore at his accession virtually the same oath Charles V would swear when he was crowned at Aachen in 1520: to secure to the estates of prelates, nobles, and cities their "freedom, ancient customs and respected rights" and not to interfere with them in any way. A contemporary observer summed up the situation when he said that "as the princes have brought the emperor to a state of dependence and allow him only certain superior rights, so in turn are they dependent on the pleasure of the Estates."[5]

During the sixteenth century, vigorous princes began to overcome these obstacles and to construct homogeneous sovereign states out of the feudal principalities they had wrested from imperial control. They worked to assure the succession of their territories according to the law of primogeniture. The Golden Bull had already established primogeniture in the electoral principalities; by the middle of the sixteenth century the succession of the oldest son to an undivided territory was common in many of the larger states. Princes also tried to consolidate, round out, and expand their territories by means of force or through suitable marriages. Most sixteenth-century German wars can be understood immediately or ultimately in terms of the princes'

---

[5]Quoted by Johannes Janssen, *Geschichte des deutschen Volkes seit dem Ausgang des Mittelalters*, ed. by L. Pastor (Freiburg-im-Breisgau, 1897), Vol. I, p. 523.

attempts to give their frontiers a rational shape and eliminate enclaves of independent territory within them. Their real problem, of course, was to make their own authority effective throughout a unified and indivisible state. To this end they began to create institutions of orderly centralized administration. They transformed their old councils of nobles and ecclesiastics into permanent and more specialized bodies staffed largely by professionals with legal training. As in the western monarchies the council, at once the supreme administrative body and the high court of justice of the principality, became the key unit of effective central government, its members appointed exclusively by the prince and responsible only to him. Princes rationalized the financial machinery of their states and regularized the collection of taxes. Their subjects, reports a sixteenth-century chronicler, "look on them as a greater curse than the robber knights of old. The knights only carried off material property, while the princes undermine the wisdom of our forefathers, change what we have heretofore held as equitable, and like a plague destroy the traditional rights of the nation."[6] a judgment which describes accurately enough the ambition of the princes, while exaggerating their success. For although German princes moved in the same direction as Francis I and Henry VIII, they moved much more slowly. The estates restricted their freedom to maneuver. They were financially dependent. Unable, like the king of France, to make consent to taxation a formality, without the colonial revenues of the king of Spain, they remained captives of tradition—under the law rather than above it. Penury circumscribed their military power. Their officers were too few to break decisively the immunities of seigneurial and municipal jurisdiction. Aristocratic opposition increased rather than diminished during the century. German princes were to exercise only in the eighteenth century the sovereign powers that the kings of France, England, and Spain had grasped two centuries before.

Charles's German dominions were just one band in the spectrum of political types formed by the component parts of his empire. If in Germany Charles was the nominal overlord of independent cities and of princes who had retained, and were consolidating, the regalian powers their predecessors had usurped from his, in Castile he ruled a compact sovereign state, enjoyed the revenues of a colonial empire rich in gold and silver, and freed by Mexican and Peruvian treasure of his financial dependence on the Cortes, dispensed with representative institutions as effectively as did Francis I and Henry II. Sicily, on the other hand, was a turbulent feudal monarchy. There a Spanish viceroy shared the attributes of sovereignty with landed magnates; on their vast estates these greater nobles monopolized civil and criminal jurisdiction, appointed local administrative and judicial officers, levied feudal dues at will, and maintained private armies. The Netherlands was a federation of semiautonomous provinces. The old nobility controlled the administration at both the central and the

[6]Ibid., p. 547.

local level. Nobles monopolized the council of state. The chief officer of local government in each province was a great noble, omnicompetent and irremovable. Charles left him full liberty.

This diversity is instructive. It reminds us that the pattern of political development in France, Spain, and England was only one among several. It emphasizes the fact that the older forms of political organization survived tenaciously—just as earlier types of economic organization continued to flourish alongside the new capitalistic types. The purely dynastic unity of Charles's empire, moreover, and its looseness of structure, warn us not to overestimate the unity of any European kingdom in the sixteenth century, a period when the difficulty and slowness of communication, and the prevalence of a pattern of human habitation in which towns and the well-populated fertile areas around them were separated by immense distances of sparsely populated forests or steppes, imposed a more or less federated structure on every large state. Spain itself was a dynastic union of kingdoms united only in the person of their sovereign, and little progress was made toward imposing a common institutional and administrative structure on Castile and Aragon before the reign (1556–1598) of Philip II. Many French provinces, especially those most recently annexed to the crown, had their own particular laws and customs, their own provincial estates, their own courts. "France" could still mean only the Île-de-France (Paris and the surrounding area), and one spoke of going from Britanny to France. Each region had its own system of weights and measures, while internal customs barriers hindered the movement of goods from province to province.

Yet the emergence of the sovereign state remains the common thread that makes diversity intelligible. Everywhere in Europe the direction of political change was toward conciliar and bureaucratic government. What varied was the rate of change and the kind and size of the territorial unit controlled by a centralized administration. In the new monarchies, sovereign states crystallized at roughly the level of the nation. In the non-Spanish territories of Charles V, smaller states crystallized more slowly around great fiefs and cities, eventually forming sovereign principalities and city-states. This gradual proliferation of sovereign states within Charles's empire explains why even its dynastic unity did not survive him. Already in 1521 and 1522 he had transferred his Austrian territories and German responsibilities to his younger brother, the Archduke Ferdinand (1503–1564). At his abdication (1555–1556) he formally divided his territories between his son and his brother. Spain (with its colonial empire and its Italian dependencies) and the Netherlands went to Philip II; Austria, Bohemia, Hungary, and the imperial title went to the Austrian Habsburgs—Ferdinand and his heirs.

But until his retirement to the Gerelamite monastery of Yuste in Estremadura, Charles dominated European politics, and his empire was the focus of a struggle for power involving every European state.

THE ITALIAN STATE SYSTEM DURING THE RENAISSANCE

Between 1450 and 1560, the crystallization of sovereign territorial states in much of Europe, the ascendancy of the house of Habsburg, the bellicose expansionism of France, and the penetration of Ottoman armies up the Danube to the gates of Vienna, created new patterns of international rivalry and, for the first time, a European state system.

Italy was the prototype of the new system and the prey of its aggressions. In the high Middle Ages the peninsula had been divided into three major spheres of power: northern and much of central Italy formed the *Regnum Italicum*, an integral part of the Holy Roman Empire of the German kings; Rome and the rest of central Italy was ruled by the papacy; southern Italy and Sicily were independent kingdoms ruled in turn by Normans, Germans, Frenchmen, and Aragonese. Imperial authority in the *Regnum Italicum* collapsed in the second half of the thirteenth century. In central Italy the withdrawal of the papacy to Avignon in the fourteenth century hastened the dissolution of the old political order. The result was an atomization of the peninsula. The Italian cities profited. As the fame and memory of the German *Imperium Romanum* declined, as papal overlordship crumbled even in Rome itself, a civilization of city-states rose on the ruins. Ever since antiquity, central and northern Italy had been exceptionally dense with towns; the type of feudal baron so common in France, England, and Germany had not developed there. Enriched by commerce, commanding resources beyond those of most feudal princes, Italian cities usurped the sovereign powers of emperor and pope; refused, like the Florentines, to draw in their horns before presumptive overlords; founded independent states; and defended their liberty by force. By the early fourteenth century, Italy north of Rome was a patchwork of autonomous city-states.

During the fifteenth century aggressive warfare simplified Italian political geography. Many smaller cities lost their independence. The more powerful ones expanded to form sizable states. By 1450, five states shared the substance of power: the kingdom of Naples in the south, the Papal States, the republics of Florence and Venice, and the duchy of Milan. Naples was a feudal monarchy; the Papal States, an ecclesiastical principality most of which was independent of effective papal control; Florence's institutions were republican, but in fact it was ruled by the merchant house of Medici; Milan was a despotism, with effective political power monopolized by the duke; Venice was an aristocracy ruled by a closed circle of families who monopolized both political and economic power. All were effectively independent of any higher authority. Milan, Florence, and Venice were sovereign states. Power and justice within their territories were exercised exclusively by their governments, whatever its constitutional form. But though they were territorial states, they were rather different from the northern kingdoms and principalities. Their peculiarity was that all a state's territory except for the mother city was regarded as a colonial hinterland, in striking anticipation of

THE ITALIAN STATE SYSTEM
DURING THE RENAISSANCE
*M. — MARQUISATE
ALPS
Milan
Verona
Venice
Padua
DUCHY OF MILAN
SAVOY
ASTI
Po R.
*M. OF MANTUA
VENETIAN REPUBLIC
ISTRIA
OTTOMAN EMPIRE
MARQUISATE OF SALUZZO
*M. OF MONTFERRAT
DUCHY OF SAVOY
Genoa
DUCHY OF MODENA
DUCHY OF FERRARA
Bologna
REPUBLIC OF GENOA
Lucca
Florence
REPUBLIC OF LUCCA
Pisa
REPUBLIC OF FLORENCE
Siena
REP. OF SIENA
PAPAL STATES
DALMATIA
ADRIATIC SEA
Tiber R.
CORSICA (to Genoa)
Rome
KINGDOM OF NAPLES
Naples
SARDINIA (to Spain)
TYRRHENIAN SEA
0
200 miles
Palermo
KINGDOM OF SICILY
MEDITERRANEAN SEA

the administration of the Portuguese and Spanish empires. Cities subject to Venice, for example, were forbidden independent commercial dealings with foreign merchants. Venetian merchants monopolized foreign trade and were the intermediaries in all transactions. Superimposed on the institutions of formerly autonomous city-states was the authority of governors appointed by the Venetian senate. No representative institutions developed, and the interests of the "colonials" rarely influenced policy. In Florence, only a small minority even of those men who lived within the city's walls were citizens and participated actively in political life. The rise of the Medicean principate in the fifteenth century and its reimbodiment in the grand duchy of Tuscany in the sixteenth resulted in the suppression not of the civic liberty of a people, but of the privileged position of an oligarchy; while beyond the walls stretched the political hinterland of the Tuscan territories, ruled by and in the interests of the citizens of Florence and their prince.

Between 1450 and 1494 the Italian states played a sophisticated diplomatic and military game in relative isolation from the rest of Europe. Rules for this game developed rapidly, concerning such matters as the role of the resident ambassador, offensive and defensive alliances, intervention and nonintervention treaties, guaranty and neutrality declarations, demarcation of spheres of influence, nonaggression pacts with provisions for action against disturbers of the peace, commercial treaties, and so on. Italians invented the modern techniques of international relations with the same fertility with which they invented techniques of business and styles of art. The regulating principle of the system was an early version of the balance of power. Francesco Guicciardini (1483–1540), whose histories of Italy and of Florence recaptured in the sixteenth century the intellectual ferocity of Thucydides, gave the new principle an early statement: "It was the aim of each [of the five major powers] to preserve its own territory and to defend its own interest by carefully making sure that no one of them grew strong enough to enslave the others; and to this end each gave the most careful attention to even minor political events or changes."[7] Since Venice was the most powerful and aggressive of the Italian states, Florence, Milan, and Naples united against Venice. The result, says Guicciardini, was a beneficent balance (*bilancia*), an equilibrium under relatively peaceful conditions. This is an early description of a closed state system regulated by the balance of power. Movement by one state necessarily called forth responses by all the other states. Equilibrium guaranteed the independence and security of all.

The governing class of every Italian state fought tenaciously to preserve this independence. There was no absence of national feeling for what Petrarch had called the "gentle Latin blood" and the "loveliest country of the earth." Everyone assumed that Italy's soil was sacred, its frontiers defined by the seas and mountains of nature herself. Italians had a common language, which printing was helping to standardize, and in the fifteenth century, a common culture which intellectuals rightly considered superior to that of the remainder of "barbarian" Europe. We call such attitudes cultural nationalism. They parallel the revived popularity in Germany in the sixteenth century of Tacitus's *Germania*, with its contrast of brave and virtuous Germans and decadent predatory Romans, and the French conviction that in language, piety, moral virtue, courage, and every other "rare and antique" virtue they surpassed all other peoples. This nationalism had no political or military significance. Nowhere in Europe did the state rest on or incarnate a national tradition. And certainly it did not do so in Italy. Although statesmen appealed to the "universal needs of Italy" and urged their rivals to be

[7]*Storia fiorentina*, ch. xi. *Opere inedite di Francesco Guicciardini*, ed. by P. and L. Guicciardini (Florence, 1859), Vol. III, p. 105.

Patterns of International Rivalry / 117

"good Italians," in their view the idea of an independent Italy implied first of all the independence of their particular states. Like the Greek city-states before their conquest by Macedonia, the Italian cities would not and could not create a unity which might assure a common and Italian independence by destroying the basis of their own particular autonomy and independence. At the end of the fifteenth century the Italian states stood disunited before the new monarchies of France and Spain.

PATTERNS OF INTERNATIONAL RIVALRY

In 1494 King Charles VIII of France (ruled 1483–1498) invaded Italy and destroyed the autonomy of the Italian state system of the Renaissance. A European system replaced the Italian. Between 1519 and 1559, on this larger stage, with more ample resources and diminished subtlety, Charles V, Francis I, and Suleiman the Magnificent, the Turkish sultan, played the diplomatic and military game invented by the fifteenth-century Italian states. Charles's empire was the predominant European power. His territories, his crusading zeal, and his dynastic claims blocked the paths of French and Ottoman expansion. The two great conflicts of the period therefore opposed Habsburg to Valois and Habsburg to Ottoman. The fundamental alliance designed to balance, and to crush, Habsburg power was between the French and the Turks.

The Habsburg—Valois Struggle

The struggle between Habsburg and Valois was personal and dynastic to a degree difficult for us to understand. The new monarchies were sovereign states, not national states. The aims of their rulers were not national aims. The state was identified with the person of the monarch and with his dynasty. The Renaissance king had sole control over the conduct of foreign affairs, and although social pressures (from the nobility, for example) and even commercial considerations sometimes influenced his policies, his purpose normally was to further no interest larger than that of his own family. It is for this reason that marriage alliances were so prominent a subject of diplomatic negotiation and so rich in consequences. The empire of Charles V, as we have seen, was the result of royal marriages; and advantageous matrimony remained a fundamental and successful object of Charles's diplomacy. In 1521 he laid the basis of the future Austrian monarchy by arranging to have his sister Mary marry King Louis of Hungary and Bohemia while his brother Ferdinand married Louis' sister, who was next in the line of succession. His own marriage to a Portuguese princess opened the way for his son, Philip II, to succeed to the throne of Portugal and in 1580 unite the Spanish and Portuguese empires under a single ruler. He married Philip II to Queen Mary of England. If a son had been born to them, England would probably not be a Protestant country today.

THE VALOIS SUCCESSION, 1461–1559

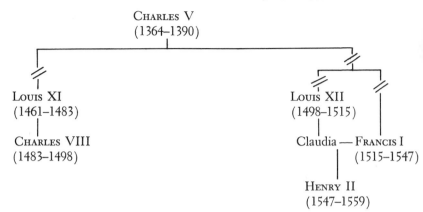

CHARLES V
(1364–1390)

LOUIS XI
(1461–1483)

CHARLES VIII
(1483–1498)

LOUIS XII
(1498–1515)

Claudia — FRANCIS I
(1515–1547)

HENRY II
(1547–1559)

Sixteenth-century wars were equally personal. Kings went to war to gain honor and profit, moved not by national interest—an anachronism in this context—but by personal ambition or resentment and by the "just" dynastic claims of their families. Charles VIII invaded Italy in order to prosecute a dubious claim to the kingdom of Naples inherited from a younger branch of the French royal family. The next French king, Louis XII, invaded the duchy of Milan in 1499, asserting that the Sforza, the reigning ducal house, were usurpers, while he himself was the rightful legal heir through his grandmother Valentina, daughter of an earlier Milanese ruling family, the Visconti. When Charles V succeeded Ferdinand of Aragon, Naples became his, to tax but also to defend. When he succeeded Maximilian as German king he became, like the German kings before him, the feudal overlord of the duchy of Milan and the inevitable opponent of French pretensions in northern Italy. Nor was Italy the only area where conflicting dynastic claims opposed Habsburg to Valois. At the death of the last duke of Burgundy in 1477, Louis XI of France (ruled 1461–1483) had seized the duchy and reincorporated it into the royal domain. Charles was determined to recover French Burgundy and reconstitute the totality of his Burgundian inheritance. Francis was equally determined to resist this fatal dismemberment of his kingdom. To the north and west, the counties of Flanders and Artois were at once fiefs of the king of France and, as two of the seventeen provinces of the Netherlands, in the actual possession of the Habsburgs. Francis considered them French, Charles viewed them as part of his empire. Similarly conflicting claims to provinces on the French and Spanish sides of the Pyrenees exacerbated relations there. Both monarchs, in short, considered their personal rights and their territories to be threatened. Charles saw France as an aggressive power attempting to rob him of his rightful patrimony, egotistically disrupting the peace of Europe, nullifying his divine vocation to lead a united Christendom against the Turk. Francis I, conversely, saw his kingdom surrounded by Habsburg territory—Spain, the Netherlands, and Germany—and believed that possessions legitimately his were threatened, that Charles wanted "to be master everywhere." The hostility between Habsburg and Valois was irreducible.

The Habsburg-Ottoman Struggle

So too was the hostility between Habsburg and Ottoman. Since the middle of the fourteenth century, Europe had looked with fear and anger, but—except for states immediately threatened—with passivity, at the rise to power of the Ottoman Turks. In the decades after the fall of Constantinople in 1453 the Turks subdued much of eastern Europe south of the Danube, including the Adriatic coast; reduced the last Genoese colonies in the East; seized large portions of the Venetian empire; and though a vigorous trade continued, broke the old commercial monopoly Italian merchants had so long enjoyed in the eastern Mediterranean. Christendom, expanding so remarkably across the western ocean, was under mounting pressure from the Moslem East. During the reign (1520–1566) of Sultan Suleiman the Magnificent, Habsburg territories bore the brunt of Turkish aggression, and the Ottomans, pushing up the Danube, became an integral part of the European state system. Suleiman took Belgrade in 1521. In August, 1526, he crushed the Hungarian army at Mohács. His diary is vividly laconic. He recorded on August 31: "The emperor, seated on a golden throne, receives the homage of the viziers and beys: massacre of 2,000 prisoners: the rain falls in torrents." And on September 2d: "Rest at Mohács: 20,000 Hungarian infantry and 4,000 of their cavalry are buried." King Louis died in the slaughter. To succeed him, his brother-in-law, the Archduke Ferdinand, was elected king of Bohemia in October, 1526, and king of Hungary in 1527. In the meantime, Suleiman pressed on to Vienna. In September, 1529, he appeared before the gates of the city. The coming of winter and the enormous overextension of his lines of communication forced his retirement. Vienna never fell. But for decades the Turks directly threatened the hereditary center of Habsburg power. Inevitably, Charles and Ferdinand dignified their defense of the hereditary lands as a defense of Europe itself against the infidel, and their determination to recover their lost Hungarian kingdom as a crusade for which they could legitimately demand men and money from all of Europe. Charles counterattacked in 1531. He resumed Portuguese and Spanish crusading probes in northern Africa, captured Tunis (in his role as "God's standard bearer"), and opened a new theater of war in the western Mediterranean, the beginning of a campaign which reached its climax many years later, in 1571, when his illegitimate son Don John of Austria (1547–1578) smashed the Turkish Mediterranean fleet at Lepanto.

Around the two fundamental lines of force and opposition generated by the conflicts of Habsburg and Valois, Habsburg and Ottoman, alliances developed according to an abstract logic of power. The first duty of any government servant, wrote Ermolao Barbaro, a Venetian noble, diplomat, humanist, Aristotelian, and cardinal, is "to do, say, advise, and think whatever may best serve the preservation and aggrandizement of his own state."[8] Two imperatives dictated international political action: first, to preserve one's own state in the face of attacks by a stronger neighbor; second, to collect allies, counterattack, defeat, and if possible, plunder that neighbor. In an age of religious enthusiasm and doctrinal nicety, motives were notably secular. One of the three great contestants was Moslem, yet the fundamental alliance of the period was between the Most Christian King of France and the infidel sultan against their common enemy, the Holy Roman emperor, the temporal head of Christendom. From Madrid, where he was kept prisoner after his defeat and capture at the Battle of Pavia (February 24, 1525), Francis wrote secretly to the sultan asking for help. The Battle of Mohács was the answer to Pavia, the fulfillment of Suleiman's promise to deliver the bey of France from the supremacy of the bey of Spain. Contemporaries denounced the "impious alliance," but it was only final evidence of the hollowness of the crusading ideal. Already in the fifteenth century the Venetians had encouraged the Turks to attack Brindisi and Otranto in order to weaken the kingdom of Naples; and they in fact occupied a part of the Apulian coast for two years (1480–1481). Even the pope received a Turkish pension, in return for keeping a rebellious brother of the sultan in captivity.

The two Christian contestants were Catholics. They fought without quarter, while the smaller states, whether Catholic or Protestant, almost invariably decided their alignment by the logic of power rather than by the text of orthodoxy. The Italians, when they were free to act, allied with the weaker against the stronger, hoping always to expel both Habsburg and Valois from the peninsula. The aim of the German princes, both Catholic and Protestant, was to keep the emperor weak, and they reacted swiftly, by forming alliances with France, against attempts to assert imperial power in Germany. Papal policy is particularly illuminating. In the crucial decades after 1520 during which Protestantism established itself in much of Europe, the temporal position of the papacy as an Italian state, and the desperate fear of successive popes that Charles V would call a church council and settle the religious question in Germany and in Europe independently of Rome, determined papal policy. After Pavia, Charles dominated both northern and southern Italy. Irresistibly the popes were drawn into a French alliance. Even the sack of Rome in 1527 by imperial troops and the captivity of the pope blunted only temporarily a necessary attraction. The result was a pattern of alignment constantly repeated during the middle decades of the century, a pattern disastrous for Catholicism but, in the logic of power, of an elegant and inevitable symmetry. On one side was the empire of Charles V; on the

---

[8]Quoted by Garrett Mattingly, *Renaissance Diplomacy* (London, 1962), p. 117.

Henry II, King of France (1547–1559). *Engraving by Niccolò della Casa, 1547. The king wears a superb suit of dress armor. National Gallery, Washington, D.C.*

other was France, allied with the Turks, the German Protestant princes, and the Roman pontiff. "How one lives," wrote Machiavelli in the fifteenth chapter of *The Prince* (1513), "is so far distant from how one ought to live, that he who neglects what is done for what ought to be done sooner effects his ruin than his preservation." Renaissance rulers rarely made that mistake.

Financial collapse brought peace and the settlement of Cateau-Cambrésis (April, 1559). The contestants, now Henry II of France and Philip II of Spain, recognized what had been plain for some time. France was not strong enough to conquer Italy and make good its claims to Milan and Naples. The long struggle for that reservoir of power and wealth, seat of the imperial dignity, and home of everything most beautiful, original, and learned in art and letters, left the house of Habsburg master of the peninsula. Spanish viceroys ruled Sicily, Naples, and the duchy of Milan. The grand duchy of Tuscany and the Papal States were Spanish satellites. Only Venice retained a limited independence of action. On the other hand, the Habsburgs were not strong enough to dismember France or seriously to weaken a kingdom relatively so tightly organized, so rich in men and resources, so strategically located. Philip II therefore renounced his claims to French Burgundy, condemning the bones of his ancestors, resting in their magnificent tombs in a Carthusian monastery near Dijon, to foreign soil. Artois and Flanders remained part of the Spanish Netherlands. By a separate treaty, the enclave at Calais, the remnant of once vast English possessions on the continent, was returned to France. Marriages cemented the dynastic truce. Continental princes turned, momentarily, from pressing their foreign ambitions to deal with the challenge of heresy at home.

CHAPTER 5

Revolution and Reformation in the Church: The Problem of Authority

MARTIN LUTHER posted his ninety-five theses against indulgences on the door of the castle church in Wittenberg in October, 1517. John Calvin died in Geneva in 1564. Within these less than fifty years a handful of religious geniuses kindled the enthusiasm of millions, created original systems of Christian doctrine, and founded new churches hostile to Rome. Inadvertently, decisively, and permanently the Protestant reformers cracked the millennial unity of European Christendom.

The word "Protestant" has a precise and well-known origin and presents no problem of meaning or usage. In March, 1529, the Catholic majority in the Diet of Speyer called on all Germans to condemn Lutheranism and to stop making changes in their religion. On April 19, the minority of princes and towns that had gone over to Lutheranism "protested" before God that they would act in no way contrary to God's will, His Word, their consciences, or the salvation of their souls. Catholics called them the "protesting Estates." Eventually, anyone who left the Catholic church was called a Protestant, and the name came to be applied to any member of a western Christian church or sect outside the Roman communion.

The origin of the modern definition of "Reformation" is more difficult to trace. In the Middle Ages the word had had two principal meanings: it could denote the inner renewal or transformation of the individual Christian, or it could refer to the correction of ecclesiastical abuses, as in the phrase "to reform the Church in head and members." Only very gradually in the sixteenth century, and exclusively by Protestants, was the word applied to the contemporary movement, begun by Luther, of opposition to Rome and the Catholic Church; and only in the seventeenth century did it become common, again among Protestants, to speak of the Lutheran "reformation" or the Lutheran "reform" of religion. In modern historiography this usage has come to express a consistent and influential interpretation of the Protestant movement and its causes. Its thesis was trenchantly put by Henry

Charles Lea, the great nineteenth-century historian of the medieval Inquisition and sacerdotal celibacy, when he wrote that "the primary cause of the Reformation is to be sought in the all-pervading corruption of the Church and its oppressive exercise of its supernatural prerogatives." The Reformation, in this view, was violent and broke the unity of Christendom because the "abuses under which Christendom groaned were too inveterate, too firmly entrenched, and too profitable to be removed by any but the sternest and sharpest remedies."[1]

This is the "abuse" theory of the Reformation. It has two difficulties. First, it masks the concern of all serious contemporary Christians, both Catholics and Protestants, with the reform of abuses. Second, it misrepresents the nature of the Protestant Reformation itself.

The Church, as all medieval and sixteenth-century men knew, was a divine institution whose head was Christ; but they knew too that it was a human institution as well, staffed by rational beings with intellects and wills vitiated by Adam's fall. Abuses were inevitable, and from the earliest times, frequent. So were efforts to narrow the gap between the ideal and the actual and to restore the Church to a nearer image of the virtues of the saints. Ecclesiastical abuses were neither more widespread nor more iniquitous in the early sixteenth century than in many earlier periods. To be sure, contemporaries concerned with the spiritual condition of the Church and the religious education of the laity deplored the secularization of the episcopacy, plurality of benefices (the possession of two or more ecclesiastical livings by one man), and clerical nonresidence (the permanent absence of priests from their parishes and bishops from their dioceses), but these were venerable abuses at every level of the hierarchy. Sixteenth-century parish priests were grindingly poor. They were often ignorant and superstitious. They kept concubines. In many convents monastic life was spiritually tepid. For the past five hundred years reformers had struggled against the same evils. The Renaissance papacy, like every contemporary monarchy, was short of money, and successive popes disdained no worldly opportunity to obtain funds. As ruler of one of the five major Italian states, many a pope used excommunication and the interdict to further his temporal ambitions. Nepotism was normal. Kings learned how to manage the sale of temporal offices by observing the traffic in ecclesiastical ones. On the other hand, the degradation of the papacy was greater in the ninth and tenth centuries than in the Renaissance. The story of the "martyrs" Rufinus and Albinus—Red Gold and Pale Silver—whose relics the pope magnificently buried "in the treasury of St. Cupidity beside the mercy seat of St. Avidity her sister, not far from the basilica of their mother St. Avarice"[2] circulated in the twelfth century,

[1]*Cambridge Modern History*, Vol. I (New York and London, 1903), pp. 678–679, 691.
[2]Quoted by R. W. Southern, *The Making of the Middle Ages* (New Haven, 1953), p. 153.

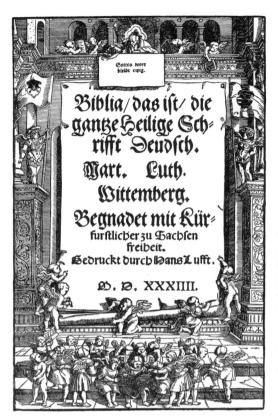

Title page of the first complete edition of Luther's translation of the Bible. *Published in Wittenberg by Hans Lufft in 1534. The source book of the German Reformation. At the top, flanked by cherubs holding the four Gospels, God the Father writes down His Word.* Gottes wort bleibt ewig; God's Word endures forever.

not in the sixteenth. Dante, writing in the early fourteenth century, put several popes in hell.

Like their medieval predecessors, sixteenth-century Christians clamored for reform and tried to achieve it. Franciscan and Dominican preachers castigated the pride, the covetousness, the secular and worldly living, of monks and priests. In moral tracts, manuals of piety, and satires, humanist intellectuals tried to temper the laity's immoderate devotion to images, relics, and pilgrimages. The magistrates of the Parlement of Paris vigorously pushed monastic reform. On occasion they used troops to impose a reforming abbot on recalcitrant monks. In 1512, the archbishop of Canterbury called a convocation of the clergy of his province to correct abuses. Between 1512 and 1517, the Fifth Lateran Council sat in Rome. At its opening session the general of the Augustinian order (Luther's order) prayed God to give the clergy strength to "restore the church to its ancient splendor and purity," and the assembled prelates passed decrees on the selection of qualified bishops and legislated against heresy, blasphemy, simony, and clerical concubinage. As the council ended, a group of distinguished Roman priests and laymen founded the Oratory of Divine Love. They took no vows; they had no papal sanction or special position. They were men of learning and religious sensibility who met from time to time in order to restore the dignity and the due observance of the divine service, participate in spiritual exercises, and awaken by their example the religious life of the city and the Church. No group of men better suggests the aims and character of a reforming movement that encompassed all of Europe. Episcopal members retired from Rome to reform their own dioceses, in Verona, Chieti, Mantua, and Carpentras in the south of France. They investigated each priest and suspended the unworthy. They encouraged preaching and the more frequent celebration of the sacraments. They insisted on clerical residence and moved against pluralities. In short, from Cracow to Toledo, from Durham to Palermo, reformers were actively engaged against entrenched corruption. In every country of Europe and in every class of society in the decades before 1517, there were men for whom *reformatio* was a matter of immediate, active concern.

The leaders of the Protestant Reformation, too, were sensitive to ecclesiastical abuses and wished to reform them. Yet the reform of abuses was not their fundamental concern. The attempt to reform an institution, after all, suggests that its abuses are temporary blemishes on a body fundamentally sound and beautiful. Luther, Zwingli, and Calvin did not believe this. They attacked the corruption of the Renaissance papacy, but their aim was not merely to reform it; they identified the pope with Antichrist and wished to abolish the papacy altogether. They did not limit their attack on the sacrament of penance to the abuse of indulgences. They plucked out the sacrament itself root and branch because they believed it to have no scriptural foundation. They did not wish simply to reform monasticism; they saw the institution itself as a perversion. The Reformation was a passionate debate on the proper conditions of salvation. It concerned the very foundations of faith and doctrine. Protestants reproached the clergy not so much for living badly as for believing badly, for teaching false and dangerous things. Luther attacked not the corruption of institutions but what he believed to be the corruption of faith itself. The Protestant Reformation was not strictly a "reformation" at all. In the intention of its leaders it was a restoration of biblical Christianity. In practice it was a revolution, a full-scale attack on the traditional doctrines and sacramental structure of the Roman Church. It could say with Christ, "I came not to send peace, but a sword." In its relation to the Church as it existed in the second decade of the sixteenth century, it came not to reform, but to destroy.

MARTIN LUTHER

Luther was the son of a prosperous mining entrepreneur of peasant stock. When he was eighteen, he matriculated at the University of Erfurt. He

Martin Luther in 1520. *Etching by Lucas Cranach the Elder. This is the earliest portrait of Luther. The inscription:* Luther himself makes known the immortal lineaments of his thought, but Lucas drew his mortal features.

mastered the Aristotelian curriculum in record time and received the bachelor's degree in 1502 and the master's early in 1505. On his father's advice he enrolled in the faculty of law, the normal path to lucrative and responsible preferment in church or state. Then in July, 1505, Luther was caught in a thunderstorm. A terrifying bolt of lightning struck near him. In fear of death and possible damnation he cried out, "St. Anne help me, I will become a monk." He fulfilled his vow by joining the mendicant order of St. Augustine before the end of the same month. The next years were punctuated by periods of tightening spiritual and psychological anguish. In the last year of his life Luther himself described very simply the problem that had brought him close to despair and blasphemy: "Though I lived as a monk without reproach, I felt that I was a sinner before God with an extremely disturbed conscience. I could not believe that he was placated by my satisfaction. I did not love, yes, I hated the righteous God who punishes sinners, and secretly, if not blasphemously, . . . I was angry with God."[3] God is just; equally certain was Luther's conviction that he himself was weak, impure, and sinful, and

[3]*Luther's Works*, Vol. XXXIV, ed. by Lewis W. Spitz (Philadelphia, 1960), pp. 336–337.

that his desperate effort to merit salvation was a failure. Appalled by the disparity between his paltry monkish "good works" and God's demand that he be just, he trembled before the prospect of deserved damnation. With the radicalism of genius Luther eventually found peace by totally transforming the problem. In 1511 he was transferred from Erfurt to the little town of Wittenberg, in electoral Saxony, and in 1512 he was appointed professor of Holy Scriptures at its new university. He lectured on Genesis (October, 1512–July, 1513), the Psalms (August, 1513–October, 1515), and finally Paul's Epistle to the Romans (November, 1515–September, 1516). He found his inspiration in Paul:

At last, by the mercy of God, meditating day and night, I gave heed to the context of the words, namely, "In it the righteousness of God is revealed, as it is written, 'He who through faith is righteous shall live.' " [Romans 1:17] There I began to understand that the righteousness of God is that by which the righteous lives by a gift of God, namely faith. And this is the meaning: the righteousness of God is revealed by the Gospel, namely, the passive righteousness with which merciful God justifies us by faith, as it is written, "He who through faith is righteous shall live." Here I felt that I was altogether born again and had entered paradise itself through open gates.[4]

The conception of an angry God faded before that of a God of mercy. Human struggle to *earn* salvation gave way to a total passivity and trust and faith in Christ. The justice of God became a free acquittal of the guilty. The result was a doctrine whose implications were devastating for the Church and for traditional Christian belief and practice as they had developed from the ninth to the sixteenth century.

Three formulas epitomize Luther's teaching: *sola fide* ("by faith alone"), *sola scriptura* ("by Scripture alone"), and *sola gratia* ("by grace alone"). They define a relationship between man and God in which as much as possible is attributed to God and as little as possible is attributed to man. Man is irremediably weak and evil.

It is not only the privation of a property of the will [wrote Luther] nor only the privation of light in the intellect, of virtue in the memory; but the absolute privation of all righteousness and of the power of all strengths, of body and soul, of the whole man interior and exterior. Further, there is in man a positive inclination to evil, a disgust for the good, a hatred of light and wisdom, a delight in error and darkness, a flight from and an abomination of good works, a race toward evil.[5]

Sola fide emphasizes the insignificance of reason and the primacy of

[4]*Ibid.*, p. 337.
[5]*D. Martin Luthers Werke. Kritische Gesamtausgabe*, Vol. LVI (Weimar, 1938), p. 312.

revelation. More radically, it insists that man is saved or justified by faith alone. This doctrine of justification by faith alone is the cornerstone of classical Protestantism. Its chief scriptural sources are two celebrated texts of St. Paul: "For by grace are ye saved through faith; and that not of yourselves: it is the gift of God: Not of works, lest any man should boast" (Ephesians 2:8–9); and "Therefore we conclude that a man is justified by faith without the deeds of the law" (Romans 3:28). No man is saved by his own merit. Man has no merit. Nothing that he can do with his own strength and by the exercise of his own will brings him closer to God. If God were just only, all men would be damned; but God is also merciful. His purely gratuitous mercy, which no one can do anything to deserve, mysteriously chooses some few men for salvation. These are the elect, predestined for salvation. They are accounted just—and thus saved—by faith; and faith itself is a gratuitous gift of grace. Therefore, to say that a man is justified by faith alone is to say that salvation is an inscrutable process over which man has no control and in which his merits and good works play no part. Man cannot cooperate in his own salvation.

Sola scriptura is a specific case of *sola fide*. It rigorously maintains that the only source of religious truth is the Word of God revealed in Scripture. Scripture is uniquely authoritative because it is the concrete locus of the Word of God, the written record of the revelation of God in Christ, the channel through which God reaches those to whom He has granted the grace of faith.

Sola gratia is a generalization of *sola fide*. Grace and nature are viewed as inalterably opposed. The natural man can neither know the truth nor will the good without the aid of grace. Human reason is deformed and blind. The unaided intellect is chained in darkness; knowledge of divine things comes from grace alone. Similarly, the human will is captive. The natural man is free to choose only between different degrees of sin; grace alone can grant him Christian freedom, the freedom to choose only the good. All power, all good, all virtue, come from God's grace; all wickedness, weakness, and evil come from nature, especially man's nature. "This doctrine," said Luther, "may seem hard and cruel, but it is full of sweetness; for it teaches us to seek humbly all assistance and all salvation, not from ourselves, but from without, through faith in Christ the Redeemer."[6]

Between 1517 and 1520—gradually, haphazardly, under the pressure of events—Luther discovered the radicalism implicit in his sweetly cruel doctrine of forgiveness. Astonished but undismayed, he found himself the leader of a revolutionary attack on the Roman Church.

The Roman Church was a monarchical, sacerdotal, and sacramental organization. Its secular power had shrunk since the crises of the Avignonese captivity and schism in the fourteenth century; but in the area of faith and

[6]*Ibid.*, pp. 89, 91, 382.

morals, Roman claims had become more comprehensive and sharply monarchical. Papal theorists identified the universal Church with the Roman Church and the Roman Church with its supreme and monarchical head, the pope. Just as the universal Church could not err in faith and morals, so also papal rulings, definitions, and interpretations were infallible. Moreover, the Church itself—defined now as that ecclesiastical hierarchy of which the pope was head, that "empire" ruled by the monarchical laws and ordinances of the pope—claimed a monopoly on grace. God's saving grace operated objectively and exclusively through the sacraments: baptism, confirmation, the Eucharist, penance, ordination, marriage, and extreme unction. The clergy, in turn, monopolized the administration of the sacraments. Separated from the laity by the indelible mark of ordination, the priest, according to the doctrine of transubstantiation, possessed the miraculous power, denied even to angels, of transforming the Eucharistic elements of bread and wine into the real body and blood of Christ. It is not an accident that this doctrine of transubstantiation was the only medieval contribution to dogma. The Mass lay at the heart of medieval sacerdotalism and sacramentalism. When the priest repeated the words "This is my body," he transformed the substance of the elements into the body and blood of Christ, while their accidents, all attributes perceivable by the senses, remained those of bread and wine. He reenacted the Incarnation and Crucifixion: God became flesh, and Christ died sacrificially upon the altar for man's salvation. Only through the mediation of the priest could this grace reach the laity. Here was the foundation of clerical power and of the unique position of the Church in society.

Luther's initial protest was against indulgences. An indulgence was the transfer by the pope of superfluous merit accumulated by Christ, the Virgin, and the saints to an individual sinner in order to remit all or some of the penalties for sin later to be suffered in purgatory. By Luther's time, papal doctrine held that such transfers of divine credit could benefit not only the living, but the dead as well. Because he believed that man is justified by faith alone, Luther denied that saints had superfluous credits or that merit could be stored up for subsequent use. He denied the power of the pope over purgatory. Finally, he branded indulgences as positively harmful because they induced a false sense of security and imperiled salvation. Peace and forgiveness of sins come only in the Word of Christ through faith. "But if anyone does not believe this word, even though he be pardoned a million times by the pope himself, . . . he shall never know inner peace."[7] The ninety-five theses against indulgences made Luther famous overnight.

The theses were the work of a reformer. Three devastating tracts published by Luther in 1520—*An Open Letter to the Christian Nobility of*

---

[7]*Luther's Works*, Vol. XXXI, ed. by Harold J. Grimm (Philadelphia, 1957), pp. 100–101.

the German Nation, *The Babylonian Captivity of the Church*, and *On Christian Liberty*—were the works of a revolutionary. In them Luther attacked every important assumption on which the medieval Church had rested. He asserted that the councils of the universal Church had erred. He called papal authority a human invention and denied the pope's infallibility in matters of doctrine. At a stroke he rejected the sacraments of confirmation, marriage, penance, holy orders, and extreme unction. In denying the sacrament of orders, Luther sought to erase the distinction between the spiritual estate (pope, bishops, the secular clergy, and the monastic clergy) and the temporal estate (princes, lords, merchants, craftsmen, and peasants), the distinction between priest and layman, thus ending, as he put it, "the detestable tyranny of the clergy over the laity." Instead Luther envisioned a priesthood of all believers. Because all of these had one baptism, one Gospel, one faith, they were all alike Christians, all alike truly members of a single spiritual estate, all priests. The alleged difference between the priesthood and the laity was, in his view, a human invention. Most important, Luther struck at the heart of sacerdotal power by redefining the sacrament of the Eucharist. He denied that the Mass was a sacrifice, a repetition of Christ's sacrifice on the cross. He denied the doctrine of transubstantiation. He denied that the sacrament worked, as medieval theologians had believed, by its own innate virtue and power. Because men were justified by faith alone, the efficacy of the sacrament was a function of the faith of the recipient. The faith that made the sacrament effective was one's own. God gave faith directly to the individual. No mediator, except the Word of Scripture, was necessary. The individual human soul stood alone before its Savior and creator.

THE FRAGMENTATION OF CLASSICAL PROTESTANTISM

Religious individualism is necessarily disruptive of established beliefs and practices. Its progress poses at once the problem of authority. By what authority, asked Luther's Catholic opponents, does a single monk presume to stand against the common faith of the entire Church and the opinion of all of Christendom? More general questions quickly followed. Where is the source of religious truth? What is our guarantee that we have found it? Luther's answers appeared to be clear. The Word of God revealed in the Bible is alone authoritative: *sola scriptura*. Scripture alone is the lord and master of all writings and doctrines on earth. No Church Father, not even St. Augustine, no theologian, not even Aquinas, no ecclesiastical dignitary, not even the pope, has the right to teach something that cannot be demonstrated from Scripture.

The difficulty with this position is that the meaning of Scripture is far from clear and that, in practice, biblical texts can be and have been interpreted in different ways. Shall we conclude that each Christian is free to interpret Scripture for himself? "God forbid," answered Luther and every responsible sixteenth-century theologian after him. Such a conclusion confuses Christian liberty with license and is, as one Protestant divine put it, "a most diabolical dogma, because it means that everyone should be left to go to hell in his own way."[8] But if the individual's reason or judgment cannot guarantee the truth and certainty of a scriptural interpretation, what can? Again Luther's answer was apparently clear. Christians must read the Bible under the guidance and inspiration of the Holy Spirit. The Holy Spirit guarantees the truth and uniformity of scriptural interpretation. The assertion was not new. What was new was that Luther denied the Spirit's authoritative guarantee to be legitimately institutionalized in the Roman Church. The objective control of interpretation by tradition and papal authority had in the past secured the doctrinal unity of western Christendom. The doctrine of *sola scriptura* dissolved this controlling link between Scripture and tradition and introduced into the definition of religious truth an element of subjectivity which not only separated Lutheran from Catholic but also gradually fragmented Protestantism itself into a multiplicity of competing faiths. The Catholic humanist Thomas More accused Luther of presuming to make his own individual interpretation of Scripture normative. (He called him an "infallible donkey.") And he predicted that once the Church's monopoly of scriptural interpretation was broken, "almost all the dogmas of the Christian faith, unchanged for so many centuries, will be called into question at the whim of upstart heretics."[9]

Events proved More right. Other reformers soon interpreted Scripture as freely and personally as Luther had done. Each claimed the guidance of the Holy Spirit. Each claimed a monopoly on Christian truth as universal as that claimed by Rome. *Sola scriptura* was the razor with which Luther cut away the "fictitious customs" and "human inventions" of the Catholic Church. Other innovators soon turned the same instrument on him; and from their divergently inspired interpretations of Holy Writ arose new varieties of Protestantism. In the sixteenth century the most important of these variant types were Zwinglianism and Calvinism.

HULDREICH ZWINGLI

Zwingli, after Luther the most creative among the Protestant theologians of the first generation, received a humanist education; he learned Greek in order to study Christ's teachings in the "original sources." In January, 1519, after several years of service as a parish priest in other towns of German

---

[8]Quoted by Roland H. Bainton, *The Travail of Religious Liberty* (Philadelphia, 1951), p. 114.

[9]*Responsio ad Lutherum*, trans. by Sister Gertrude J. Donnelly (*The Catholic University of America Studies in Medieval and Renaissance Latin*, Vol. XXIII, Washington, D.C., 1962), p. 147.

Switzerland, he began to preach the Gospel in the Grossmünster, or principal church, of Zurich. First Erasmus, then Luther, influenced his doctrinal development. As early as 1520, in marginal notes in his copy of the Psalms, he stated clearly the doctrine of justification by faith alone. He accepted the unique authority of Scripture, and like Luther and against all evidence, believed that the Bible was simple, clear, and easy to understand. In his view, the true Christian had to try every doctrine and usage by the touchstone of the Gospel and the fire of the apostle Paul. What agreed with Holy Writ was true; what conflicted with it, detestable. He followed Luther, too, in many of the consequences he drew from these assumptions. He disputed the efficacy of good works as a means to salvation, denied the existence of purgatory, and attacked monasticism and sacerdotal celibacy; he denied free will, and defended the predestination of the elect; he reduced the sacraments to two, and simplified the liturgy. When on Maundy Thursday, 1525, Zwingli celebrated the Lord's Supper instead of the Mass in the Grossmünster, Zurich's break with Rome was complete.

Zwingli's contribution was to push liturgical and sacramental simplification beyond the point to which Luther was prepared to go. Zwingli wished to reduce religion to its essentials, to achieve what he called a *summa religionis* (a "quintessence of religion"). Because he nursed a marked prejudice against any corporeal conception or representation of divine things, his passion for simplicity led him to an ascetic rejection of images and of every sensuous detail in the traditional ceremonial of the Church and to a denial of the Real Presence of Christ in the sacramental elements of the Eucharist. The congregation, he believed, should have ears only for the Word of God, not for the "trills" of music, and should have eyes only for the Scripture, not for female saints "luxuriously and sleekly" painted, as though their very purpose were to incite lasciviousness. Under Zwingli's influence his fellow citizens broke up the organ in the Grossmünster, removed and destroyed the stained glass windows, statues, and pictures of Zurich's churches, and whitewashed the interior walls. Zwinglians renounced liturgical magnificence and reduced their vernacular services to a reading and exposition of the Word of God. As a Catholic priest in Glarus, Zwingli had used at Mass a magnificently decorated golden chalice. As a Protestant minister in Zurich, he celebrated the Supper with a simple wooden cup.

From the same impulse came Zwingli's "sacramentarianism," his conviction that the Communion service was not a physical partaking of God, but only a commemorative, spiritual, and symbolic eating. Both Luther and Zwingli rejected the Catholic Mass, regarding it as a form of sacrificial magic. But Luther retained the Real Presence, maintaining that the actual flesh and blood of Christ coexisted in and with the natural substance of bread and wine and that the virtue of the sacrament depended on the faith of the recipient. Zwingli was more radical and more consistent. He denied the objective presence of the Eucharistic Christ in the sacrament of the altar

From Catholic Mass to Protestant Supper. *On the left, the chalice Zwingli used when he was a Catholic priest at Glarus; on the right, the wooden cup with which he celebrated the Lord's Supper.*

because it contradicted, in his view, the primordial idea of justification by faith alone. The bread and wine of the Supper were not the means of salvation, but only tokens of communion and symbols of duty. They conferred no grace, for the distribution of grace appertained to the Spirit alone. The Lord's Supper was a memorial service, celebrated in memory of the redemptive death of Christ.

Luther and Zwingli broke on this issue. No confrontation illuminates more clearly the problem of authority than the debate on the sacrament of the altar, or Eucharist, between Lutherans and Zwinglians at Marburg, in Hesse, in October of 1529. Zwingli came to the colloquy with Johannes Oecolampadius (1482–1531), the reformer of Basel, and the great Strasbourg theologian Martin Bucer (1491–1551). Luther came with Philip Melanchthon (1497–1560), his right-hand man and ultimately his sucessor. Luther began the debate by writing on a table in large letters Christ's words of institution: *Hoc est corpus meum* ("This is my body"—Matthew 26:26). Oecolampadius replied that the word *est* ("is") should be understood symbolically to mean *significat* ("represents"). To prove this point he cited a text from the sixth chapter of John (verses 48–54). Here Jesus says that he is the bread of life, and continues, "Whoso eateth my flesh and drinketh my blood, hath eternal life; and I will raise him up at the last day." But the Jews and disciples take him literally, and Jesus hastens to explain, "It is the spirit that quickeneth; the flesh profiteth nothing" (verse 63). Oecolampadius concluded, "Is it not then clear that Jesus would have nothing to do with the physical eating of his body?" In his splendidly one-track way, Luther answered: "I won't argue about whether *est* means *significat*. I rest content with what Christ says, and He says: *This is my body*. Not even the devil can change that. Therefore believe in the pure word of God and glorify Him." The end came in a rapid dialogue between Luther and Zwingli:

ZWINGLI: We urge you too to give up your preconceived opinion and glorify God. I do not give up my text either, and you will have to sing another song.
LUTHER: You are speaking in hatred.
ZWINGLI: Then let John 6 cure your ignorance.
LUTHER: You are trying to overwork it.
ZWINGLI: No! No! This text will break your neck.
LUTHER: Don't brag. Our necks don't break so fast. You are in Hesse now, not in Switzerland.[10]

Luther concluded that he and Zwingli each had a different kind of spirit. "I myself," he wrote later, "will in no wise hearken to aught that is contrary to my doctrine; for I am certain and persuaded through the Spirit of Christ, that my teaching . . . is true and certain."[11] He was equally persuaded that Zwingli was the victim of spiritual witchcraft. The Catholics, of course, were certain that Luther himself was inspired by the devil. With a scatological wit entirely typical of Reformation polemic, Sir Thomas More pointed out that though Luther talked as if he were "safe in Christ's bosom," in reality "he lies shut up in the devil's anus."[12]

JOHN CALVIN

Calvin was born in Noyon, in northern France, a quarter of a century later than Luther and Zwingli. He was a reformer of the second generation. Inevitably he was not an innovator in the same sense that each of them had been. But he too was certain that he read and understood the Bible under the direction of the Holy Spirit, that his own interpretation of Scripture was therefore true, that "what I have taught and written did not grow in my brain, but that I hold it from God." The result was a third variety of

[10]D. *Martin Luthers Werke*, Vol. XXX.3 (Weimar, 1910), pp. 110–123.
[11]A *Commentary on St. Paul's Epistle to the Galatians*, ed. by P. S. Watson (Westwood, N. J., n.d.), p. 195.
[12]*Responsio ad Lutherum*, p. 127.

Protestantism, an independent theology midway between Luther's and Zwingli's. Calvin's achievement was to organize Protestant doctrine into a clear, comprehensive theological system, to weld the insights of Luther, Zwingli, and Bucer into the last, and one of the greatest, of the *summae* of theology—the *Institutes of the Christian Religion*. In due course, he won over the magistrates of Geneva. In November, 1552, after long opposition, the highest secular authority in the city-state declared the *Institutes* "to be well and saintly made, and its teaching to be the holy doctrine of God."[13]

A constructive intellect, autocratic self-confidence, and an admirable education equipped Calvin supremely well for his task. He mastered scholastic philosophy at the University of Paris, read massively in patristic, medieval, and contemporary theology, studied law at Orléans and Bourges, and learned and used the humanist's historical and philological techniques of textual criticism (his first book was a commentary on Seneca's *De clementia*). When the first edition of the *Institutes* appeared in 1536, he was only twenty-six. The book is beautifully written, organized, and argued; it is clear and pungent, as sharp and well turned as a brilliant legal brief. Calvin expanded and reworked it in successive editions throughout his life. Designed to be a complete account of Christian teaching, it is the most dynamic and influential synthesis of sixteenth-century Protestant thought.

Rarely has the Protestant vision of the relation between God and man been more majestically defined. God is just and good, powerful and glorious. His will is free, sovereign, and omnipotent. Man is ignorant, vain, infirm, depraved, radically corrupt. His shameful nakedness exposes a "teeming horde of infamies." For Calvin, therefore, as for Luther, justification by faith alone is the principal article of the Christian religion. Because man is morally helpless, he cannot reestablish contact with God. God must reestablish contact with man. He does so through the Incarnation of His Son. He justifies man by mercifully and gratuitously granting him faith in His Word, that Word which is alternatively referred to as Wisdom, Christ, the Redeemer, the second Person of the Trinity, and the canonical Scriptures. Christ is the Word by whom all things were created. Christ is also the author of the written scriptural Word. In the written Word, the eternal Word is known. For this reason the Bible is the infallible book of truth when it is read under the direction of the Holy Spirit. But the Word does not move equally all who hear it preached. The action of the Holy Spirit and of God's grace is independent of man's will and works. Therefore predestination is inseparable from justification by faith alone, illuminating and reinforcing that central truth.

No fact more powerfully exalts the glory of God or more persuasively teaches humility to man than the existence of predestination. From eternity,

[13]Quoted by François Wendel, *Calvin. The Origins and Development of His Religious Thought*, trans. by P. Mairet (New York, 1963), p. 92.

God has decided the salvation or reprobation of every man. By His eternal and immutable counsel He freely ordains some to eternal life, others to eternal damnation. With respect to the elect, God's counsel is founded on His free mercy, without regard to human merit. He wills the rest of humanity to damnation according to a just and incomprehensible, but irreprehensible, judgment. Why, we may ask, does God take pity on some but not on others? There is, says Calvin, no other answer but that it pleased Him to do so. Nor can one argue that God's foreknowledge of a man's faith or faithlessness, of his merits or lack of them, determines His choice. The divine will is never dependent on the good will of man. God's will is free; man's is in bondage. Election does not depend on faith; faith makes election manifest. Man cannot choose faith or reject it, for grace is irresistible. God freely chooses some and rejects the rest, again "for no other reason than that he wills to exclude them." But this is not all. By definition every action of God's will is just, although man's puny reason cannot grasp this justice. The reprobate are incomprehensibly but justly condemned. And because the reprobate are justly condemned, they are condemned by their own fault. "Accordingly, man falls according as God's providence ordains, but he falls by his own fault." Calvin himself confessed the doctrine a horrible one: *Decretum quidem horribile fateor.*[14] All the more strikingly it measures the gulf between the secular imagination of the twentieth century and six-teenth-century Protestantism's intoxication with the majesty of God. We can only exercise historical sympathy to try to understand how it was that many of the most sensitive intelligences of a whole epoch found a supreme, a total, liberty in the abandonment of human weakness to the omnipotence of God.

ANABAPTISM

The crystallization of classical Protestantism into three distinct systems of doctrine—Lutheran, Zwinglian, and Calvinist—did not exhaust the six-teenth-century consequences of the idea that Scripture alone is normative in faith and morals. The classical reformers—Luther, Zwingli, and Calvin—tended to see the Bible primarily as a guiding authority in matters of doctrine. More radical groups, the most important of whom were the Anabaptists, understood *sola scriptura* to mean a minute ordering of human life according to the commandments of the Sermon on the Mount, a literal restitution of New Testament Christianity by a covenanted community of believers separated from the world and its evil works.

Anabaptism arose in Zurich among members of Zwingli's circle who protested his gradualism and demanded a complete and immediate break

---

[14]*Institutes of the Christian Religion,* ed. by J. T. McNeill, trans. by F. L. Battles (*Library of Christian Classics,* Vols. XX–XXI, Philadelphia, 1960), Vol. 11, pp. 955, 957.

Huldreich Zwingli at the age of forty-eight. *Woodcut by an unknown artist, 1531.*

with all antiscriptural ceremonies and doctrines. It crystallized as a distinct variety of Protestantism on January 21, 1525, when the layman Conrad Grebel, the son of a wealthy patrician merchant, rebaptized a former priest named Georg Blaurock, who in turn rebaptized the other men and women present in his house. Its first important doctrinal statement was the Schleitheim Confession, produced by a Synod of Swiss Brethren in February, 1527. After two decades of persecution, sporadic excesses, and near disintegration, the sect was given by Menno Simons (1496–1561) both its permanent doctrinal and organizational form and its name. (Anabaptists initially called themselves Brethren, or simply Baptists. Their enemies named them Anabaptists, or "rebaptists," in order to bring them within the jurisdiction of an ancient law of the Justinian Code carrying the death penalty for rebaptism. They were first called Mennonites in 1545.)

Jesus said, "If ye love me, keep my commandments." Anabaptists did so literally, presuming to live in the perfection of Christ. They read Matthew 5:34, "Swear not at all," and they obeyed. This seemingly innocuous refusal to take oaths isolated them in a society accustomed to confirm by oath innumerable transactions and contracts, and placed them in a posture of civil disobedience, for Swiss and south German cities normally required their inhabitants to swear a yearly oath of obedience to the municipal authorities. They read in Paul's Epistle to the Corinthians that Christians should not go to law, so they avoided lawyers and refused to go to court. They read that the early Christians had held all property in common, and in order to conform to this New Testament standard they broke the locks on the doors of their houses and cellars and lovingly shared their goods with one another. Some Anabaptists practiced evangelical communism. Because Christ said, "Resist not evil," and commanded Peter to put his sword into the sheath, Anabaptists were usually pacifists, and in the face of persecution, nonresistant. "True Christian believers," wrote Conrad Grebel, "are sheep among wolves, sheep for the slaughter; they must be baptized in anguish and affliction, tribulation, persecution, suffering, and death; they must be tried with fire, and must reach the fatherland of eternal rest, not by killing their bodily, but by mortifying their spiritual enemies. Neither do they use worldly sword or war, since all killing has ceased with them."[15]

Revolutionary biblical literalism of this kind could lead to picturesque excess. Some Anabaptists actually preached from the rooftops, or obeying Christ's command to become like little children, played and babbled like infants, or ran about naked because of a verse in Isaiah, or practiced polygamy in imitation of the Old Testament patriarchs, or persuaded credulous women that it was impossible for them to be saved without sacrificing their virtue, for, they argued, the Lord said that only he who was willing to part with all he held most dear would enter the Kingdom of Heaven. In 1532, demented by persecution, millenarian enthusiasm, and expectations of eschatological revenge, Anabaptists captured the episcopal city of Münster, in northwestern Germany, and briefly established a heavenly Jerusalem—communist, polygamous, and violent.

But these were occasional aberrations. Typically Anabaptists were peaceful, humble, patient, honest, and temperate. They originated the movement for total abstinence from alcoholic beverages. They wore coarse cloth and broad felt hats. Any brother or sister who fell into sin was first admonished, then openly disciplined or banned, that is, excluded from the sacrament of communion until he had repaired his life. Their worst enemies agreed that their lives were exemplary. Luther called them "work saints," and regarded them as legalists who disowned the principle of justification by faith alone and sought salvation through good works. Anabaptists answered that they tried to fulfill God's will not in order to be saved, but in order to obey God's express commands and to give proof of their faith by its fruit in good works. Yet fundamentally Luther was right. A profound moralism was at the heart of Anabaptism. It is for this reason that Anabaptists rejected as the "abomination of all abominations" one of the central doctrines of classical Protestantism—predestination and the bondage of the will. Like the humanist Erasmus they believed in free will, and they did so for the same reason: both considered it the indispensable basis for a responsible moral life, newly and freely chosen in Christ.

[15]*Spiritual and Anabaptist Writers*, ed. by G. H. Williams and A. M. Mergal (*Library of Christian Classics*, Vol. XXV, Philadelphia, 1961), p. 80.

Such a life, Anabaptists believed, was possible only apart from the world. The authors of the Schleitheim Confession put it like this: "A separation shall be made from the evil and from the wickedness which the devil planted in the world; in this manner, simply that we shall not have fellowship with them [the wicked] and not run with them in the multitude of their abominations. . . . For truly all creatures are in but two classes, good and bad, believing and unbelieving, darkness and light, the world and those who [have come] out of the world, God's temple and idols, Christ and Belial; and none have part with the other."[16] Anabaptists were separatists. They considered the state and society to be outside the perfection of Christ, and regarded themselves as citizens only of heaven. They concluded, therefore, that the realm of civil government and civil coercion must be entirely separate from the realm of conscience, religious discipline, and polity, and they rejected the possibility of a Christian magistracy. Thus Anabaptists refused to hold civil office, just as they refused to bear arms. Conversely, they denied that the civil authorities could legitimately interfere in matters of faith. Anabaptists withdrew from the world as effectively as medieval monks had done. Or rather, they moved the monastery into the world and transformed it into the "segregated Protestant community."

It is precisely because their conventicles were voluntary congregations of believers separated from the world that Anabaptists rejected infant baptism and practiced instead adult or believer's baptism. Baptism is the sociological sacrament. It links the individual Christian to society; while the manner of its definition and administration reveals at once whether he belongs to a church or a sect. Infant baptism presupposes a church that includes the entire population of a community or territory. Babies, without explicit faith or voluntary choice, are born into the church. Adult baptism creates a sect, a voluntary congregation of true Christians, a gathered society of the regenerate. It is the sign of mature repentance and rebirth in Christ, the symbol of membership in a society of believers who have consciously chosen Christ. Luther, Zwingli, and Calvin founded churches. Anabaptism was the first sixteenth-century sect.

THE CITY OF THE SAINTS

Lutherans, Zwinglians, Calvinists, and Catholics all feared, detested, and persecuted the Anabaptists. One fundamental tendency of Anabaptism penetrated classical Protestantism nonetheless: its reformist impulse, its drive to maintain the ethical purity of the segregated community by an elaborate discipline, its concern with every detail of morals and manners. When puritanical aspirations and practices of this sort, associated among Anabap-

[16]John C. Wenger, "The Schleitheim Confession of Faith," *Mennonite Quarterly Review*, Vol. XIX (1945), p. 249.

John Calvin at the age of fifty. *Woodcut by an unknown artist, 1559. In the frame*: John Calvin, faithful minister of the Word of God. *Below, Proverbs, 1, 7*: The fear of the Lord is the beginning of knowledge.

Prouerbes j.
La crainte du Seigneur eſt le commencement de Science.

tists with voluntary adherence to a sect, became a central concern of "magisterial" Protestants—that is, Protestants like Zwingli and Calvin, who retained and defended the ecumenical and authoritarian conception of the church they had inherited from the Middle Ages, regarded the church as an ally of the Christian state, and believed that reformation should proceed with the cooperation and under the protection of the secular power—the result was a penetrating and comprehensive system of social control.

The most conspicuous example of such a disciplinary system in operation was the city-state of Geneva during the long period of Calvin's ascendancy (1541–1564).

Every member of the civic community of Geneva was also a member of the church. To Anabaptists, who argued that in the visible church, as in the eternal and invisible church, membership must be restricted to true believers, to those with faith, Calvin answered that no adequate criteria exist for distinguishing the few true Christians from the hypocritical majority. Any such distinction was the more difficult because even true Christians remained sinners throughout their lives on earth. Everyone, therefore, must have an opportunity to hear the Word of God purely preached by a minister of the church. By infant baptism every child must be snatched from Satan and initiated into the ecclesiastical community, just as under the old covenant circumcision initiated infants into the holy community of Israel. Every adult must attend the Lord's Supper.

Calvin considered a comprehensive effort to discipline the beliefs and manners of the entire population necessary not only because membership in church and in state were inseparable, but also because every adult must attend the Lord's Supper worthily, unspotted by heresy, blasphemy, or wickedness. Wrong belief and immoral behavior dishonor God; since the church is the body of Christ, it "cannot be corrupted by such foul and decaying members without some disgrace falling upon its Head."[17] The purpose of Calvinist discipline was to keep the sacrament from profanation by making sure that the beliefs of every member of the community conformed to the teaching of the *Institutes* and that everyone's life and manners were exemplary. To this end, transgressors were identified and warned. If they did not mend their ways, the ministers publically denounced them. Refractory sinners were excommunicated, for just as a heretical member must be cut away so that it cannot infect the healthy body, so too must the wicked be excluded from the church to prevent the corruption of the good by the company of the bad. Cut off from his fellows and from the sacraments by excommunication, the excluded sinner was supposed to feel shame, repent, and reform; if he laughed at excommunication, he was handed over to the secular authority for punishment.

Discipline was institutionalized in the Consistory, composed of twelve elders—members of the city council, laymen of good life and good repute— who met with the pastors once a week to hear the reports of informers and busybodies about their neighbors. No man or woman, however highly placed, could escape the "fraternal correction" of the Consistory. It prosecuted a bewildering variety of offenses, from the gravest moral lapses to the most frivolous. A major category of offense was private immorality—fighting, fornication, adultery, swearing, and so on. Another concerned behavior in church. There were penalties for making a loud noise or laughing during service, and for unseemly behavior on the sabbath. The elders controlled all amusements, prohibiting promiscuous bathing, card playing, gambling, dancing. They forbade theatrical performances and tried to close the taverns and replace them with state eating houses furnished with French Bibles. Many infractions involved the remnants of popery. A goldsmith was punished for making a chalice for the Mass, a barber for tonsuring a priest, another man for saying that the pope was a good man—every "reformed" Genevan knew that the pope was Antichrist. Geneva's ecclesiastical discipline created a holy commonwealth, a city whose end was to glorify God, with the life of every citizen sanctified to that high purpose. The Scottish reformer John Knox (1505–1572) has recorded the pious astonishment of the faithful: Geneva, he wrote home in December, 1556, "is the maist perfyt schoole of Chryst that ever was in the erth since the dayis of the Apostillis. In other places, I confess Chryst to be trewlie preachit; but maneris and religioun so sinceirlie reformat, I have not yit sene in any uther place."[18]

CATHOLIC REFORMATION AND COUNTER-REFORMATION

While Protestant revolutionaries founded and ordered new churches and sects, Catholic reformers repaired the fabric of the old Church. Already before 1517, as we have seen, the reformation of abuses preoccupied dedicated clerics and laymen in every country of Europe. Their efforts to reform the church gathered momentum after 1517, and became in the 1530's a vast movement of spiritual, moral, and ecclesiastical renewal, independent of Protestantism and not necessarily directed against it. This movement is appropriately called the Catholic Reformation. It was an increasingly successful effort, at every level of the hierarchy—papacy, cardinalate, diocese, parish, and monastery—to correct ecclesiastical abuses within the traditional sacramental and institutional framework of the Church. Catholic reformation culminated in mid-century in the decrees of the Council of Trent concerned with the correction of abuses. Although Catholic sovereigns enforced the decrees at the local level with more deliberation than speed, much progress was made in rationalizing Church government and jurisdiction, eliminating the chaos in ecclesiastical appointments, and improving the discipline and education of priests and monks. Such reforms made possible the revitalization of the Church which is so striking a fact of the later sixteenth century.

Intertwined with the reforming impulse of sixteenth-century Catholicism were policies and practices which took their origin from the need to repel Protestant attack, and in due course, to counterattack and recover the ground steadily being lost to Protestantism between the beginning of the Lutheran revolt and 1560. This long, and in the end remarkably successful, struggle against Protestantism is appropriately called the Counter-Reformation. It was fought on many fronts and with a variety of weapons. As Protestant ideas spread, the need to protect the faithful against heretical proselytizing and propaganda became ever more urgent. Local authorities tightened censorship; and to guide them the papacy began to issue more elaborate indexes of prohibited books. In 1542, in order more effectively to discover heretics and to try and judge them, the pope established the Roman Inquisition, which successfully rooted out every trace of Protestantism in Italy. A lively concern to bolster the doctrinal reliability of clergy and laity and to convert Protestants in Europe and heathens overseas encouraged the foundation and proliferation of new orders. The most famous was the Jesuit

[18]*The Works of John Knox*, ed. by David Laing (Edinburgh, 1864), Vol. IV, p. 240.

order, founded by the great Spanish soldier-mystic St. Ignatius of Loyola (1491–1556) and officially approved by Pope Paul III in 1540 in a bull beginning with the stirring words, *Regimini militantis ecclesiae* ("For the order of the church militant"). The best-known paragraph in Loyola's *Spiritual Exercises* (written 1522–1542) catches perfectly the commitment, passion, and discipline of mid-century Catholic militancy: "To arrive at complete certainty, this is the attitude of mind we should maintain: I will believe that the white object I see is black if that should be the decision of the hierarchical Church, for I believe that linking Christ our Lord the Bridegroom and His Bride the Church, there is one and the same Spirit, ruling and guiding us for our souls' good. For our Holy Mother the Church is guided and ruled by the same Spirit, the Lord who gave the Ten Commandments."[19]

But the most important and interesting development in sixteenth-century Catholicism was neither the reform of abuses within the Church nor the Church's successful effort to stem the spread of Protestantism; it was rather the emergence during the decades before the end of the Council of Trent of the doctrine and style of piety that have stamped Roman Catholicism in modern times.

The medieval Church was more ecumenical, more genially encompassing, more permissive doctrinally, then either the sixteenth-century Protestant churches or the post-Trentine Catholic Church. There was more room in it for doctrinal maneuver. More possibilities existed for disagreement and debate among the orthodox. Most of the doctrines propounded in Calvin's *Institutes* and all of the doctrines embodied in the decrees and canons of the Council of Trent had coexisted peacefully in the Middle Ages. Intellectual clerics could and did debate them, question them, believe them, and defend them. In a word, all the bits and pieces that were to make up the sixteenth-century theologies of Protestantism and Catholicism were in solution in medieval thought. What so dramatically happened during the age of the Reformation is that they crystallized into two distinct and opposed systems, each more exclusive, more consistent, and more rigid than the medieval theological tradition from which they both derived. First, Protestants built up a systematic theology based on Luther's three *solae*: faith, grace, and Scripture. Inevitably, Catholics felt the need to redefine and reorganize Catholic doctrine in response to this challenge. This was the task and accomplishment of the Council of Trent.

The council sat in three sessions. The first lasted from 1545 to 1547; the second met in 1551–1552; the third, in 1562–1563. The dogmatic decrees of the first and second sessions left no doubt about what Catholicism was, and little subtlety was required to distinguish it from Protestantism. Protestants

[19]*The Spiritual Exercises of Saint Ignatius*, trans. by Thomas Corbishley, S.J. (New York, 1963), p. 122.

Tomb of Pope Paul III. *Guglielmo della Porta. The Counter-Reformation took shape in Rome during the reign of this decisive and magnificent pontiff. St. Peter's, Rome.*

admitted only one authority—Scripture. The fathers at Trent reestablished two—Scripture and tradition. Moreover, they declared the Latin Vulgate translation to be an authentic text of the Bible, and they stressed the exclusive right of Holy Mother Church "to judge of the true sense and interpretation of the holy Scriptures." Protestants asserted that men were justified by faith alone, without the works of the law; in a masterly exposition, the fathers at Trent decreed that men were saved by faith in combination with good works. The decrees and canons concerning the sacraments sharply distinguished the Catholic interpretation from the views of Lutherans, Zwinglians, and Calvinists. The last session of the council redefined and reaffirmed almost every belief and practice that Catholic humanists like Erasmus had considered superstitious half a century before: the making of vows, the belief in purgatory, the invocation of saints, the veneration of relics, and the giving of indulgences. On November 13, 1564, the pope summed up the Catholic faith as taught at Trent in the Creed of Pope Pius IV.

Growing differences in their devotional practices and styles of piety and feeling created a psychological gap between Catholics and Protestants even wider than the doctrinal gap so precisely defined by Calvin and the Trent fathers. An unusually heated emotionalism is the most noticeable characteristic of Catholic piety by the mid-century. Contemporary religious paintings suggest the ideal attitudes of worship: copious weeping, distorted features, extravagant gestures, eyes turned up dramatically to heaven. A medieval literary genre, the poem of tearful contrition, was revived and enjoyed a great vogue. The purpose of such verses was to describe, for example, the remorseful tears of St. Peter after he had denied Christ, or those of St. Mary Magdalene deploring her early life, in order to provoke the tears of the faithful and freshen their faith and piety. To encourage the spectator to relive the sufferings of Christ on the Cross or the torments of the martyrs, the Church asked its artists to picture these holy agonies in gruesome detail: St. Agatha with her breasts being torn away, St. Dorothy branded, St. Fidelis scourged, St. Edward with his throat cut. A revival of the late medieval preoccupation with death is another aspect of this holy enthusiasm. Representations of skulls are regularly found on tombstones after Trent. Epitaphs take on a more somber tone than they had had during the fifteenth-century Renaissance. On the tomb of a cardinal who died in 1451 in Rome was inscribed, "Why fear death, which brings us rest?" but a typical epitaph of the later sixteenth century reads: "My turn yesterday, yours today."

At the heart of Catholic religious emotion was mysticism. No other period, except possibly the fourteenth century, has produced so abundant a crop of attractive visionaries as the age of the Council of Trent. One reason for this development is the harmony between the dogmatic decrees of Trent and the assumptions of mysticism. The mystic assumes that man, with the aid of God's grace, can gradually perfect himself and briefly see God face to face. Mysticism—how unlike classical Protestantism—is optimistic about God and about man. With its emphasis on planned and ordered meditation, spiritual exercises, and a rigorous training of the will, sixteenth-century mysticism admirably complemented a theology built on an affirmation of the freedom of the will, man's ability to cooperate in his own salvation, and the efficacy of charity and good works. It answered too the need of devout men and women for a more personal, warmer piety and a more direct relation between God and man. Protestantism met this need by eliminating hierarchical and sacramental intermediaries between God and man; Trentine mysticism offered an ascending ladder of contemplation and perfection on whose upper rungs men experienced brief moments of ineffaceable sweetness and joy.

Perhaps the most striking characteristic of the new Catholic piety was its stress on just those elements in the traditional inheritance of Christian devotion which were rejected or minimized by Protestants. Protestants minimized the religious significance of the Virgin Mary and the saints. In late sixteenth-century Catholicism, on the other hand, devotion to the Virgin gained a popularity it had enjoyed at no time since the thirteenth century. The doctrine of the Immaculate Conception of Mary, vigorously attacked by late medieval and Renaissance Dominican theologians as a popular superstition, was now officially defended in Rome. New and related devotions appeared: of the Holy Family, of St. Joseph (a figure of ribald fun in the Middle Ages), of the Child Jesus. Correspondingly, increased attention was paid to the saints, and especially to St. Peter. At St. Peter's in Rome, frescoes painted during this period show him walking on the waters, raising the dead, healing sick people with his shadow, meeting Christ at the gates of Rome, vanquishing the magician Simon Magus, all episodes designed to illustrate and defend the primacy of the papal see. Protestants denied the existence of purgatory. Catholics multiplied confraternities to pray for the dead. In the *Spiritual Exercises* Loyola urged his readers to speak with particular approval of religious orders, of virginity and celibacy, of the relics of the saints, "showing reverence for them and praying to the saints themselves," of pilgrimages, indulgences, jubilees, Crusade bulls, fasting and abstinence in Lent, and the lighting of candles in churches. The iconography of the Last Supper changed, reflecting the renewed emphasis on the doctrine of the Real Presence. The normal medieval and Renaissance depiction of the Last Supper (Leonardo da Vinci's is a good example) shows Christ and the apostles at the moment when Christ says, "One of you shall betray me." After the middle of the sixteenth century, painters chose the moment when Christ says, "This is my body," that is, the institution of the Eucharist. Protestants, finally, had rejected much of the sensuousness and beauty of the medieval liturgy and of earlier church decoration. The Trentine Church did everything possible to make the Catholic service as splendid as possible. A vivid symbol of the growing differences in feeling, taste, and habits between Protestants and Catholics is the contrast between the whitewashed inside walls of the Grossmünster in Zurich and the interior of the Jesuit church in Rome—theatrical, brilliantly painted and gilded, filled with magnificent frescoes and sculptures, sounding with the serpentine polyphony of Palestrina and the massed brasses of Gabrieli.

By 1560 the religious unity of Europe had been irreparably shattered. A vigorous Catholic church, a Lutheran church, Zwinglian and Calvinist churches, an Anglican church, and a variety of sects competed for men's minds and loyalties. For the first time in many centuries, problems of religious choice and conversion became of major concern for ordinary men and women.

CHAPTER 6

Revolution and Reformation in the Church: The Problem of Conversion

FROM WITTENBERG AND ZURICH, Strasbourg and Geneva, in books, through personal contact between churchmen, commercial travelers, and students, by public and secret preaching, Protestant ideas penetrated every state in Europe.

Printing played the most important role in the spread of Protestantism. Some two thousand different editions of Luther's books and sermons appeared between 1517 and 1526 alone. To those we must add the flood of popular pamphlets, broadsides, and cartoons attacking the pope as Antichrist, satirizing the Mass, calling for the secularization of monasteries, urging the incompatibility of serfdom and Christian liberty. These simple texts and vivid images touched every social and intellectual level of the population.

Preaching was the second important channel for the communication of the new ideas. The Reformation was a doctrinal crisis. It began as a debate among professionals who took doctrine seriously. In the early sixteenth century, as in the thirteenth, almost all such men were clerics. It is not surprising, therefore, that Protestantism's earliest converts were priests and monks—members of Luther's own Augustinian order, Franciscans and Dominicans, and parish priests like Zwingli. As soon as these men heard and believed the good news of justification by faith alone and the wonderful authority of God's scriptural Word, they went forth and preached it to others. At first they had no organization, no church. In the countryside and in the towns, Lutheran and traditional practices and beliefs existed side by side. The situation was fluid, upsetting, and confusing. Ideas ordinarily confined to theological faculties were now propagandized by pastors and ministers, officially debated before princes, magistrates, and citizens, and discussed at home and in the streets by merchants, craftsmen, knights, peasants, students, bishops, and dukes.

In short, religious doctrines were in public competition, and individuals

Luther preaching. *Woodcut by Lucas Cranach the Elder. Lying before Luther is the Bible. His right hand points to the crucified Christ; his left consigns the Roman clergy to Hell. The congregation is receiving communion in both bread and wine.*

had the freedom (progressively limited, as we shall see, by persecution and the religious preferences of their rulers) to choose among them. What determined their choices? Why did some men remain attached to the old faith? Why did others become Lutherans or Calvinists? What attracted still others to Anabaptism?

Making a choice involved a personal drama of conscience. By and large, the evidence suggests that most men chose a religion among the several competing for their allegiance because they believed it was true rather than because it was in some way useful. It has sometimes been supposed that direct correspondences can be found between particular systems of theological doctrine and the interests of particular social classes, but the validity of this assumption is illusory. Luther found converts at every level of the social structure and among men of widely divergent social and economic interests. Calvinism was not in the sixteenth century a middle-class religion. It appealed equally, perhaps more, and certainly with greater political effect, to the aristocracy. This is not to say that conversion is unintelligible except in terms of personal religious psychology. A sociology of conversion is possible and can be useful—but only if it is alert to the concrete variety of local circumstances.

THE PEASANTS

The response of the peasantry offers an initial perspective on the spread of Protestantism. In 1524–1526 tension between German peasants and their landlords erupted in a peasants' revolt, the last and most desperate of a series of uprisings that had begun in the later Middle Ages. Peasant grievances were not new. The most famous peasant manifesto, the so-called Twelve Articles (January–February, 1525), listed complaints familiar for over a century—against tithes, serfdom, the invasion by landlords of the common fields, forests, streams, and meadows, the lords' disregard of manorial customs and their efforts to raise rents and increase labor services. Nor was it unusual for peasants to associate their economic and social demands with evangelical and millenarian expectations, or to justify them by scriptural texts. Lutheranism, that is, did not cause the armed and revolutionary outburst of some 300,000 peasants, miners, artisans, journeymen, and disaffected knights against their lords; on the other hand, Luther's intransigence concerning the Gospel clearly magnetized them. And of course some of his ideas could be given a radical social twist. The freedom of the Christian man, for example, though a purely religious conception in the context of Luther's theology, could be extended to mean freedom from

Peasants plundering the monastery of Weissenau. *Drawing by an unknown artist, 1525.*

serfdom. The idea of a priesthood of all believers suggested a more secular egalitarianism. Luther's repudiation of monasticism suited peasant covetousness. Here, at least, was one body of landlords who could be justifiably pillaged. Luther's primitive economic ideas, his blasts against usury and what he called *Fuggerei*, after the Augsburg bankers, harmonized with a widespread resentment. Above all, perhaps, Luther offered hope, hope that religious reformation was the initial step toward a new and juster society, one in which evangelical precepts were less obviously contradicted by reality than they had been in the past.

Peasant spokesmen therefore rephrased traditional demands in the language of evangelical Lutheranism. The first of the Twelve Articles demanded for every congregation the right to choose its own pastor to "preach to us the Holy Gospel purely and clearly, without any human addition, doctrine or commandment." Another attacked the small tithe, a traditional cattle tax due the parish priest, on the grounds that "God the Lord created cattle for the free use of men, and we regard this as an improper tithe which men have invented; therefore we will not give it any longer." The most important article was against serfdom: "It has been the custom hitherto for men to hold us as their own property; and this is pitiable, seeing that Christ has redeemed and bought us all with the precious shedding of His blood, the lowly as well as the great, excepting no one. Therefore, it agrees with Scripture that we be free, and will to be so." The peasants swore to obey the commandments of Scripture and their legitimate rulers, and concluded with unfounded optimism: "We have no doubt that, as true and real Christians, [our lords] will gladly release us from serfdom, or show us from the Gospel that we are serfs."[1]

In April, 1525, Luther answered in his *Admonition to Peace: A Reply to the Twelve Articles of the Peasants in Swabia*. The peasants, he said, had seriously misinterpreted the Gospel. Their attitude was carnal, not spiritual. They sought to give their enterprise an evangelical appearance, although in fact their single purpose was to make their properties and bodies free. His commentary on the article condemning serfdom struck bluntly home: "That is making Christian liberty an utterly carnal thing. Did not Abraham and other patriarchs and prophets have slaves? . . . Therefore this article is dead against the Gospel. It is a piece of robbery by which every man takes from his lord the body, which has become his lord's property. For a slave can be a Christian, and have Christian liberty, in the same way that a prisoner or a sick man is a Christian, and yet not free. This article would make all men equal, and turn the spiritual kingdom of Christ into a worldly external kingdom."[2] Few passages in Luther's works underscore so heavily his con-

[1]*Works of Martin Luther*, Vol. IV (Philadelphia, 1931), pp. 210–216 gives the Twelve Articles in an English translation by C. M. Jacobs.
[2]*Ibid.*, p. 240.

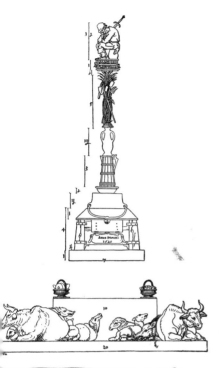

Project for a monument commemorating the Peasant War. *Woodcut from Dürer's* Unterweisung der Messung, *published in 1525.* "Should someone wish to erect a victory monument because he has defeated the rebellious peasants," *wrote Dürer,* "let him use this design." *Base and shaft assemble the fruits and attributes of peaceful labor. At the top, on a cage of chickens, sits a peasant with a sword plunged between his shoulder blades.*

tempt for secular aspiration; his conservatism and authoritarianism; his insistence that the kingdom is supernatural and in heaven, not of this earth; his refusal to draw any social inferences from the Gospel except that man's external life in this world properly consists in suffering wrong, patience, and contempt for temporal wealth and life; the utter primacy that religion had for him and his single-minded concern for its purity.

This was not Luther's last word on the peasant war. A month later, in May, he published his tract *Against the Robbing and Murdering Hordes of Peasants,* the only unforgivably shameful thing he ever wrote. He said the peasants were guilty of three sins: perjury, rebellion, and blasphemy. "Therefore let everyone who can, smite, slay, and stab, secretly or openly, remembering that nothing can be more poisonous, hurtful, or devilish than a rebel. It is just as when one must kill a mad dog; if you do not strike him, he will strike you, and a whole land with you."[3]

Virtually without exception princes and nobles, secular and lay, Catholic and Lutheran, combined to crush the peasants. The gruesome repression strengthened every despotic tendency in German political and social development. At a crucial moment, the leaders of the new religion chose not the people, but the princes. Luther had no illusions about the princes. He called

[3]*Ibid.,* p. 249.

them "furious, raving, senseless tyrants." But in his terror of other men's revolutions he tied his own irremediably to the princes and laid the foundations of the Lutheran church of later centuries: a state church dependent on the secular ruler, profoundly conservative, its membership drawn primarily from the upper and middle classes. The attachment of the German peasantry to Lutheranism was dealt a fatal blow when their appeal for a justice compatible with evangelical teaching was answered by the slaughter, it is estimated, of a hundred thousand of their number. Peasants became apathetic conformists, whether Catholic or Lutheran. When they had freedom of choice, they preferred to join a sect, apart from the state and the established church.

THE BURGHERS

The Protestant penetration of the urban population illustrates other aspects of the interplay of ideas and interests in the Reformation era. The pattern of reformation in the imperial city of Augsburg provides an instructive example. In the first half of the sixteenth century, Augsburg was one of the greatest financial and trading centers of the continent. (The kings of Scotland, remarked an Italian visitor, would wish to be as well housed as the simple burghers of Augsburg.) Both its social structure and the antagonisms dividing its inhabitants were typical of contemporary urban life. At the top were a small group of wealthy merchant-bankers. The Fuggers are the best known, but they were not alone. The firm of Anton Welser and Conrad Vöhlin traded with Venice, lent money to the Habsburgs, dabbled in Tyrolese silver, and helped finance the first Portuguese voyages. In 1505, Welser sent three merchant ships to India with the fleet of the king of Portugal and made a profit of 175 per cent on the return cargo. The Hochstetters were the most hated monopolists of their time. Herwarts and Gossembrots, Paumgartners and Rems, were other merchant-bankers of the same stamp. In the stratum below this wealthy elite were the manufacturers of linen cloth and fustian, clothes, books, and shoes; while below these independent entrepreneurs were the very much more numerous dependent journeymen, workers, and servants. Journeymen and workers were pitted against the masters of the guilds. The masters fought on two fronts, against their workmen and against the great merchant-bankers who were coming to dominate the city's economic and political life. Themselves capitalist innovators in their relations with their journeymen, they stubbornly defended the fixing of a "just price" and the cooperative limiting of competition against what they considered the unscrupulous machinations of the oligarchs, who through their commercial and financial pressures threatened to undermine the independence of the masters in the same way as the masters had undermined that of the journeymen.

The religious choices made by the inhabitants of Augsburg reflect this pattern of competing interests and discontents. Most of the great mercantile and financial families remained Catholic. Ambrosius Hochstetter was "entirely against the Lutherans." So were the Fuggers, the Welsers, and the others. It is equally evident that the majority of independent masters, and in the early 1520's many of their workmen, were eager converts to Lutheranism. Manufacturers of fustian listened with respect to Lutheran preachers. Augsburg printers published Luther's translation of the Bible into German, as well as many of his other works. A former Franciscan preached against Rome and high prices, caused, he cried, by Jakob Fugger. When the council expelled him from the town, 1,800 weavers and journeymen tailors demonstrated in front of the town hall for his return. In Augsburg, in this first phase of its reformation, the Lutheran attack on Catholicism was inseparable from the attack on monopoly and *Fuggerei*.

During the peasants' revolt the situation changed. Anabaptist missionaries entered the city, preached secretly in cellars and gardens, and recruited some eight hundred converts, principally among the mass of impoverished weavers, the *armen Weber*. The arrival of Zwinglian preachers in 1526 complicated the religious life of the city even further. By 1530 Catholicism was in full retreat, and the council had broken Anabaptism by executions and expulsions. Lutherans remained numerous. The sympathies of the government were Zwinglian.

It is one thing to notice that in Augsburg the *armen Weber* were attracted to Anabaptism, the small-scale manufacturers were often Lutheran, and the merchant-bankers preferred to retain their old religion. It is quite another to argue that this particular pattern of correspondences is a necessary one, reflecting intrinsic affinities between certain religious beliefs and certain social classes. It was not an innate harmony between sixteenth-century Catholic teaching and the higher forms of capitalist enterprise that caused the merchant oligarchy to remain Catholic. A more plausible explanation can be found in the commitment of Augsburg merchant-bankers to the emperor. Charles V needed them; and once they had lent him money, they needed him even more. Every interest which held them to the Habsburgs held them to the traditional faith as well. It is equally hazardous to argue any inherent affinity between the principal doctrines of Luther and the psychological and ethical needs of petty manufacturers. As we have seen, Luther appealed just as much, in certain circumstances, to peasants and workers.

Moreover, other cities of Europe offer patterns of religious choice different from Augsburg's. In Lyons, for example, men of substance normally remained Catholic, while many journeymen and workers became in turn Lutheran and Calvinist. In 1529 unrest among workers in the silk and printing industries crystallized in serious social disturbances. Contemporaries attributed the difficulties to the "wicked sect," that is, to the Protestants. In the early 1550's large groups of printing and silk workers (sons of poor artisans and of agricultural laborers in the surrounding provinces or impover-

View of Augsburg. *From Hartmann Schedel's* Liber chronicarum *with wood-cuts by Michel Wohlgemuth and Wilhelm Pleydenwurff, published in Nuremberg, 1493.*

ished immigrants from Germany and Italy) customarily assembled in the streets to sing "Calvinist" psalms. In 1573 a Lyons cleric attributed the high incidence of Protestantism among the *menu peuple*, or plebeians, to their hopes for freedom from ecclesiastical government and taxes and their expectation of sacking the houses of the rich under the sanction of religion. Elsewhere the pattern was either reversed—with the urban ruling class sympathizing with Zwinglianism or Calvinism while a majority of the workers remained Catholic—or more commonly, as in Paris, modified. During the night of October 17–18, 1534, Protestants plastered the walls of Paris with placards attacking the Mass. The government reacted by burning as many of the culprits as it could catch. The fragmentary lists of men and women burned or condemned to death in absentia record their ranks or occupations. These lists suggest that the social composition of Parisian Protestantism was exceedingly varied. Most of the individuals listed were members of the working, lower-middle, and middle class. Among them were relatively small groups consisting on the one hand, of journeyman dyers, weavers, masons, cooks, and carpenters, and on the other, of substantial entrepreneurs, goldsmiths, printers, and minor civil servants. A larger group was made up of modest artisans and retail traders: bookbinders, engravers, hatters, cobblers, illuminators, cabinetmakers, bakers, grocers, and four singers from the royal chapel choir. The lists also record a scattering of quite different types: a theologian and four Augustinian monks, the poet Clément Marot, several aristocrats and their wives, and a handful of rich merchants.

What can we conclude? In the first place, in the early decades of the Reformation, Protestantism frequently mobilized social and economic discontent. The peasants of southwestern Germany, German knights making a last stand against the encroachments of princely power, journeymen and artisans in the larger European cities, all understood the Gospel "carnally" and pursued their material aspirations with evangelical zeal. This simple response gradually yielded to another as the logic of conflicting interests created more complicated patterns of religious diversity: as long as men had a reasonable freedom of choice among competing churches and sects, the members of different social groups tended to choose different religious affiliations. What particular religion a particular group in a particular place in fact adopted was accidental—the result of specific local conditions. The generalization that can be made is that the religion of the poor was very often different from the religion of the rich. By 1540 the wealthier citizens were Catholic in some towns, Lutheran in others, Zwinglian or Calvinist in still others. And in each town a religion different from that of the wealthy and dominant attracted the petty artisans, journeymen, and workers. The sixteenth-century religions possessed no inherent economic or social biases, but within the range of exceptions suggested by such statistics as those from Paris, social divisions assumed religious dimensions and men extended rivalries of class into the novel area of religious ideology.

PERSECUTION AND LIBERTY

From the very beginning of the Reformation, however, the possibility of free choice among competing faiths was limited by persecution. This forcible pressure to conformity was ultimately to be a decisive factor in the shaping of the religious geography of Europe.

Lutherans, Zwinglians, Calvinists, Anglicans, and Catholics all forcibly repressed dissent. Anabaptists were the first martyrs of Protestant persecution. As early as 1525 the Zurich authorities, with Zwingli's approval, condemned Anabaptists to death by drowning. In 1529, at the imperial Diet which met at Speyer, six Protestant princes and the representatives of fourteen Protestant south German cities joined with the Catholic majority and the Emperor Charles V in approving the revival and enforcement of an ancient law of the Justinian Code punishing rebaptism by death. The result was inhuman. Here is how Menno Simons described it:

How many pious children of God have we not seen during the space of a few years deprived of their homes and possessions for the testimony of God and their conscience; their poverty and sustenance written off to the emperor's insatiable coffers? How many have they betrayed, driven out of city and country, put to the stocks and torture? How many poor orphans and children have they turned out without a farthing? Some have they hanged, some have they punished with inhuman tyranny and afterward garroted them with cords, tied to a post. Some they have roasted and burned alive. Some, holding their own entrails in their hands, have powerfully confessed the Word of God still. Some they beheaded and gave as food to the fowls of the air. Some have they consigned to the fish. They have torn down the houses of some. Some have they thrust into muddy bogs. They cut off the feet of some, one of whom I have seen and spoken to. Others wander aimlessly hither and yon in want, misery, and discomfort, in the mountains, in deserts, holes, and clefts of the earth, as Paul says. They must take to their heels and flee away with their wives and little children, from one country to another, from one city to another—hated by all men, abused, slandered, mocked, defamed, trampled upon, styled "heretics." Their names are read from pulpits and town halls; they are kept from their livelihood, driven out into the cold winter, bereft of bread, pointed at with fingers. Yes, whoever can wrong a poor oppressed Christian thinks he has done God a service thereby, even as Christ says.[4]

Anabaptists were not the only victims of Protestant persecution. The case of Michael Servetus (1511–1553) is exemplary. In the eyes of virtually every contemporary Christian, this Spanish physician was a notorious and obstinate heretic. He rejected infant baptism and embraced the Anabaptist idea of the church as a voluntary society of the regenerate. Going even further, he attacked the Trinity, thereby embracing the second doctrinal deviation to carry the death penalty in Roman law. He was an antitrinitarian on scriptural grounds. By demonstrating the *Comma Johanneum* to be a late interpolation, Erasmus had shown that the doctrine of the Trinity had no clear scriptural foundation (p. 71). In 1523 Sir Thomas More had tried to show the absurdity of Luther's contention that nothing should be believed with certainty unless it could be proved from a clear scriptural text by pointing to the belief in the Trinity: "Nowhere in all scripture," he remarked, "is the Father called 'uncreated'; the Son nowhere called 'consubstantial'; nowhere is the Holy Spirit indicated with enough clarity as 'proceeding from the Father and Son.' "[5] Why, he asked, had Luther, having rejected so much else because it had no scriptural authority, not rejected the Trinity also?

Servetus dared to take the step at which all the great reformers balked. Because it had no biblical foundation, he called the Trinity a "three-headed Cerberus" and asserted that the Son was not coeternal with the Father. Melanchthon condemned his "detestable heresies." Calvin judged his work "a rhapsody patched together from the impious ravings of all the ages"; and when in early 1553, after living and practicing in Lyons for twenty years under an assumed identity, he secretly published his masterpiece, the *Restitution of Christianity*, and imprudently sent Calvin a copy under his own name, Calvin denounced him (through a third person) to the Catholic authorities in France. Servetus was jailed, but escaped. The Inquisition in Lyons garroted his effigy, then burned it. He planned to take refuge in Naples, but a suicidal vanity led him to travel from Lyons to Naples by way of Geneva. The day after he arrived, he went to hear Calvin preach. He was recognized, and Calvin at once instructed one of his disciples to lodge against

[4]*The Complete Writings of Menno Simons*, ed. by John C. Wenger, trans. by Leonard Verduin (Scottdale, Pa., 1956), pp. 599–600.
[5]*Responsio ad Lutherum*, trans. by Sister Gertrude J. Donnelly, (*The Catholic University of America Studies in Medieval and Renaissance Latin*, Vol. XXIII, Washington, D.C., 1962), p. 141.

him before the magistrates the capital charges of blasphemy and heresy. Within three weeks the council condemned him. On October 27, 1553, he was burned alive, suffering the penalty prescribed by Roman law for antitrinitarianism and antipedobaptism.

Catholics persecuted dissenters with equal vigor. The most celebrated engine of persecution in all of Europe was the Spanish Inquisition, established in 1478. Theoretically, the inquisitorial process was not a trial at all. The inquisitor was not a judge, but a father confessor whose object was not to punish the body but to save the soul; to plead guilty was to obtain mercy. Consequently the Inquisition did not punish. It imposed penances appropriate to the guilt confessed: a pilgrimage, flogging (generally one to two hundred lashes administered publicly), exile, imprisonment of from a few months to life, service on the galleys of the royal navy. Needless to say, penitents were excluded from all public office and their property was confiscated by the state.

For the obdurate the penalty was death, with the following classes of offender "relaxed" to the secular arm for burning: the pertinacious heretic who refused to recant (there were never many of these); the *negativo*, who persistently denied that he held any erroneous beliefs although the tribunal was satisfied that he did; and most numerous of all, the relapsed, who had once recanted and become reconciled and had then fallen back into their former errors. It is impossible to determine exactly how many thousands of persons the Inquisition relaxed to the secular arm. But there can be no doubt of its success. It ferreted out backsliders among the *conversos*, Jews converted to Christianity, many of whom had married into the first families in Spain (King Ferdinand had Jewish ancestors; so did St. Teresa of Avila) and occupied prominent positions in church and state. By 1530 no Marranos (outwardly conforming Christians who secretly remained faithful Jews at home) were left in Spain. Protestantism too found Spain uncongenial. Inquisitors suspicious enough to jail the founder of the Jesuit order and the archbishop of Toledo, primate of Spain, easily discovered and burned the few "Lutherans" there.

It is reasonably easy to understand what the victim of religious persecution died for. He died for the truth of an individual interpretation of Scripture, and to maintain the integrity of his own conscience. But why, for example, did Calvin and the magistrates of Geneva, with the unanimous approval of the Lutheran authorities in Wittenberg and the churches of Basel, Bern, Schaffhausen, and Zurich, think it necessary and desirable to kill Servetus? Why did the Catholic authorities in France strangle and burn him in effigy? Why did Servetus' own brother, an agent of the Spanish Inquisition, make a special trip out of Spain to collect evidence against him? Why did Servetus himself consider death the proper penalty for other men's heresy?

Persecution was justified by a variety of persuasive arguments. A father legitimately restrains a child from playing with fire; a son may forcibly prevent his crazed father from jumping off a cliff; the doctor rightly amputates a diseased limb in order to save the rest of the body; the good gardener removes rotten branches to save the tree. In the same way, the heretic must be constrained for his own good and the good of others.

Scripture confirmed these rational analogies; for by the end of the thirteenth century, theologians had attached the Old Testament penalty for apostasy—death—to the New Testament crime—heresy. They argued that the enormity of an offense depended on the rank of the person against whom the crime was committed. Since heresy was a crime against God, death was the only adequate penalty. St. Thomas Aquinas illustrated this argument by comparing the heretic to a false coiner. As the false coiner corrupted the currency, which was necessary for temporal life, so the heretic corrupted the faith, which was necessary for the life of the soul. Death was a penalty justly meted out by the prince to false coiners; how much more just was the death penalty for heretics, whose sin was graver to the extent that the life of the soul was more precious than the life of the body.

But the persecutor did not only believe that heresy was a heinous crime against God and rightly punishable by death; he also passionately believed that his interpretation of the Bible was the only true one and that he, and the church he represented, had a monopoly of religious truth. Commonly allied to this conviction was the assumption, shared by virtually everyone in Europe before the outbreak of the religious wars of the second half of the century, that the security of the body politic demanded religious as well as temporal obedience, religious as well as secular loyalty and uniformity. The heretic, consequently, was more than a shameless distorter of God's truth; he was a rebel and a political subversive as well. These convictions were accompanied by the equally prevalent belief that coercion was effective and that it benefited the coerced; the result, in the opinion of every man of common sense, was an impregnable justification of persecution.

The persecutor's intransigence—and it was the intransigence also of his victim and of his age—ultimately rested on his refusal to betray the Holy Spirit, the guarantor of his doctrinal impeccability. Every religious leader was persuaded that a man who denied his interpretation of Scripture, or what he considered a fundamental doctrine of Christianity like the Trinity, was giving the lie to God. Wrong belief is a monstrous crime against God. It insults the Most High. We punish the slanderer. Shall we permit a blasphemer of the living God to go unscathed? Treason against a temporal prince is punished by death. Shall the man who reviles God, the sovereign emperor, suffer a less punishment? We justly execute murderers, who kill the body. Shall we not execute blasphemers, who kill the soul? We muzzle dogs. Shall we leave men free to open their mouths as they please and contaminate their fellow citizens and the church with their pernicious books? "God makes plain that the false prophet is to be stoned without mercy," wrote Calvin in a commentary on the thirteenth chapter of Deuteronomy. "We

The Water Torture. *Engraving from Milles de Souvigny, Praxis criminis persequendi, published in 1541. A widespread method of interrogation, used in both criminal and inquisitorial procedures. The victim's mouth was stuffed with a cloth, his nose held, and the cloth saturated with water. The result was intermittent suffocation.*

are to crush beneath our heel all affections of nature when his honor is involved. The father should not spare his child, nor the brother his brother, nor the husband his own wife or the friend who is dearer to him than life. No human relationship is more than animal unless it be grounded in God. If a man be conjoined to his wife without regard to God, he is worthy to be cast out among the brute beasts. If friendship is contracted apart from God, what is this union but sheer bestiality?"[6] Servetus was rightly killed because he was a false prophet. His views were wrong, they might bring other souls to perdition, they disrupted the unity of the civic and ecclesiastical communities, above all, they were a scandalous blasphemy against the majesty of God.

Not quite everyone agreed that Servetus had been rightly burned. His death provoked the most eloquent defenses of toleration written in the sixteenth century: two works by the Protestant humanist Sebastianus Castellio (1515–1563): *Concerning Heretics and Whether They Should Be Punished by the Sword of the Magistrate* and *Contra libellum Calvini*

[6]Quoted by Roland H. Bainton, *The Travail of Religious Liberty* (Philadelphia, 1951), p. 70.

(1554). His conclusion is justly remembered: "To burn a heretic is not to defend a doctrine, but to kill a man."[7]

THE RELIGIOUS PREFERENCES OF THE GERMAN PRINCES

As the coercive governments of city-states, principalities, and kingdoms enforced religious uniformity within their territories—some with rapid success, some only very gradually—the religious preferences of the magistrates and princes overbore those of the citizens and subjects. Almost without exception the religion of a territory became identical with the religion of its prince; the individual's freedom of religious choice was reduced to a single right, that of emigration to a state whose ruler was a coreligionist. Just as the personal decisions of sovereigns determined war and peace, so did their personal theological convictions determine the success or failure of the Reformation in their territories. Although the consciences of emperor, kings, and princes have no more intrinsic interest than those of peasants and merchants, they have had a far larger historical importance. The conversions of princes were as important for the religious history and geography of sixteenth-century Europe as their marriages and dynastic claims were for its diplomacy and wars.

In his *Open Letter to the Christian Nobility of the German Nation*, published in August, 1520, Luther had thanked God for awakening his heart once more to hope now that He had given Germany in Charles V a young and noble ruler to reign over it. How unfounded this hope was to be became clear at the dramatic confrontation of Luther and the young emperor at the Diet of Worms. On the evening of April 18, 1521, Luther appeared in the great torchlit hall before his king and the representatives of the German nation. He was asked whether he was prepared to recant his books. He replied briefly in German. His closing words are justly famous. Turning to Charles V and the imperial electors and princes, he said:

Unless I am convinced by the testimony of the Scriptures or by clear reason (for I do not trust either in the pope or in councils, since it is well known that they have often erred and contradicted themselves), I am bound by the Scriptures I have quoted and my conscience is captive to the Word of God. I cannot and I will not retract anything, since it is neither safe nor right to go against conscience. May God help me! Amen.[8]

The next day, April 19, Charles V answered. His statement is as passion-

---

[7]Quoted by Joseph Lecler, *Toleration and the Reformation*, trans. by T. L. Westow (New York and London, 1960), Vol. I, p. 355.

[8]*Luther's Works*, Vol. XXXII, ed. by George W. Forell (Philadelphia, 1958), pp. 112–113.

ate, as moving, as true to the essential character and vision of the man who spoke it, as Luther's:

> You know that I am descended from the most Christian emperors of the noble German nation, from the Catholic kings of Spain, the archduke of Austria and the dukes of Burgundy. To the honor of God, the strengthening of the faith, and the salvation of souls, they all have remained up to death faithful sons of the church and have always been defenders of the Catholic faith, the sacred rituals, decrees, ordinances and holy customs. After death they have left to us by natural right and heritage these holy Catholic observances, to live according to them and to die according to their example, in which [observances], as true followers of these our predecessors, we have up to now lived. For this reason I am determined to support everything that these predecessors and I myself have kept, up to the present. . . . For it is certain that a single friar errs in his opinion which is against all of Christendom and according to which all of Christianity will be and will always have been in error both in the past thousand years and even more in the present. For that reason I am absolutely determined to stake on this cause my kingdoms and seignories, my friends, my body and blood, my life and soul. For it would be a great shame to me and to you, who are the noble and renowned German nation, who are by privilege and pre-eminent standing singularly called to be defenders and protectors of the Catholic faith, if in our time not only heresy but suspicion of heresy or decrease of the Christian religion should through our negligence dwell after us in the hearts of men and our successors to our perpetual dishonor. And after having heard the obstinate answer which Luther gave yesterday, April 18, in the presence of us all, I declare to you that I regret having so long delayed to proceed against this Luther and his false doctrine and I am no longer willing to hear him speak more. . . . I am determined to proceed against him as a notorious heretic, requesting of you that you conduct yourselves in this matter as good Christians as you have promised it to me and are held to it.[9]

Charles spoke in French, a reminder that the German king was a foreigner in Germany. He had grown up in the Netherlands, nurtured in the French culture of the Burgundian court. He matured outside of Germany, and by the time of his death was a Spaniard in sensibility, language, and taste. To the extent that the Lutheran revolution was an expression of German cultural and religious nationalism, it was utterly foreign to him. To the extent that it expressed specifically German political aspirations, it was the ally of princely and urban particularism and threatened to limit still further his authority in Germany. Charles's policy could never be German. Taken as a whole it was imperial and therefore larger than any national German policy; with respect to specifically German matters it was locally territorial, like that of any other German prince, and therefore smaller than a national policy. His imperial policy, moreover, was inevitably rooted in Catholicism, its ideology inevitably Roman. Charles could hardly be a Catholic in Spain

[9]*Ibid.*, p. 114, note 9.

and a Protestant in Germany. Every personal and dynastic interest, every conviction and aspiration, bound Charles to Rome. He considered himself the secular head of Christendom. To abandon the traditional faith would have been to reduce the meaning, purpose, and justification of his empire, to turn it into an accident of power. The emperor remained Catholic, condemned Luther, and put him under the ban of the empire, making him an outlaw.

In practice, throughout his reign Charles was powerless to act effectively in Germany. He failed to strengthen the royal power and curtail the power of the princes. His efforts to extirpate heresy and restore the religious unity of the empire by means of a national council and then by military force also failed. His struggle against the Valois kept him almost continuously out of Germany. Constant Turkish pressure compromised the anti-Protestant zeal of his brother Ferdinand, who found it impossible to reconcile his need for subsidies from Protestant princes to fight the Turk with his Catholic duty to prosecute them for heresy. Even Charles's victory over the Protestant princes at Mühlberg, in 1547, was illusory. A league of princes, in alliance with France, immediately rose against him to defend German "liberty" against Spanish "despotism," reversed the military situation, and drove Charles across the Alps into Italy. In short, from the Diet of Worms until his abdication thirty-five years later, the independent power of the princes disarmed Charles's hostility to Luther and to the Reformation; and the princes' preferences, not the emperor's, determined in the end the religious geography of Germany.

No simple formula can explain the religious choices of the German princes. The economic and political advantages of a Lutheran conversion were substantial. The act of becoming a Protestant added religious sanction and motive to a prince's claim to be independent of the Catholic emperor. The prince's opposition to imperial interference in his territory became a defense not only of his jurisdictional autonomy but of evangelical truth as well. Furthermore, conversion to Protestantism was economically tempting. Luther condemned monasticism; a secularization of Church property, especially monastic property, was a "reform" that could lead to a significant increase in revenue. Typical is the disposition of Church wealth by Landgrave Philip of Hesse (1504–1567), one of the most important Protestant princes, after he dissolved the monasteries and nunneries in his territories. Too many vested interests were involved for him to appropriate all monastic revenue for himself; he therefore allocated 59 per cent to educational and charitable purposes—to hospitals, as dowries for poor noble ladies, to found the first German Protestant university at Marburg. But 41 per cent remained for him. Clearly, Philip's financial gain was considerable. Above all, by introducing the reformation in his state the German prince increased his control over the church. As early as the fourteenth century it had been the stated ambition of German princes to be "pope, archbishop, bishop, archdeacon, and deacon" in their own territories. Breaking openly with Rome was one way to achieve this ambition. The prince usurped the authority of pope and bishops. His courts absorbed the jurisdiction of the ecclesiastical courts. The enforcement of family law and the supervision of morals became prerogatives of the state. The prince extended his control of ecclesiastical patronage and appointments. Ecclesiastical commissioners appointed by the prince reformed abuses and dealt with the finances and physical needs of the various congregations. They enforced uniformity of faith and liturgy on the prince's subjects. In practice they even defined doctrine. Acquisition of authority over these activities increased enormously the power of the prince.

Protestant princes did not secure these advantages without risk. During the crucial decades between 1520 and the Peace of Augsburg in 1555, Catholic princes were in a majority in the Diet. Until his death in 1546 Luther remained an excommunicated heretic under the ban of the empire. To embrace Lutheranism and transform the ecclesiastical organization of a territory was a revolutionary act, an open defiance of imperial authority and the decisions of the Diet. Charles V was determined to suppress heresy, by force if necessary. In such a struggle, Protestant princes risked their lands and titles. How real that risk could be is illustrated by the fate of the Saxon elector John Frederick (1503–1554). In 1547 Charles invaded the electorate with Spanish troops and defeated the Saxon army at Mühlberg. The elector was captured and imprisoned. Forced to choose between his lands and his faith, he chose his faith. He lost his title and much of his territory.

Nor must one suppose that the religious crisis did not offer Catholic princes similar increments of power and ecclesiastical control—with less risk. The duchy of Bavaria was a bastion of Catholicism in southern Germany. The religious policy of the Bavarian dukes was supple. They remained attached to the old faith. They saw in Lutheranism a threat to law and order. "Do not fail to realize," wrote Duke William to his brother in 1527, "that a creed which allows each man to interpret his faith according to his taste and will must breed civil disobedience and ultimately rebellion and bloodshed."[10] They were prepared to stamp it out; but in their own time and way. Each move against heresy extracted concessions from Rome: an expansion of ducal jurisdiction over clerics, curtailment of jurisdictional appeals to Rome and of the competence of the ecclesiastical courts, a bull empowering the dukes to visit monasteries and remove unworthy abbots and priors, increased control over ecclesiastical appointment, permission to tax the clergy at the rate of a fifth of their yearly incomes (henceforth a pillar of the Bavarian financial system). The dukes reinforced their monopoly on the formation of religious policy. Their agents conducted the reform of ecclesiastical abuses. They reserved to themselves alone the power to arrest and

[10]Quoted by Gerald Strauss, "The Religious Policies of Dukes Wilhelm and Ludwig of Bavaria in the First Decade of the Protestant Era," *Church History*, Vol. XXIII (1959), p. 368.

The Pope as Antichrist. *Drawing by Melchior Lorch, dedicated to Luther; dated 1545.* Crowned with the papal tiara and with a tree-trunk cross in one hand and the corroded keys of Peter in the other, the satanic beastman spreads fire, destruction, and abomination over the earth. It is an image of the violence, fanaticism, and cruel hatreds never far below the surface of sixteenth-century life.

examine suspected heretics. Catholic doctrine was preserved at the expense of clerical "liberties" and papal authority. The result was a Bavarian territorial church very largely under ducal control.

The absence of any striking difference between the secular advantages secured by Lutheran princes and those obtained by Catholic princes during the religious revolution in Germany suggests that princely motives for remaining a Catholic or becoming a Lutheran were seldom exclusively political or economic. Placed in similar circumstances, with identical political and economic interests, one elector of Brandenburg was a zealous Catholic, while the next—his son—became a Lutheran. For some princes reform was cynically indistinguishable from secularization. In 1525 Albert of Hohenzollern (1490–1568) grand master of the Order of Teutonic Knights, on Luther's advice, renounced his clerical calling, secularized the order's lands, and made himself the first duke of Prussia. Another prince became a Lutheran because his wife was one. But others embraced the new faith for a simpler reason—because they were persuaded that what Luther said was true. Princes remained Catholics for reasons equally various. Duke George of Saxony was a sincere Catholic, but there seems no doubt that his attachment to the old faith was fortified by the fact that the elector of Saxony—his kinsman, rival, and bitter foe—was Luther's secular protector. Some Catholic princes, such as the dukes of Bavaria, were influenced by the fear that religious revolution would become the signal for social revolution. Few ecclesiastial princes followed the example of Albert of Hohenzollern; but even those who did not were quite prepared to use Luther against Rome—to blackmail the papacy into concessions with respect to finance, jurisdiction, and appointments—relying on their Catholicity to protect them from those elements in Lutheranism they believed to threaten their own positions. Others again were as certain as Charles V "that a single friar errs in his opinion which is against all of Christendom," and would as willingly have renounced their states as their religion. Princely conversion, in short, was a matter of conscience, dozens of individual choices molded by a complex variety of pressures, some secular, some religious, different in each particular case and harmonized by the infinite capacity of human beings for self-deception.

By the middle of the century the princes, in order to safeguard the independence, free choice, and faith of each, had agreed to build a measure of religious diversity into the German constitution. The result was the Religious Peace of Augsburg, hammered out by the imperial Diet between February and September, 1555. The Diet subordinated religious principle and the ecumenical claims of the Catholic and Lutheran churches to political expediency. The settlement allowed electors, princes, imperial knights, and cities to choose between Catholicism and Lutheranism. It excluded sacramentarians (Zwinglians and Calvinists) and sectarians (Anabaptists). Cities which had both Catholic and Lutheran citizens were required to allow each group to practice its religion freely. In the princely territories, on the other hand, the religious preferences of the ruler were binding on his subjects. The Catholic subjects of a Lutheran prince, and the Lutheran subjects of a Catholic ruler, were free only to sell their property and go. The *ius reformandi*, the right to order the religious affairs of a territory, became an attribute of princely sovereignty; the subject enjoyed the *ius emigrandi*, the right to emigrate. Lawyers of a later generation defined the principle of the settlement in an expressive phrase: *cuius regio, eius religio* ("he who rules a territory determines its religion"). Princely "liberty" was victorious in religion as in politics, and for the first time in the history of western Europe, secular law recognized two religious confessions.

THE TRIUMPH OF THE TERRITORIAL CHURCH

During the sixteenth century the unity of Roman ecclesiastical organization collapsed not only in Germany but in all of Europe. The Church, which in the high Middle Ages had been a European corporation, broke apart into a congeries of local territorial churches, their boundaries determined by the geography of political power; there were national churches, princely churches, provincial churches, even churches confined to the population of a single

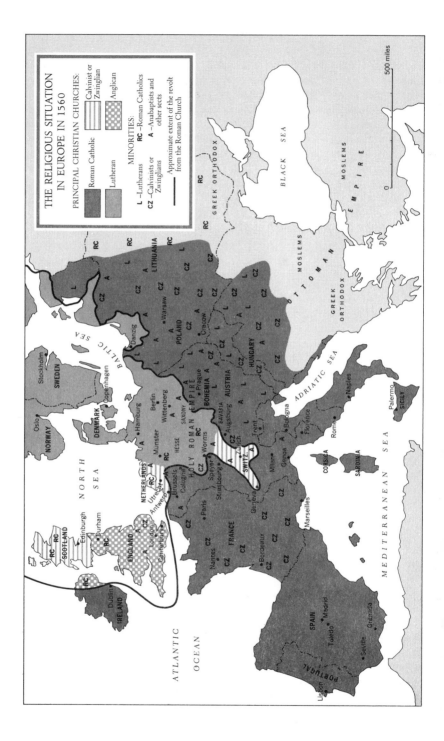

THE RELIGIOUS SITUATION
IN EUROPE IN 1560

PRINCIPAL CHRISTIAN CHURCHES:

Roman Catholic   Calvinist or Zwinglian

Lutheran   Anglican

MINORITIES:

L –Lutherans   RC –Roman Catholics
CZ –Calvinists or Zwinglians   A –Anabaptists and other sects

—— Approximate extent of the revolt from the Roman Church

city or, as in Poland, to the population of a single aristocratic estate. Doctrinal variety made this consolidation of secular control of the church at the level of the territorial state more obvious than in the past, but it did not alter its essential character: the concentration of ecclesiasical appointments, taxation, jurisdiction, administration, and discipline in the hands of the secular authorities. In this context the Reformation is another aspect of the emergence of the sovereign state.

Circumstances peculiar to the Iberian peninsula, in addition to the personal devotion of Charles V to the faith of his ancestors, assured the Catholicity of the Spanish monarchs. Medieval Spanish history had been characterized by perpetual crusades, climaxed by the reconquest of Granada in 1492. The long struggle against the Moslems and the presence in the kingdom of a large Jewish population created a self-consciously Christian sensibility that was fervently Catholic and uniquely aggressive, suspicious of foreign beliefs, fearful of heresy, unswerving in its doctrinal loyalty to Rome. The same year that Granada fell and Columbus sailed for "India," the Spanish government expelled the Jews. In succeeding decades the victorious fight of the Inquisition against Marranos and "Lutherans" gradually created a doctrinal unity and an intellectual conformity unique in Europe.

The passionate orthodoxy of crown and country did not prevent the kings of Spain from asserting their authority over a powerful and wealthy church. By 1523 the crown had secured the right to present to every bishopric in Spain. In America it exercised a universal *Patronato* over the church, including a monopoly of appointments to all ecclesiastical benefices. The king also widened his authority over the Church in a second way, by limiting ecclesiastical jurisdiction. The royal council examined every papal bull received in Spain in order to make sure it contained nothing contrary to the prerogatives of the king or his kingdom. When Pope Paul IV (in office 1555–1559), as a temporary diplomatic maneuver, excommunicated Charles V and Prince Philip, the council "retained" the bull and forbade its publication on pain of exemplary chastisement. The crown severely curtailed appeals from Spanish ecclesiastical courts to the Roman curia. After the creation in 1527 of the *Nunciatura*, a high court staffed by the papal nuncio and six Spanish judges, the vast majority of cases that had formerly gone to Rome remained in Spain. The council reviewed the court's decisions as well as the nuncio's own instructions from the Vatican. Finally, the government increased its control of the Church's wealth by limiting payments to Rome and taxing the clergy far more heavily than in the past. Throughout the sixteenth century, taxation of the Church was one of the most important sources of royal revenue. By the time of the reign of Philip II, the king was head of the church in Spain almost as effectively as Henry VIII was head of the Church of England.

The situation in France was similar. By 1515, when Francis I ascended the throne, the French church claimed three kinds of liberties: administrative liberty, the right to staff itself according to the canonical principle of election; fiscal liberty, the right to tax itself for its own purposes; and jurisdictional liberty, the right to judge and discipline its own members. The French, or Gallican, clergy defended these liberties against both pope and king. They considered virtually any papal interference in the internal affairs of the French church an abuse, and with the backing of the royal courts repulsed papal efforts to appoint to French benefices, limited appeals to the Roman curia, and refused the payment of "annates," a sum equivalent to a year's income from a benefice, due in Rome when the pope confirmed the appointment. But the Gallican church presumed to be independent not only of Rome but of the crown as well. It failed to preserve its liberties against this nearer threat. In 1516 Francis I negotiated the Concordat of Bologna, a compromise between papal and royal interests achieved at the expense of the autonomy of the French church. Over the furious opposition of the clergy, the University of Paris, and the royal courts, the concordat suppressed elections and made the king master of every important ecclesiastical appointment in France. He nominated whom he chose; the pope rarely failed to confirm his choice. The pope's *quid pro quo* was financial—the restoration of annates; in this transaction the pope, the spiritual power, took the temporalities for himself and gave the spiritualities to a temporal prince. Of course, Francis had no intention of allowing the pope a monopoly on plucking the golden feathers of the Gallican goose. He tightened royal control of the Church's property and wealth and instituted policies which led to the regular taxation of the clergy by the end of the century. The Gallican church had resisted papal interference only to fall the more completely under the domination of the king.

The settlement at Bologna, just a year before the publication of Luther's theses on indulgences, became a powerful cement binding the French crown to Rome. Assured of practical supremacy over their own church, Francis I and his successor, Henry II, had little inducement to follow the example of the king of England. The logic of power also bound French kings to Rome in another way. The widening success of imperial armies in Italy during the 1520's both frustrated French ambition and curtailed papal independence. The result, as we have seen, was a Franco-papal alliance. A small price, willingly paid, was continued royal loyalty to the Catholic faith. There was to be no danger of a Protestant succession as long as the Valois occupied the throne.

THE ENGLISH REFORMATION

Unlike Francis I and Charles V, Henry VIII of England, who ascended the throne in 1509, did break with Rome. The circumstances of his defection illustrate yet another aspect of the complex interplay of politics and reformation. No religious motive complicated Henry's ecclesiastical policy. He was conservative in religion and disliked doctrinal innovation. In 1521 he wrote a book against Luther, and a grateful pope conferred on him the title *Defensor fidei* ("defender of the faith"). Before his death in 1547 Protestantism made little headway among his subjects. To be sure, many laymen were anticlerical, outspokenly hostile to abuses such as the granting of benefices to minors, burial fees, the excessive number of holy days during harvest time, and the pretensions of the ecclesiastical courts. But no more than their king did they stomach doctrinal change. Except for the rejection of papal supremacy, the official teaching of the Anglican Church during Henry's reign remained Catholic in every important respect.

Nor was this Catholic monarch initially tempted to break with Rome because his grip on the English church and clergy was any weaker than that of the kings of France and Spain on theirs. Papal authority was as limited in England as in the continental monarchies. Parliament had passed, and the crown enforced, statutes designed to strengthen the secular power and protect the king's rights against ecclesiastical usurpation. The Statute of Provisors (1351) limited papal appointments in England, guaranteeing the autonomy of the English church and the rights of lay and ecclesiastical patrons. The complex of laws known as the *praemunire* (passed between 1352 and 1393) restricted appeals to the papal court and protected the royal courts from papal and clerical interference. The crown had significant control over ecclesiastical revenues and over persons and documents sent from Rome. As early as 1420 the pope wryly observed, "Not the pope but the king of England governs the church in his dominions."

Henry's motive for the break with Rome was more specific: it was personal and dynastic. He wished to be rid of his wife, Catherine of Aragon. He was passionately in love with Anne Boleyn and determined to marry her. More important, Catherine had produced no male heir, only a daughter, Mary Tudor, and the absence of a male heir raised the specter of dynastic crisis. England had never been ruled by a queen. In any case, having a queen as sovereign was known to result in almost insuperable dynastic and international problems—threats of aristocratic rivalry, faction, and even civil war if she married one of her own subjects; the threat of foreign domination if she married a prince from abroad. A scruple was conveniently at hand to disturb Henry's conscience about the validity of his marriage. Scripture forbids a man to marry his brother's wife, and Catherine was the widow of Henry's older brother, Arthur. Only a papal dispensation had made it possible for Henry to marry her. Henry now wished the pope to annul the marriage his predecessor had sanctioned, and under ordinary circumstances he would have had no difficulty in securing this papal annulment. But circumstances were not ordinary; Catherine was the aunt of Charles V. In 1527 Rome fell to imperial troops, and during the next few years the pope was so securely in the emperor's power that it was impossible for him to grant Henry's request.

After failing to secure the "divorce" by negotiations with the pope between 1527 and 1529, Henry hesitated. Then, early in 1532, under the influence and guidance of his great minister Thomas Cromwell (c. 1485–1540), he set a course which by 1534 was to make him pope in his own dominions. His purpose was to create a legal authority in England that could and would annul his marriage. He had already neutralized ecclesiastical opposition by forcing the clergy to recognize him as head of the church in England "as far as the law of Christ allows" (1531). Parliament then authorized him to cut off the payment of annates to Rome (1532). Combining the threat of financial pressure with diplomatic finesse, he extracted from the curia the bulls necessary to confirm Thomas Cranmer (1489–1556), a candidate wholly sympathetic to his cause, as archbishop of Canterbury. The pregnancy of Anne Boleyn in January, 1533, made it necessary to hasten events; her issue had to be made legitimate. In February, Parliament passed the great Act of Appeals, cutting every judicial link with Rome and making Cranmer's archiepiscopal court the highest and only legitimate ecclesiastical tribunal for English cases. In May, Cranmer granted the annulment. The future Queen Elizabeth was born in the autumn. An Act of Succession confirmed her legitimacy and the rights of hoped-for sons to succeed to the throne. A final piece of legislation, the Act of Supremacy, crowned the revolutionary edifice in November, 1534. Henry became without qualification the "only supreme head in earth of the Church of England called *Anglicana Ecclesia*."[11]

Although the crucial inducement to break with Rome was thus personal and dynastic—if not for the problem of the "divorce," the Reformation in England would at least have been long delayed—its result was the decisive subordination of church to state. The English Reformation subjected the clergy to a royal will independent of Rome. At last, after centuries of papal "usurpation," England had become a "true monarchy" and an "empire" owing allegiance to no authority except its king's. The king now exercised every power formerly wielded by the pope. He controlled the church's courts, appointments, and revenues. He made ecclesiastical law and determined doctrine. Like the German Protestant princes, he was *summus episcopus*—a lay bishop—in his dominion. It followed that the religion of the people must be the religion of the church's head: *cuius regio, eius religio*. Deviation was at once heretical and treasonable, and Henry established the Anglican "middle way" by burning heretics in pairs—papists on the one hand, Anabaptists and "Lutherans" on the other. During the last years of his reign, and again during the reign of Mary, committed Protestants found it expedient to emigrate to Switzerland and the Rhineland. Not surprisingly, the consciences of the vast majority of Englishmen were more elastic than theirs. They followed with apparent docility the rapidly altering doctrinal preferences of their sovereigns, and many thousands lived long enough to be

[11]G. R. Elton, *The Tudor Constitution* (Cambridge, Eng., 1962), 355.

Roman Catholics in 1529, Henrician Catholics from 1534 to 1547, moderate, then extreme, Protestants under Edward VI (1547–1553), Roman Catholics once more under Mary (1553–1558), and again moderate Protestants under Elizabeth I.

The very triumph of the territorial church and the emergence of the secular rulers of Europe as the religious arbiters of their dominions gave the religious struggle a new political violence. Just as economic and class tensions took on a religious coloration, so too did the fundamental political opposition of the age—that between royal and princely efforts to unify the state and centralize its administration, on the one hand, and the defense of local and corporate privilege, the "liberties" of nobles and clergy, monasteries and universities, provinces and cities, on the other. With the exception of the Tudors, the most important European monarchs ultimately became the allies of a reformed and reinvigorated Catholicism. Protestantism, by contrast, normally secured its political base at a lower level, that of the smaller principality, the province, or the city, and was supported by groups resisting the encroachments of centralizing sovereigns. In the sixteenth century, Catholicism gradually became the religion of "absolutism"; Protestantism the ideology of the feudal, urban, and corporate opposition. However, the opposition did not choose Protestantism because some political principle favorable to liberty was inherent in it; the competing religions were as neutral politically as they were economically and socially. The defenders of local autonomy and local privilege were so often Protestant simply because the Habsburgs and the Valois were Catholic. Like those German princes who found in Lutheranism and its affirmation of the rights of conscience another bulwark against imperial authority, many nobles and urban oligarchs in the Netherlands and France, in Germany, Poland, and Hungary, discovered an affinity between Calvinism and their ambition to defend, augment, or recover their political independence. But the case of England indicates clearly enough that opposition to the crown did not have to be Protestant. There, feudal reaction (for example, the rebellion under Henry VIII known as the Pilgrimage of Grace and the revolt of the northern earls under Elizabeth), this time against a Protestant prince, found an ideological program in the restoration of Catholicism. Once the struggle between centralizing "absolutism" and the defense of local "liberties" fused with the struggle between Protestantism and Catholicism, the most potent secular antagonism of the age acquired a religious dimension and the certainties of faith mixed inextricably with the passions of politics. The struggle became absolute, incapable of compromise. Europe stood on the threshold of a century of civil and religious war.

SUGGESTIONS
FOR FURTHER READING
(Books marked * are available in paperback.)

GENERAL

Several good manuals survey the period: W. K. Ferguson, *Europe in Transition, 1300–1520* (Boston, 1962); Erich Hassinger, *Das Werden des neuzeitlichen Europa, 1300–1600* (Braunschweig, 1959); *Denys Hay, *The Italian Renaissance* (Cambridge, Eng., 1962) (Cambridge University Press); *Myron P. Gilmore, *The World of Humanism, 1453–1517* (New York, 1952) (Harper Torchbook); *The Reformation, 1520–1559*, ed. by G. R. Elton *(New Cambridge Modern History*, Vol. II, Cambridge, Eng., 1958).

European history in the fourteenth, fifteenth, and sixteenth centuries raises unusually interesting problems of terminology and periodization. When does modern history begin? Does the word "Renaissance" usefully describe a particular historical period? What are the dates of the "late Middle Ages"? W. K. Ferguson, *The Rennaissance in Historical Thought* (Boston, 1948) studies the answers historians have given these and similar questions between the fifteenth century and the present. Two collections of papers read at symposia in 1951–1952 and in 1959 supplement Ferguson and introduce the reader to current literature and debate in the fields of economic, political, and intellectual history and the history of literature, art, and science: *The Renaissance. Six Essays* (New York, 1962) (Harper Torchbook) and *The Renaissance. A Reconsideration of the Theories and Interpretations of the Age* (Madison, Wis., 1961) (Univ. of Wisconsin Press).

POLITICAL HISTORY

Historians continue to organize their narratives of European political history on national lines. The following histories lay the groundwork nicely: *J. H. Elliott, *Imperial Spain, 1469–1716* (New York, 1964) (Mentor); John Lynch, *Spain under the Habsburgs*, Vol. I (Oxford, 1964); *S. T. Bindoff, *Tudor England* (London, 1950) (Penguin Pelican); Hajo Holborn, *The Reformation* (New York, 1959), vol. I of his *History of Modern Germany;* Robert Mandrou, *Introduction à la France moderne, 1500–1640* (Paris, 1961). *Karl Brandi, *The Emperor Charles V*, trans. by C. V. Wedgwood (London, and New York, 1939) (Humanities), surveys the Netherlands, Spain, Italy, Germany, and indeed all Europe from the perspective of the dominating political personality of the age.

Beneath the rapid flow of the political narrative is the rocky bed of political institutions.For England, see Kenneth W. M. Pickthorn, *Early Tudor Government*, 2 vols. (Cambridge, Eng., 1934) and *G. R. Elton, *The Tudor Revolution in Government* (Cambridge, Eng., 1953) (Cambridge Univ. Press). For France, Gaston Zeller, *Les Institutions de la France au XVIe siècle* (Paris, 1948); J. Russell Major, *Representative Institutions in Renaissance France* (Madison, Wis., 1960); and William F. Church, *Constitutional Thought in Sixteenth-Century France* (Cambridge, Mass., 1941). For Germany, F. L. Carsten, *Princes and Parliaments in Germany* (Oxford, 1959). For Spain, J. Gounon-Loubens, *Essais sur l'administration de la Castile au XVIe siècle* (Paris, 1860).

*Garrett Mattingly brilliantly describes the peacetime relations of these states in his *Renaissance Diplomacy* (New York, 1955) (Penguin Peregrine). J. R. Partington, *A History of Greek Fire and Gunpowder* (Cambridge, Eng., 1960), gives a most interesting account of the changes in military technology which revolutionized their wartime relations and put \so intense a pressure on sixteenth-century political and financial institutions. See also F. L. Taylor, *The Art of War in Italy, 1494–1529* (Cambridge, Eng., 1921) and Sir Charles Oman, *The Art of War in the Sixteenth Century*, 2 vols. (London, 1937).

ECONOMIC AND SOCIAL HISTORY

The best guide is W. K. Ferguson, "Recent Trends in the Economic Historiography of the Renaissance," *Studies in the Renaissance*, Vol. VII (1960), pp. 7–26; while the *Cambridge Economic History*, especially Vol. IV (Cambridge, Eng., 1967), on the sixteenth century, provides an admirable synthesis of present knowledge. A stimulating introduction to many of the problems preoccupying social historians today is *J. H. Hexter's *Reappraisals in History. New Views on History and Society in Early Modern Europe* (New York, 1961) (Harper Torchbook). Some exceptional monographs offer more detailed treatment of salient features of a complicated and fascinating social and economic landscape: *Raymond de Roover, *The Rise and Decline of the Medici Bank, 1397–1494* (Cambridge, Mass., 1963) (Norton); Richard Ehrenberg, *Capital and Finance in the Age of the Renaissance* (New York, 1928); J. U. Nef, "Industrial Europe on the Eve of the Reformation," *Journal of Political Economy*, Vol. XLIX (1941), pp. 1–40, 183–224; Florence Elder de Roover, "Andrea Banchi, Florentine Silk Manufacturer and Merchant in the Fifteenth Century," *Studies in Medieval and Renaissance History*, Vol. III (1966), pp. 223–285; Frederick C. Lane, *Andrea Barbarigo, Merchant of Venice, 1418–1449* (Baltimore, 1944); Henri Lepeyre, *Une Famille de marchands: les Ruiz* (Peris, 1955); Emile Coornaert, *Les Français et le commerce international à Anvers, fin du XVe–XVIe siècle*, 2 vols. (Paris, 1961); Goetz Freiherr von Pölnitz, *Die Fugger* (Frankfurt am Main, 1960).

Three dynamic factors in sixteenth-century economic life were demographic expansion, the spice trade, and the great price rise. For orientation see E. F. Rice, "Recent Studies on the Population of Europe, 1348–1620," *Renaissance News*, Vol. XVIII (1965), pp. 180–187; the chapter on the spice trade in Donald F. Lach, *Asia in the Making of Europe* (Chicago, 1965), Vol. I (1), pp. 91–147;

and E. J. Hamilton, "The History of Prices before 1750," *XIe Congrès International des sciences historiques, Rapports,* Vol. I (Stockholm, 1960), pp. 144-164. All three are closely linked to the discoveries and European expansion in the New World and in the Far East. *Boise Penrose, *Travel and Discovery in the Renaissance, 1420–1620* (New York, 1962) (Atheneum) is a readable and authoritative survey.

There is a large and important literature on the meaning, origins, and development of capitalism. One may usefully begin with *Maurice Dobb, *Studies in the Development of Capitalism,* second ed. (New York, 1963) (New World Paperbacks). *Kurt Samuelsson, *Religion and Economic Action,* trans. by E. G. French (New York, 1961) (Harper Torchbook) is a recent discussion of the relation between capitalism and religion and of the controversial literature the problem has provoked since the publication in 1905 of Max Weber's celebrated essay on the Protestant ethic and the spirit of capitalism. At the heart of the controversy was the idea and practice of usury. See the illuminating book of Benjamin N. Nelson, *The Idea of Usury* (Princeton, N.J., 1949).

INTELLECTUAL HISTORY

The best introductions to Italian Renaissance thought are *W. H. Woodward, *Vittorino da Feltre and Other Humanist Educators* (Cambridge, Eng., 1897) (Teachers College Press); Eugenio Garin, *Italian Humanism. Philosophy and Civic Life in the Renaissance,* trans. by Peter Munz (New York, 1965); and two books by *Paul Oskar Kristeller: *Renaissance Thought. The Classic, Scholastic, and Humanist Strains* (New York, 1961) (Harper Torchbook) and *Eight Philosophers of the Italian Renaissance* (Stanford, Calif., 1964) (Stanford Univ. Press).

Among the many books on humanism in northern Europe, the following are reliable and attractive: *R. W. Chambers, *Thomas More* (London, 1935) (Ann Arbor Books); Fritz Caspari, *Humanism and the Social Order in Tudor England* (Chicago, 1954); Lewis Spitz, *The Religious Renaissance of the German Humanists* (Cambridge, Mass., 1963); *Hajo Holborn, *Ulrich von Hutten and the German Reformation,* trans. by Roland Bainton, (New Haven, 1937) (Harper Torchbook); Augustin Renaudet, *Préréforme et humanisme à Paris pendant les premières guerres d'Italie (1494-1517),* second ed. (Paris, 1953); Lucien Febvre, *Le Problème de l'incroyance au XVIe siècle. La religion de Rabelais* (Paris, 1942); *Johan Huizinga, *Erasmus and the Age of the Reformation* (New York, 1957) (Harper Torchbook).

Readers interested in historical writing will consult with profit Felix Gilbert, *Machiavelli and Guicciardini. Politics and History in Sixteenth Century Florence* (Princeton, N.J., 1965). For the history of science, see *Alistair C. Crombie, *Medieval and Early Modern Science,* 2 vols. (New York, 1959) (Doubleday Anchor); *Herbert Butterfield, *The Origins of Modern Science, 1300–1800* (London, 1949) (Free Press); and *Thomas S. Kuhn, *The Copernican Revolution* (Cambridge, Mass., 1957) (Random House Vintage). Pierce Butler, *The Origins of Printing in Europe* (Chicago, 1940) is an expert introduction to a technological innovation with profound consequences for European intellectual life.

Finally, a regrettably small selection of important and exciting books on the history of art: *Bernard Berenson, *The Italian Painters of the Renaissance* (London, 1952) (Meridian); Erwin Panofsky, *Renaissance and Renascences in Western Art*, second ed. (Stockholm, 1965); *Jean Seznec, *The Survival of the Pagan Gods. The Mythological Tradition and Its Place in Renaissance Humanism and Art*, trans. by Barbara Sessions (New York, 1953) (Harper Torchbook); Rudolf Wittkower, *Architectural Principles in the Age of Humanism*, third ed. (London, 1962); *Walter Friedländer, *Mannerism and Anti-Mannerism in Italian Painting* (New York, 1957) (Schocken); Otto Benesch, *The Art of the Rennaisance in Northern Europe* (London, 1965); *Kenneth Clark, *The Nude. A Study of Ideal Form* (New York, 1956) (Doubleday Anchor).

CHURCH AND REFORMATION

On the late medieval and Renaissance church, see W. K. Ferguson, "The Church in a Changing World," *American Historical Review*, Vol. LIX (1953), pp. 1–18; A. C. Flick, *The Decline of the Medieval Church*, 2 vols. (London, 1930); *G. Mollat, *The Popes at Avignon, 1305–1378*, trans. by Janet Love (New York, 1963) (Harper Torchbook); Walter Ullmann, *The Origins of the Great Schism* (London, 1948); Hubert Jedin, *A History of the Council of Trent*, trans. by Ernest Graf, 2 vols. (London and New York, 1957–1961).

A vivid introduction to the Protestant revolution is *Hans Hillerbrand, *The Reformation. A Narrative History Related by Contemporary Observers and Participants* (New York, 1964) (Harper Torchbook). *Roland Bainton, *The Reformation of the Sixteenth Century* (Boston, 1952) (Beacon) sketches the development of Protestant doctrine with sympathy and precision. *Norman Sykes, *The Crisis of the Reformation* (London, 1946) (Norton) clarifies the issues of faith and practice at the heart of the theological controversy. For the lives and teachings of the principal reformers, see *Bainton, *Here I Stand. A Life of Martin Luther* (New York, 1950) (Mentor); *Erik H. Erikson, *Young Man Luther* (New York, 1958) (Norton); E. G. Rupp, *Luther's Progress to the Diet of Worms* (London, 1951); P. S. Watson, *Let God Be God* (London, 1947), a well-balanced presentation of Luther's theology; Oskar Farner, *Zwingli the Reformer. His Life and Work* (London, 1952), a short account by the author of the definitive biography (4 vols., Zurich, 1943–1960); J. V. Pollet, *Huldrych Zwingli et la Réforme en Suisse d'après les recherches récentes* (Paris, 1963); François Wendel, *Calvin. The Origins and Development of His Religious Thought*, trans. by P. Mairet (New York, 1963); George H. Williams, *The Radical Reformation* (Philadelphia, 1962).

The following books survey the history of the Reformation in Europe and in individual countries: Emile G. Léonard, *A History of Protestantism* (London, 1965) Vol. I; A. C. Dickens, *The English Reformation* (London, 1964); G. Donaldson, *The Scottish Reformation* (Cambridge, Eng., 1960); Jean Viénot, *Histoire de la Réforme française des origines à l'Edit de Nantes* (Paris, 1926); Lucien Febvre, *Au Coeur religieux du XVIe siècle* (Paris, 1957).

Index

Aeneid (Virgil), 6, 73, 74
Africa
  gold trade in, 26, 27–29
  Portuguese expansion in, 26–29
*Against the Robbing and Murdering
  Hordes of Peasants* (Luther), 151
Agricola, *see* Bauer, Georg
Albert of Hohenzollern, 164, 165
Alcabala, 100
Alberti, Leon Battista, 79
Albuquerque, Alfonso de, 31
Alexander VI, 10
Allegory of Philosophy (Dürer), 79–81
America, Spanish, 26, 32, 107
  discovery and exploitation of, 32–37
  mining industry in, effect on conquest
    and settlement, 32, 35
  effect on European economy, 37
  exploitation of Indian labor, 32, 35
  German technology and, 35–36
  gold and silver discovered, 32, 33,
    35
  mercury-amalgamation process, 35–
    36, 37
  silver deposits at Potosí and Zaca-
    tecas, 35, 36, 37
Anabaptism/Anabaptists, 17, 148, 153,
  165
  doctrines of, 136, 137–38, 139
  origins of, 136–37
  persecution of, 139–40, 155
  way of life, 138–39
Anatomy of Melancholy (Burton), 76
Anglican Church, formation of, 104, 168–
  71
Apollonius, 22
Aquinas, St. Thomas, 6, 54, 74, 77, 81,
  158
Arabs, 3, 11, 50
Archimedes, 22
Ariosto, Lodovico, 15
Aristotle, 20, 25, 54, 73, 75, 77, 78, 88
  theory of motion, 19
Art, *see* Humanism
Augsburg, Diet of, 110
  pattern of religious choice in, 152–53
  Religious Peace of, 165
Augustus, Emperor, 70
Augustine, St., 68, 74
Avalos, Fernando de, 13
Aztecs, 75
  conquest of, 33–34

Babylonian Captivity of the Church, The
  (Luther), 130
Bacon, Roger, 10–11
Banalités, 64
Barbaro, Ermolao, 120
Barbary Coast, European trading on, 28
Bauer, Georg, 23, 25
Bavaria, duchy of, 163–64, 165
Bembo, Pietro, 85
Berlichingen, Götz von, 62
Black Death (1384–1349), 59
Boccaccio, Giovanni, 67
Bodin, Jean, 71, 76, 93–95
Boethius, 80
Bohemia, 6
Böhm, Hans, 65
Boleyn, Anne, 169, 170
Bologna, Concordat of, 168
  University of, 25, 73
Books, *see* Printing
Bourgeoisie, *see* Merchant-capitalist(s)
Bovelles, Charles de, 78
Bramante, Donato, 84
Brantôme, Pierre de, 63
Brüderschaften, 49
Bruni, Leonardo, 71, 72
Bucer, Martin, 133, 135
Budé, Guillaume, 67
Burgundy, ducal court of, 107
Burton, Robert, 76

Calvin, John, 55, 125, 143
  biographical, 134, 135
  death, 122
  denounces Michael Servetus, 156–57
  doctrines of, 135–36
  justifies persecution of dissenters, 158–
    59
  on relation of church and state, 140–41
Calvinism, 131, 144, 145, 146, 148, 153–
  54, 165, 171
Capitalism
  cleavage between capital and labor, 53–
    54
  defined, 46–47
  effect on agrarian society, 58–65
  first labor unions and strikes, 49
  journeymen transformed to wage la-
    borers, 48–49, 52
  secularization of economic ethic of
    churches, 54, 55–56
  state-controlled, 47, 48
  see also Europe, industrial organization;
    Merchant-capitalist(s)

176

178 / Index

capture of Indian Ocean spice trade
29–32
significance of, 26, 32
takeover of African gold trade, 26–29
Prester John, 26
Prince, The (Machiavelli), 121
Principia (Newton), 18
Printing
block, 2–3
and book censorship, 9–10
diffusion of images and ideas through,
9, 147
expansion of from 1460 to 1500, 6, 8
first printed books, 5–6
importance of paper manufacture to, 3
influence on scholarship, 8–9
invention of, 1–2
Chinese contributions to, 2–3
technical development of, 3–4
type, invention of, 4
Protestantism, 56, 77, 120, 145
conversion to and class rivalries, 152–55
and the Counter-Reformation, 142–44,
145–46
fragmentation of, 130–39
origin of term "Protestant," 122
persecution of dissenters by, 155–60
as religion of local autonomy and local
liberties, 171
spread of, problem of conversion, 147–
48
the burghers, 152–55
the German princes, 160–65
the peasants, 149–52
as system of social control, 139–42
see also individual sects and their
founders
Ptolemy, 81
Puerto Rico, 33, 37

Ranke, Leopold, 106
Raphael, 74, 85–86
Reformation, Catholic, 142
Reformation, Protestant, 8, 9, 61, 70, 110
"abuse" theory of, 122–23, 125
the Anglican Church, 168–71
aims of, 125
gives rise to territorial church, 165–61
see also Luther, Martin; Protestantism
Regnum Italicum, 114
Reichskammergericht, 110–11
Reichstag, 110
Reuchlin, Johann, 67
Rems, the, 152
Representative assemblies
question of taxation and principle of
consent, 102–5
Republic (Plato), 76
Resolution and composition, method of,
18–20

Restitution of Christianity (Servetus), 156
Roman Catholic Church, 57, 62
attacks Lutheranism at Diet of Speyer,
122
breaks into territorial churches, 165–68
Counter-Reformation, 142–43
doctrinal openness in Middle Ages, 143
doctrine of transubstantiation, 129, 130
ecclesiastical abuses, 123–25
and the English Reformation, 168–71
in Germany during Reformation, 163–
65
humanist view of, 69–70
indulgences, 129
infallibility in faith and morals, 128–29
interpretation of scripture, 130–31
Luther attacks doctrines of, 129–30
mysticism in 16th century, 145
and pattern of conversion to Protestantism, 153, 155
persecution of dissenters by, 155, 158–
60
prohibition of usury, 54, 55
as religion of absolutism, 171
sacerdotalism, 129, 130
sacramentalism, 129, 130
see also Reformation, Catholic; Trent,
Council of
Roman Empire, 1, 47
Roman Index of Prohibited Books (1559),
10
Roman law, 93

Salamanca, University of, 67
Schleitheim Confession, 137, 139
Schöffer, Peter, 1, 3, 4, 5
Scholastics/Scholasticism, 21, 25, 77, 81
attitude toward experimentation, 20
limited mathematical knowledge of, 20
method of resolution and composition,
18–20, 25
Scientific method
humanists and, 22–23
importance of mathematics in, 22–23,
25
Italian artist-engineers and, 20–22, 23,
25
scholastics and, 18–20, 23, 25
three procedures combined in, 18, 23–
25
Scientific revolution, foundations of, 18–
25
Seneca, 6, 73
Servetus, Michael, 156–57, 159–60
Sicily, 112, 114
Simons, Menno, 137, 155–56
Sovereign territorial state, 15, 16, 65, 114
churches become subject to, 165–71
continued reliance on powerful nobility,
99